"What a fantastic piece of work! . . . Towns and Bird have given church leaders a great gift. They provide a solid conceptual framework, illustrate their ideas with concrete examples, offer thought-provoking questions for further reflection, and deliver their message with an interactive format that enables the truths to find a home with others. The work is a comprehensive compendium, a state-of-the-church, both in issues and challenges. It will give every growing leader new ideas to continue his or her ministry development."

—Reggie McNeal, director, Leadership Development Department

"This work leapfrogs to the front of the pack. . . . Elmer Towns and Warren Bird's treatment of postmodern thought is worth the price of the book. . . . A changing world demands changing methods. This books shows us how."

—Josh Hunt, author, *You Can Double Your Class in Two Years or Less*

"Our culture has been a 'Jerusalem' culture sharing a basic biblical worldview. Now it is an 'Athens' culture in which different approaches to church planting and evangelism are needed. Towns and Bird explore this 'brave new world' and offer practical approaches. . . . The book is a gold mine of insights, suggestions, and resources."

—Murray Moerman, coordinator, Church Planting Canada (DAWN Strategy)

"This incredibly innovative and prophetic book leads us as the body of Christ to look with compassion upon those who are in need. It is challenging and opens our heart to be more Christlike."

—Cindy Jacobs, cofounder, Generals of Intercession

"This is a first-rate book. It is exactly what is required to help struggling churches make the most of the opportunities that they have, and even those churches which are not yet struggling. The book is full of practical ideas based on clearly enunciated principles. . . . The book is as relevant to the situation in the UK as it in the USA. I have no hesitation in recommending it 1,000 percent!"

—Peter Brierley, executive director, *Christian Research*

"*Into the Future* . . . deserves our attention. This book is full of insights that will help American churches minister more effectively in the twenty-first century."

—Franklin Graham, president, Samaritan's Purse

"This excellent book is a must-read for those who are committed to seeing the church continue its relevancy in this new century. The authors have given us not only their thorough research but also resources that will facilitate healthy discussion for those who are serious about taking a creative look at the church of the future."

—Robert H. Schuller, Crystal Cathedral Ministries

"Elmer Towns and Warren Bird . . . are more than futurists; they give practical principles for church leaders to plan a strategy to take local churches into a fruitful future. . . . They believe in the church, and they believe in the future; and I agree with them that the future is bright for those who trust God and plan for it."

—C. Peter Wagner, Colorado Springs, Colorado

"Some of the most useful church leadership information I've read in years. . . . This is a truly marvelous book—I want my whole staff to read it."

—Ted Haggard, senior pastor, New Life Church

"Each chapter is a rich stewpot, ch⸻⸻⸻⸻⸻⸻⸻⸻ quotations, lists, and insights, which provide t⸻⸻⸻⸻⸻⸻⸻⸻ors and thinkers."

⸻litor, *Leadership*

Into the Future

Other books by Elmer Towns

Biblical Meditation for Spiritual Breakthrough
Developing a Giving Church (with Stan Toler)
Fasting Can Change Your Life
Fasting for Spiritual Breakthrough
My Angel Named Herman
The Everychurch Growth Book: How to Break Growth Barriers
   (with C. Peter Wagner and Thom Rainer)

Other books by Warren Bird

How to Break Growth Barriers (with Carl George)
Nine Keys to Effective Small-Group Leadership (with Carl George)
Prepare your Church for the Future (with Carl George)
Real Followers: Beyond Virtual Christianity (with Michael Slaughter)
The Coming Church Revolution (with Carl George)
The Comprehensive Guide to Cassette Ministry (with Johnny Berguson)

Into the Future

Turning Today's Church Trends into Tomorrow's Opportunities

Elmer Towns
& Warren Bird

Foreword by Dr. Leith Anderson

Fleming H. Revell
A Division of Baker Book House
Grand Rapids, Michigan 49516

© 2000 by Elmer Towns and Warren Bird

Published by Fleming H. Revell
a division of Baker Book House Company
P.O. Box 6287, Grand Rapids, MI 49516-6287

Second printing, November 2000

Printed in the United States of America

Library of Congress Cataloging-in-Publication Data

Towns, Elmer L.
    Into the future : turning today's church trends into tomorrow's opportunities
/ Elmer Towns & Warren Bird.
        p.   cm.
    Includes bibliographical references and index.
    ISBN 0-8007-5725-4 (pbk.)
    1. Church renewal. I. Bird, Warren. II. Title.
BV600.2 .T69 2000
262'.001'7—dc21
                                                        00-024860

For current information about all releases from Baker Book House, visit our web site:
http://www.bakerbooks.com

Contents

List of Church Profiles   7
List of Expert Commentators   8
Foreword   9
Acknowledgments   11
Introduction   13

Part 1: Churches Move toward Church Health and Quality

1 Get Help Becoming More Healthy   23
   Focus attention on becoming a healthy church.
2 Keep the Bible in One Hand and a Cup of Cold Water
   in the Other   35
   Be unapologetic about showing social concern.

Part 2: Churches Move toward Relational Communication

3 Enter the World of *Cheers, Friends,* and *Seinfeld*   55
   Communicate through multisensory and relational frameworks.
4 Learn the Language That Connects with Postmoderns   67
   Use relevance and credibility to spur interest in the gospel.

Part 3: Churches Move toward Targeted Outreach

5 Turn On Your Daytime Running Lights   81
   Remember that it's better to do a few things well.
6 Set Benchmarks for Reaching the Unchurched   93
   Think outside the box to find and reach unchurched people.

Part 4: Churches Move toward New Forms for Faith Transfer

7 Make More Room for Truth   107
   *Expect the next generation to be raised in our country's most secularized
   culture yet.*

8   Go Confidently to Mars Hill   119
Look for a new generation that is both rigorously academic and unabashedly Christian.

Part 5: Churches Move toward Greater Appreciation of Worship

9   Maximize the Strong Points of Your Worship Service   131
Don't insist that one worship style has to fit all congregations.
10   Cash In on Two Millennia of Good Ideas   149
Remember that people really want to participate.

Part 6: Churches Move toward Empowerment of Lay Leadership

11   Learn to Be a Leader-Maker   163
Rejoice that the people of God are truly becoming ministers.
12   Look Underneath the Megachurch Movement   177
Discover how churches grow by becoming the "biggest little church around."
13   Make the Church Better Than a Business   189
Capitalize on the uniqueness of your church's spiritual resources and eternal mission.

Part 7: Churches Move toward New Stewardship Motives

14   Free People to Give from the Heart   201
Discover the specific reasons why people are willing to give money to their church.

Conclusion   217
Notes   225
Subject Index   237
Name Index   241

List of Church Profiles

 1 Community Church of Joy—Glendale, Arizona   24
 2 Fellowship Bible Church—Little Rock, Arkansas   36
 3 Vineyard Community Church—Cincinnati, Ohio   56
 4 Ginghamsburg Church—Tipp City, Ohio   68
 5 Skyline Wesleyan Church—Lemon Grove, California   82
 6 Redeemer Presbyterian Church—New York, New York   94
 7 McLean Bible Church—Tysons Corner, Virginia   108
 8 Mosaic (formerly The Church on Brady)—Los Angeles,
    California   120
 9 Centre Street Evangelical Missionary Church—Calgary,
    Alberta, Canada   132
10 Scottsdale Family Church—Scottsdale, Arizona   150
11 Trinity Baptist Church—Kelowna, British Columbia,
    Canada   164
12 New Hope Christian Fellowship—Honolulu, Hawaii   178
13 Georgian Hills Baptist Church—Memphis, Tennessee   190
14 Windsor Village United Methodist Church—Houston,
    Texas   202

Into the Future is a book for wheat-growers. It is for those who want to answer the fantasy question in heaven, saying, "Yes, I was there. God did wonderfully amazing things. Let me tell you my exciting share!"

Leith Anderson
Wooddale Church
Eden Prairie, Minnesota

Acknowledgments

This book would be unnecessary if we didn't serve such a wonderful God, who alone knows the future and who grants wisdom as we ask. As the Bible affirms, he is at work through human history and invites his children to be part of that unfolding drama: "For it is God who works in you to will and to act according to his good purpose" (Phil. 2:13).

Warren thanks:

Carl George and Dale Galloway as the two people who have mentored me most in what it means to be a pastor;

Bob Cushman, Michael Slaughter, and David Jankowski as three terrific pastors who have allowed me to be part of the breakthrough churches that you lead;

the many people who each took a major risk in asking me to write for you, including Sara Robertson, Julie Smith, Dan Pawley, H. Robert Cowles, and Elmer Towns; and

my amazing wife, Michelle, and our two outstanding children, Gretchen and Nathan, who graciously stepped around several big piles of books in my office until this manuscript was finally finished.

Elmer thanks:

all those who have given me insights into the church—Jerry Falwell, Jack Hayford, Bill Hybels, Rick Warren, Cecil Hodges, John Maxwell, Doug Porter, Dave Seifert, David Yonggi Cho, Charles Ryrie, Howard Hendricks, and Donald McGavran; and

the one who perhaps influenced me most, W. A. Criswell.

We also thank Linda Elliott, Lee Vukich, Renee Grooms, and Matthew Chittum for their assistance with proofreading, compiling footnotes, and correspondence. We appreciate Janet L. Dales's excellent help with the application points. Finally, thanks to our long-standing friend at Revell, Bill Petersen, who suggested this book and kept encouraging us through the process.

Introduction

On the outskirts of Kelowna, British Columbia, one of the local roads features a 90-degree turn at the end of a long straight stretch. A huge swamp lies on the outside curve of that turn.

The straight, level quality of the road makes it a favorite for teens who like to drag race. Too often, they don't slow down enough to make the curve. Swerving off the pavement, they end up in foot-deep water and require a tow truck to extract them.

Tim Schroeder, senior pastor of Trinity Baptist Church in Kelowna, is a volunteer chaplain with the local police. He was on duty one evening when the police received a report about a car stranded in the swamp.

Tim waded out into the foot-deep waters and opened the car door expecting to find a slightly intoxicated teenager. Instead he found a rather embarrassed elderly couple.

"How did this happen?" Tim asked after he and his partner had safely escorted the couple to the police car. The man who had been at the wheel began explaining about his difficulties in using his new trifocals. He simply couldn't get used to making the necessary mental adjustments.

In short, he said, "I couldn't see, so I kept going the way I was going."

The next Sunday, Tim Schroeder used that real-life story as an illustration related to church life. "How often does that man's circumstance parallel what we do with the church?" he asked. "When we forget our call, when we don't see the mission clearly, when we don't understand the changing times, when we lose our passion for seeing new people come to Christ, and when we get content with the status quo, then instead of negotiating the turn and making the necessary changes and corrections, we just keep going the way we are."

> *"I couldn't see, so I kept going the way I was going."*

Missing the Turn?

A lot of churches land in the "swamp" before they gain enough focus on the future to realize that the road turned another way. It's amazing how far a church can go with unquestioned habits (i.e., "business as usual") before realizing that we completely missed a "turn."

When we attempt to accomplish our mission on the basis of faulty information, however, that's exactly what will happen. If we assume that the best course of action is to continue to do everything the way we have always done, we may be mistaken.

Many of our customs, attitudes, and strategies are dead. Instead of clinging to dead, man-made traditions, we need to embrace what God blesses today.

This book marshals many specialists who love the Lord and love his church. None want to make fun of the church. Rather, all are passionate that a business-as-usual approach is inadequate for focused mission in the twenty-first century. Each wants to help us find the things we are doing that aren't going anywhere.

If the Horse Is Dead: Dismount?

Dakota tribal wisdom says that when you discover you are riding a dead horse, the best strategy is to dismount. In contrast, here's how many in the church respond when they find out their "horse" is dead:

1. Say things like, "This is the way we always have ridden this horse."
2. Appoint a committee to study the horse.
3. Buy a stronger whip.
4. Change riders.
5. Arrange to visit other churches to see how they ride dead horses.
6. Raise the standards for riding dead horses.
7. Appoint a tiger team to revive the dead horse.
8. Create a training session to increase our riding ability.
9. Compare the state of dead horses in today's environment.
10. Change your definitions or rules by declaring, "This horse is not dead."
11. Hire new staff members to ride the dead horse.
12. Harness several dead horses together for increased speed.
13. Declare that "No horse is too dead to beat."
14. Provide additional funding to increase the horse's performance.
15. Do a cost-analysis study to see if riding dead horses is cheaper.
16. Purchase a product to make dead horses run faster.
17. Declare that the horse is "better, faster, and cheaper" dead.
18. Form a quality circle to find uses for dead horses.
19. Revisit the performance requirements for horses.
20. Say this horse was procured with cost as an independent variable.
21. Promote the dead horse to a supervisory position.

Nelson on Trends

As a student of organizations and future church trends, I'm thrilled at this colorful collage of what the twenty-first-century church looks like. The grand benefit of this book is a big-picture view of the various systems present in healthy congregations.

Like a car without a transmission or gas tank, a church without certain values and structures will not function in the future, even if a few of the necessary parts are present.

As the opening story in the book illustrates, it's amazing how long a church can continue doing what it has always done, totally unaware that it has missed a crucial "turn" in the road. With the authors, I am passionate that a business-as-usual approach is inadequate for focused mission in the twenty-first century.

New-paradigm ministry is significantly different than old-paradigm ways. This book, like a scout into the future, points the way for us who dare to lead dynamic ministries that are relevant beyond the twentieth century.

Alan Nelson
director, Leading Ideas
pastor, Scottsdale Family Church, Scottsdale, Arizona
author, *The Five Star Church* (Regal, 1999)

are at the heart of the gospel? Around what principles of our faith can all Christians feel confident in helping each other rally? A church that unifies around the right ideals and principles experiences maximum impact for evangelism.

Tremendous Evangelistic Opportunity

As our society lives in the cusp of a postmodern era (see chapter 4), common acceptance of Christian ideals is at an all-time low. Western culture is more non-Christian in its outlook than at nearly any other time in history. Our challenge is to present the gospel to people who look at Jesus Christ through secular, skeptical, and technical eyes.

Unless we are steeped in our faith, we will miss tremendous opportunities to show the relevance of Christ to a world that increasingly strays from any association with the things of God. Evangelists must ask themselves how to present Jesus Christ to those who have been "burned over" or disillusioned by their perception of Christianity. The entire postmodern world presents unique challenges for evangelism.

In short, the challenge of this book is to help you present the gospel, by word and deed, in a society that has changed the meaning of such concepts as values, truth, and character. This book can help you develop a healthier church (part 1), increase your skills in relating to your unchurched neighbor (part 2), anticipate the next window of spiritual openness that might emerge (part 3), gain new tools for communicating your faith (part 4), model the kind of worship that God deserves (part 5), develop the gifts and motivations that he has put into you (part 6), and position your worldly goods for maximum eternal impact (part 7).

Are You a Difference Maker?

In the coming year, do you envision yourself making more or less of a difference for Christ and his kingdom? What dreams does your congregation have for new ministry in the future? "A church without dreams is a dead church,"[3] Len Sweet often says.

May God use the information in this book to lead you into your most fruitful chapter of ministry ever for him. May he help you look forward to the future as a time of your greatest impact, even "immeasurably more than all we ask or imagine, according to his power that is at work within us" (Eph. 3:20).

Part 1

Churches Move toward Church Health and Quality

Get Help Becoming More Healthy

Christians are moving away from a numbers-driven church growth emphasis to focus on growing healthy churches.

Keep the Bible in One Hand and a Cup of Cold Water in the Other

A significant number of churches are becoming unapologetic about showing social concern without losing sight of the gospel.

one

Get Help Becoming More Healthy

Trend #1: Christians are moving away
from a numbers-driven church growth emphasis
to focus on growing healthy churches.

୶

Baseball's Mark McGwire made home-run history in 1998, but he wasn't born a natural hitter. McGwire's eyesight is 20/500. "Without his contacts he is Mr. Magoo," comments a *Sports Illustrated* article. "His glasses have lenses that could have been pilfered from the Hubble telescope."[1] McGwire's poor eyesight didn't stop him, though, from achieving a tremendous season.

Like McGwire for the St. Louis Cardinals, your church can have a championship season for Jesus, despite noticeable handicaps. Your congregation can reach its maximum potential and be everything God calls it to be.

In addition to overcoming his poor eyesight, McGwire used some questionable methods—such as taking drugs to enhance his performance. We must limit your church's journey toward maximum health to methods and strategies that are firmly based in God's Word, even if we, like McGwire, know we'll never bat 1.000.

Haddon Robinson, author of *Biblical Preaching: The Development and Delivery of Expository Messages,* has devoted his life to helping pastors

Core Values Keep Congregation from Becoming Distracted

Community Church of Joy

Denomination: Evangelical Lutheran Church in
                 America
Location: Glendale, Arizona (metro
                 Phoenix)
Senior pastor: Walt Kallestad (since 1979)
Recent goal: Expand the lay leadership
                 base; improve communication;
                 revisit core values.
Church vision: That all may know Jesus Christ
                 and become empowered
                 followers.
Year founded: 1974
Attendance: 3500 (current)
                 2700 (5 years ago)
                 2000 (10 years ago)
Internet address: www.joyonline.org and
                 www.joylead.org

Community Church of Joy is one of the most in-novative congregations in North America. "If we in the church have the most important, the most exciting, the most revolutionary news in all history, then why don't we find the most creative, in-novative, and irresistible ways to capture people's attention so they will line up to hear, see, and ex-perience it?" asks the senior pastor, Walt Kallestad, in his book *Entertainment Evangelism*.

Year after year, Kallestad has pressed the congre-gation to think like missionaries and act like mar-keters. He regularly asks his leadership team, "Are our people still inviting their friends who have no connection with a church, or is the 'holy huddle' dilemma creeping in?"

You would expect nothing but joy to have sur-faced in 1998 when this growing congregation moved to a two-hundred-acre ministry campus that will eventually include a teen town, chil-dren's center, senior resort, international leader-ship and prayer center, school and a community park. "In our relocation, we stirred up a hornet's nest," reports Kallestad. "We say we're an out-of-the-box mission center," he says, "but we had become too comfortable. Too many people got the crabbies over the changes they needed to make."

His solution was to return to the issue of core val-ues. At the one-year anniversary on the new cam-pus, he began a new message series. "I'm telling our people once again who we are, and what our mission is," he says. He finds that when change occurs, it's easy for everyone to become dis-tracted. "You have to constantly fight to keep your focus on the mission," he concludes.

*Walt Kallestad, *Entertainment Evangelism* (Nashville: Abingdon Press, 1996), 7.
An earlier version of this case study appeared in "Leadership on the Edge," catalogue 11, January 1999, and is used by permission from The Interna-tional Centre for Leadership Development and Evan-gelism, Winfield, BC, http://www.GrowingLeader-ship.com, 800-804-0777.

communicate better. He points out the obvious when he says, "If you want to learn to hit a baseball, it is better to study one .300 hitter than three .100 hitters."[2] Is your church hitting closer to .100 or to .300 in its effectiveness? This chapter is designed to help you identify values that contribute to the health of your congregation and to guide you in evaluating the steps you must take toward optimal church health in the context of tomorrow's world.

Focus on a Healthy Relationship with God

Steve Macchia, a pastor who now heads an organization called Vision New England (formerly the Evangelistic Association of New England), once flew to a town in Canada named St. John's. He had been invited to speak to a church group and had been given instructions to look for an eye-catching Howard Johnson's hotel sign in the baggage claim area. He had been told there would be a courtesy phone near the bright sign. From there, he was to call the hotel shuttle, get a good night's sleep, and then meet the group he was to address first thing in the morning.

A church must be God-centered to be healthy.

He looked in vain for a HoJo's sign. Finally, he asked for help, and an airline official politely informed him there was no Howard Johnson's in their town. Macchia waved his reservation sheet in her face and insisted that she was wrong.

As they studied the correspondence together, Macchia reached a startling conclusion. He was not only in the wrong airport, but in the wrong city. Even more significantly, he was in the wrong province of Canada. He had gone to St. John's, Newfoundland, and needed to be in St. John (no *s*), New Brunswick.

That experience became a picture of his life. He had been figuratively hopping on one wrong airplane after another, landing in one wrong town after another. "They were all good planes and good locations," he says, "but they were the wrong planes and destinations for me."[3] He was going everywhere and nowhere, lacking an awareness of what was really most important.

For the next several months he sought as never before to realign his life according to God's principles. Although he had been in pastoral ministry for more than a decade, he had not previously gone through such an intense self-evaluation. He emerged with a stronger sense of where he needed to place his energy and priority to really make a difference for Christ.

Spiritual Health Can't Happen without Being God-Centered

Steven Macchia's survey used a scale with rankings of 1 (lowest) to 9 (highest). Notice the common thread in the five top-ranking values:

8.84 *Reliance upon God's power and the authority of his Word*

8.78 *God's empowering presence*

8.71 *Pervasive prayerfulness*

8.43 *God-exalting worship*

8.31 *Spiritual disciplines*

8.21 Learning and growing in community

8.19 Commitment to loving and caring relationships

8.02 Development of servant-leadership

7.90 Outward focus

7.56 Wise administration and accountability

7.03 Networking within the body of Christ

6.94 Stewardship and accountability

From Stephen Macchia, *Becoming a Healthy Church* (Grand Rapids: Baker, 1999), 14–26.

This assessment led Macchia on a larger journey. Working for Vision New England, he spent years trying to profile a truly healthy church. He set out to identify principles and values that have application across New England, and presumably across the continent.

To do so he talked with scores of theologians, pastors, and longtime lay leaders, hoping to pinpoint the primary emphasis of a healthy church. Is it strong preaching? A great choir? Lots of wealthy executives in the pews? An effective Sunday school program? A thriving missions emphasis? Or something else—perhaps simply healthy leadership?

Macchia conducted an extensive study that included two major surveys. His overall findings were consistent across race, gender, denomination, and age groups: No single factor significantly outpaced others as the mark of a healthy church. The leading factors did, however, have a common denominator: A church must be God-centered to be healthy.

According to God's people across many denominations, the first mark of spiritual health is a congregation's reliance on God's power and the authority of his Word. Likewise, experiencing God's presence is of utmost importance.

A healthy church actively seeks the Holy Spirit's direction and empowerment for daily life and ministry. It gathers regularly as the local expression of the body of Christ to worship God in ways that engage the heart, mind, soul, and strength of the people. And it provides training, models, and resources for members of all ages to develop daily spiritual disciplines in their life in Christ.

Macchia finds great reassurance in these principles and values. "If a church is to be healthy and vital, it needs to be led by a pastor and leadership team who are themselves pursuing health in their personal lives and in their shared leadership capacity. Only then will a local church become the vibrant, healthy entity God intends," he says.[4] Henry Blackaby's *Experiencing God* echoes Macchia's call for a God-centered focus: Find and join what God is doing. Know him. Experience him. Find his agenda for your church and life, and get plugged into it.

Don't Assume Size Indicates Health

In perhaps the world's most comprehensive study of church health, German researchers Christian Schwarz and Christoph Schalk have processed more than 4 million survey responses from several thousand churches across more than fifty countries covering six continents. Like Steve Macchia, they found that not one but many essential qualities are required for a church to be healthy. Schwarz's *Natural Church Development* outlines the leadership, gift-oriented ministry, passionate spirituality, effective structures, inspiring worship services, holistic small groups, need-oriented evangelism, and loving relationships that characterize a church that is naturally healthy.[5]

What finding surprised these researchers the most? "On average, the smaller churches are the better churches," say Schwarz and Schalk. In terms of church health: "The larger, the worse."[6]

What do they mean by that statement? While there are many notable exceptions, the larger a church becomes, the less involved most of its laity are. People in bigger churches easily fall through the cracks if they are not involved in a small service team, fellowship group, or Sunday school class. In public ministry "professionalism" can replace passionate spirituality. Evangelism can also wane. Often as a church continues to grow, its newcomers tend to be transfer Christians rather than new converts unless the congregation's leadership continually challenges the church to remain outwardly focused.

Whatever its size or history, your congregation can become more healthy. You don't have to reach a certain size first.

How to Experience God

#1 God is always at work around you.

#2 God pursues a continuing love relationship with you that is real and personal.

#3 God invites you to become involved with him in his work.

#4 God speaks by the Holy Spirit through the Bible, prayer, circumstances and the church to reveal himself, his purpose, and his ways.

#5 God's invitation for you to work with him always leads you to a crisis of belief that requires faith and action.

#6 You must make major adjustments in your life to join God in what he is doing.

#7 You come to know God by experience as you obey him and he accomplishes his work through you.

From Henry Blackaby and Claude V. King, *Experiencing God: How to Live the Full Adventure of Knowing and Doing the Will of God* (Nashville: Broadman and Holman, 1994), 50.

Develop a Passion to Reach Lost People

Dale Galloway is perhaps best known for his role as founding pastor of New Hope Community Church in Portland, Oregon. For its first two decades, 80 percent of the new members identified themselves as previously unchurched. As a result, this innovative church experienced minimal sheep swapping and minimal reshuffling of saints from area churches to New Hope.

Galloway observes that underneath every breakthrough church is a strong priority on evangelism. He says, "Cutting-edge churches have different styles and looks, but their senior pastors all share one common characteristic: passion for reaching the lost. When I listen to them, I get big tears in my eyes for the lost. I like to hang around passionate people because it builds my excitement. The same thing happens for the people of those churches!"[7]

Evangelist Luis Palau takes the same perspective. "Jesus made His mission very plain: 'For the Son of Man came to seek and to save what was lost' (Luke 19:10). We know His final command to 'go and make disciples of all nations' (Matthew 28:19) as the Great Commission, not the great suggestion." Yet Palau believes Jesus' commission is "largely ignored" in churches today. "There are pockets of action, thank God, but evangelism isn't *a* priority, let alone *the* priority, for thousands of churches and Christians in America" (emphasis added).[8]

Their senior pastors all share one common characteristic: passion for reaching the lost.

Pollster George Barna confirms Palau's observation. His video "Ten Myths about Evangelism"[9] tallies the differences between what churches say and what we do. For example, a church may score 100 percent in verbally affirming that evangelism is essential. Yet when asked to list its top goals or to itemize its budget, its claims about evangelism often become noticeably hollow. Through ten different measuring points, Barna emphasizes that most congregations struggle with church health issues because they lack evangelistic vitality.

Barna further observes that during the opening years of this new century, if trends continue unchecked, some 250 million unchurched people will live in North America. "To complete such a task of sharing the gospel with those people is going to consume every ounce of energy and every resource we can muster."[10] According to evangelist Billy Graham, the mobilization of the whole church for evangelism—including both the clergy and the laity—is something Christians today must focus on more intently if churches are to be healthy. Graham summarizes: "It means we repent of our compromises and our failure to demonstrate the transforming power and love of Christ in our lives, and we learn afresh what it means to be salt and light in a decaying and dark world."[11]

Professor Michael Green has rightly said that "whenever Christianity has been at its most healthy, evangelism has stemmed from the local church and has had a noticeable impact on the surrounding area."[12]

Without new life, any church will eventually stagnate and die. A passion for evangelism contributes to church health.

Follow the Ministry Model of Jesus

As a youth pastor, Dann Spader spent almost a decade analyzing the Gospels to learn how Jesus developed his ministry. His study ended with the conclusion that "Christ gave us not only a message of reconciliation, but also the method."[13] Spader, along with Gary Mayes, mapped out four phases in Jesus' ministry that provide a guideline for ministry today:

1. Build—build an environment for growth.
2. Equip—train a team for ministry.
3. Win—mobilize for evangelism.
4. Multiply—multiply your leadership base.[14]

These four stages of spiritual growth lead to optimal health in a church. An awareness of these stages helps eliminate the mistake of forcing new Christians into service that overwhelms them or of leaving the mature Christian unchallenged. The focus is on life change at each point: "Doing everything possible to help every person possible pursue Christ more completely and consistently."[15] As Spader and Mayes point out, "Our culture measures success by educational degrees, statistical gains, big buildings, and hefty bank accounts. God measures success by changed lives and leaders who are producing them."[16] A healthy church, according to Spader and Mayes, is one characterized by Ephesians 4:13: "all reach unity in the faith and in the knowledge of the Son of God and become mature, attaining to the whole measure of the fullness of Christ." The best route to increased health, they believe, is for a church to saturate itself with Jesus' example of ministry training.

God measures success by changed lives and leaders who are producing them.

Identify Your Purpose

When he was in seminary, Rick Warren had no idea that God would use him to lead the fastest-growing Baptist church in the history of North America. He had enrolled in school because God had called him to serve as a pastor. While there, he sensed God directing him to discover "the principles—biblical, cultural, and leadership principles— that produce healthy, growing churches." He remarks, "It was the beginning of a lifelong study."[17] Upon graduation, Warren and his wife, Kay, moved to southern California where he planted and grew a church designed to reach unbelievers.

When congregations are healthy, they grow the way God intends.

When Saddleback Community Church surpassed ten thousand in attendance, with 80 percent of the growth consistently coming from unchurched newcomers, Warren compiled his knowledge in a book. Despite the publisher's modest expectations of 40,000 copies for the first year, the book climbed to the "top 20" list for religious books and remained there. It crossed the 100,000 bestseller status within months and sold almost 500,000 copies of the English edition by the end of 1999 and 500,000 more translated copies.

The emphasis of the book, evidenced by its title, demonstrates how every congregation is a *Purpose-Driven Church*. Clearly the idea of identifying one's purpose hit a felt need with pastors and lay leaders across the land.

Some churches are driven by the phrase, "We've always done it this way." Others follow a financial purpose, with the watchword being "How much will it cost?" or "How much will we save?" Others let their buildings drive them, in keeping with Winston Churchill's observation, "We shape our buildings, and then they shape us."

Instead, Rick Warren teaches that Christ has five purposes for his church. Drawing from Jesus' Great Commission (Matthew 28:18–20) and Great Commandment (Matthew 22:37–40), Saddleback organizes itself around these five purposes:

Membership: "Baptizing them" (incorporating into fellowship)
Maturity: "Teaching them to obey" (discipleship)
Ministry: "Love your neighbor as yourself" (service)
Mission: "Go and make disciples" (evangelism)
Magnification: "Love the Lord with all your heart" (worship)

Saddleback's purpose statement puts these all together: "to bring people to Jesus and *membership* in his family, to develop them to Christlike *maturity*, and to equip them for their *ministry* in the church and life *mission* in the world, in order to *magnify* God's name."[18]

How does a church identify its purpose? According to Warren, first study what the Bible says. Then seek to answer four questions: Why do we exist? What are we to be as a church? What are we to do as a church? and How are we to do it? Finally, put your findings in writing and summarize your conclusions in a single sentence.

This ongoing process will lead a congregation to greater health. As Warren says, "The key issue for churches in the twenty-first century will be church health, not church growth. . . . When congregations are healthy, they grow the way God intends."[19]

Saddleback's Summary of Christ's Five Purposes for the Church[20]

Purpose	Outreach	Worship	Fellowship	Discipleship	Service
Task	evangelize	exalt	encourage	edify	equip
Acts 2:42–47	"added . . . those being baptized"	"devoted themselves to . . . praising God"	"devoted to the fellowship"	"devoted . . . to the apostles' teaching"	"they gave to anyone as he had need"
Objective	mission	magnify	membership	maturity	ministry
Target	community	crowd	congregation	committed	core
Life Component	my witness	my worship	my relationships	my walk	my work
Basic Human Need	purpose to live for	power to live on	people to live with	principles to live by	profession to live out
The Church Provides	a focus for living	a force for living	a family for living	a foundation for living	a function for living
Emotional Benefit	significance	stimulation	support	stability	self-expression

▶ Determine to Remain Culturally Relevant

If you lined up a hundred people in front of a certain church building on Manhattan's Fifth Avenue and asked them why a cast-iron fence was built around the church, the majority might guess that it's to protect the building from vandals. Or they might suspect it's there to keep people from entering the building when it's not open or to match an architectural style. Most likely no one would guess the real reason. The fence was originally designed to keep cattle out of this New York City worship site.

The church in question, America's oldest Protestant church with a continuous ministry, was organized in 1628 under a charter from the King of England. At the time it was surrounded by a rural area where livestock grazed and farmers came to worship.

Marble Collegiate Church, as it is known today, hasn't had a cow near it for decades, perhaps centuries. Yet this gorgeous facility has kept its fence through several renovations. It meets the future well protected from any invading herd of cows that might amble across the industrial corridors of West Twenty-ninth Street at Fifth Avenue.

We don't include this story to poke fun of this congregation or any other church facility. In reality, every single congregation across North America faces the same dilemma: making sure its words and actions speak meaningfully to us today. As author and radio Bible teacher R. C. Sproul says, "The gospel is news to each generation, and we must seek new ways to address our times."[21] Rick Warren says it this way: "Jesus never lowered his standards, but he always started where people are."[22] He concludes, "The message must never change, but the methods *must* change with each new generation."[23]

Top Ten Insights about Culturally Relevant Ministry

#10 Cultural relevance is the rationale for why worship should be contemporary.

#9 All church ministries are contemporary to *some* generation, but most are contemporary to an era other than the 1990s.

#8 Cultural relevance is one way we extend incarnational, indigenous Christianity.

#7 Employing culturally relevant forms is desirable because God's revelation takes place through culture.

#6 When the gospel is expressed in a people's indigenous cultural forms, then and only then do most of them perceive that Christianity is for "people like us."

#5 Many churches have come a long way in agreeing that ministry in the people's language is necessary to reach them.

#4 However, many churches in whom the battle for language has been substantially won have not yet discovered that "culture is the silent language" (E. T. Hall).

#3 Furthermore, traditional churches do not yet perceive how deeply culture shapes personality and the way people view life and the world—that "culture is the software of the mind."*

#2 Consequently, the leaders and people of certain churches resist making the changes needed to become culturally relevant. Why? (a) Most people have not learned to distinguish between the gospel and the cultural forms in which they received it, and (b) they assume that to be faithful requires following the forms in which they received the gospel.

#1 Most culturally irrelevant churches cannot engage pre-Christian people meaningfully, nor do they plan to in significant numbers.**

*Geert Hofstede, *Culture and Organizations: Software of the Mind Intercooperational and Its Importance for Survival* (New York: McGraw-Hill, 1997), 4.

**George Hunter, "The Culturally Relevant Congregation," November 1996. Audiocassette of a presentation to the American Society of Church Growth.

✎ Murren on Healthy Churches

We got a lot of national publicity for launching a Seattle congregation that by 1996 grew to four thousand in weekend attendance. During my fifteen years there, the church's ministries registered more than seventeen thousand decisions for Christ.

Our hearts were in the right place, but I don't think I always modeled church health as described in this chapter while I was at Eastside Foursquare Church.

As I look back, I believe I paid a tremendous toll for working too long in my secondary giftings. I knew all along I was more an artist than a CEO type, but it took me a long time to understand how I could work more out of my main strengths.

If I had it to do all over again, I would strive for the congregation to be 80 percent more lay driven. I was too staff-focused.

Perhaps my deepest regret surrounds something I saw but didn't seriously act upon for almost a decade—the power of small group community for evangelism, discipleship, and leadership development.

Maybe I'd even try not to grow as fast as we did, if it causes us to burn out too many people. If ministry sacrifices the health of good people, it's not worth doing.

I left Eastside to start churches and do evangelism. The aim of my new outreach ministry, called "Square One Live," is to reach one million boomers and busters by 2013, and to train ten thousand churches in how to do effective outreach.

As I help these younger and newer pastors, I want them to be healthier than I was, shining brightest for Jesus by maximizing who they are in him.

Doug Murren
director, Hope Community Church Network, Seattle, Washington
author, *Churches That Heal* (Howard Publishing, 1999)

George Hunter, a theologian at Asbury Theological Seminary who authored several chapters in a book entitled *Making Church Relevant*, looks for one overriding motivation in a church. If a church is to remain healthy, this motivation must be there, he asserts. At issue is the level of a church's love and concern for people who are different, both because they don't know Christ and because they dress, talk, or behave in ways that make church people uncomfortable. Such people are often "searching in all the wrong places for something upon which to base their lives," according to Hunter.[24]

"The ultimate test facing the twenty-first century church will be whether we really believe the 'new barbarians' matter to God," Hunter says. "If we lift up our eyes, see the harvest, and enter it in appropriate terms, Christianity in the twenty-first century has a magnificent future. But if we continue looking only for people who are like the people we already have, we probably do not have much of a future. We probably do not deserve one."

? APPLICATION QUESTIONS
FOR INDIVIDUAL RESPONSE OR GROUP DISCUSSION

1. The chapter opened by stating that "Christians today put more priority on becoming a healthy church than in achieving numerical growth." Is this a step forward or backward? Why?
2. What are the healthiest qualities about the church you serve? What could you do to help lead your congregation (or one of its ministries) to greater health?
3. Just how different is the "old" emphasis on church growth and numbers from the "new" emphasis on church health that leads to growth?

PASTORS 4. Many of the books cited in this chapter contain or offer a "health-assessment" tool. For example, *Natural Church Development* supports an easily conducted congregational survey designed to rank different areas of church health. Track down one of these tools (see www.GrowingLeadership .com), present it to your membership or board, and then use the results to identify next steps needed in your journey toward congregational health.

two

Keep the Bible in One Hand and a Cup of Cold Water in the Other

Trend #2: A significant number of churches are becoming unapologetic about showing social concern without losing sight of the gospel.

✑

Despite what secular elites may say, Christianity has been and still is the most powerful force for good in Western culture.

A few years ago, a major Gallup study called "The Saints Among Us" found that people deeply and personally committed to the Christian faith are, in Gallup's words, "a breed apart." Statistics show they are happier, more charitable, more ethical, more likely to help the needy, and even more tolerant.[1]

What critics often fail to see is that churches, for all their faults, real and imagined, have been a highly positive force in Western society. Jesus' command to love our neighbor has inspired a steady outpouring of social and philanthropic work. In fact, historian William G. McLoughlin goes so far as to say that the great spiritual awakenings

The fact remains, however, that the record of Christian charity is so impressive that even John Dewey, a founder of modern humanism, praised believers for their social conscience. Criminologists today, such as political scientist John Dilulio, have studied data on urban crime and concluded that the best hope for urban youth is found in gospel-centered churches and faith-based ministries.[5]

Across the world, Christians continue to provide what Jesus called "a cup of cold water" (Matt. 10:42) to those in greatest need, both within the church and without. Habitat for Humanity International has built homes together with some 80,000 families in need in more than 1,500 U.S. cities and sixty other countries. This they have done "because of Jesus," says Habitat's founder, Millard Fuller. "We are putting God's love into action."[6] Through Slobodan Milosevic's 1999 reign of terror, Christians provided food, supplies, or sponsorship to tens of thousands of Muslim Albanians. In response to recent U.S. tragedies, from airplane crashes to high school shootings, churches have played a significant role in providing emotional and physical support, as well as spiritual counsel, to victims and their families.

In short, from the time of Christ to the present, many segments of orthodox Christianity have served human need as an outgrowth of their love for God and their understanding of the gospel. In the process, questions often arise about the definition and boundaries of the Christian faith.

Consider Concerns about a Watered-Down Gospel

Many readers are encouraged as they are reminded of this whole-person application of the gospel across the centuries. "Who would object to Christians being known as people who put feet to their faith?" they might ask.

The two-pronged emphasis of the gospel in both word and deed, however, has not been without its problems. In some cases, "too much talk and not enough action" has become too much social gospel and not enough evangelistic gospel. Others complain, "Great deeds of love, but you've lost the message behind it." They see churches that have done too much humanitarian work and too little work to get people in right relationship with God. Some, for example, criticize the YMCA, originally a great soul-winning agency, that has almost entirely lost its emphasis on evangelism.

The two-pronged emphasis also raises issues about Christianity in relation to culture. "Too much world in the church," say some. "Not enough church out in the world," say others. As Richard Niebuhr's book *Christ and Culture* asked in the aftermath of the front-page fundamentalist–modernist disputes of the early 1900s, is Christ "of" culture, "above" culture, the "transformer" of culture, "against" culture, or "in paradox" with culture?[7]

Such concern is not just theory. Exactly one hundred years ago, a debate raged across North America and Europe. A movement known as theological liberalism emphasized that the church should have a strong social influence. At the same time it rejected the idea that people go to heaven or hell when they die based on how they have responded to the message of Jesus Christ. This movement also threw out the idea of supernatural miracles such as Jesus' virgin birth or bodily resurrection from the dead. It also denied that God had supernaturally inspired the writers of the Bible.

> **Os Guinness on Four Steps Toward Compromising Your Faith**
>
> 1. Assumption: entertaining or acknowledging an idea as having merit or truth.
> 2. Abandonment: giving up anything that proves to be incompatible with the new assumption or practice.
> 3. Adaptation: altering your faith to fit in with the new assumption or practice.
> 4. Assimilation: absorbing truths of faith into the new assumption.
>
> From Os Guinness, *Dining with the Devil: The Megachurch Movement Flirts with Modernity* (Grand Rapids: Baker, 1993), 56–57.

Perhaps the most important and influential theologian at the start of the twentieth century was Adolph von Harnack (1851–1930). His best-selling book, *What Is Christianity?*, was highly controversial because of how it redefined the gospel. Theologian Walter Rauschenbusch (1861–1918) released *A Theology of the Social Gospel* in 1917. He believed that when Jesus spoke about the kingdom of God this meant not the community of the redeemed, but the transformation of society on earth. To him, the gospel meant social reform and political action.

Unfortunately, a polarization occurred during the next several decades. Theological liberals emphasized right actions, while fundamentalists emphasized right beliefs. The regrettable public stereotype (which wasn't entirely true) showed historic Christianity as suspicious of anyone who promoted the doing of the gospel over the preaching of the gospel. Mid-century the tide began to turn toward a biblical balance with the publication of Carl F. H. Henry's *The Uneasy Conscience of Modern Fundamentalism*, but some fear any sense of social gospel to this day.[8]

An example of the "slippery slope" concern today surfaces in those who point out the shortcomings of the church growth movement. "Christians are free to plunder the Egyptians, but forbidden to set up a golden

Checklist of Concerns, Based on Questions about the Church Growth Movement

1. Are we teaching a practical atheism? (compromised theology)
   We are if we make little reference to God and show little dependence on the Holy Spirit.
2. Are we more controlled by methodology than by theology? (unbiblical principles)
   We are if our theological understanding is superficial and our primary interest is in methodology.
3. Are we ignoring the warnings of history? (naive view of culture)
   We are if we display a minimal sense of historical awareness from similar situations in the past.
4. Are we overly concerned with numbers and bigness? (inappropriate methods)
   We are if our goal is anything less than fully committed followers of Jesus Christ growing toward maturity in the community of a local church.
5. Are we allowing carnal motives to corrupt our testimony for Christ and his kingdom? (unholy view of human nature)
   We are if we fail to say no to ever-present temptations of pride, arrogance, envy, and deceit in our dreams to build great churches for God's glory.

calf," affirms Os Guinness in *Dining with the Devil: The Megachurch Movement Flirts with Modernity*. "Could it be that the church-growth movement in its present expansionist phase is also a movement waiting to be undeceived?" he asks.[9] He is not alone (see the sidebar on this page).

"The gospel of Jesus Christ . . . is being supplanted by a new 'gospel of consumer orientation,'" concludes a book entitled *Selling Out the Church: The Dangers of Church Marketing*.[10] "Judas was only the first person to sell Jesus out," claims a hard-hitting book entitled *Selling Jesus: What's Wrong with Marketing the Church*.[11]

H. B. London and Neil Wiseman warn:

You can build a big-attendance church without much help from God . . . Almost anyone, from a human point of view, can do the right things and people will be attracted to a church. . . . If you succeed in your own strength, however, your church will be a shallow, misguided, self-indulgent, muddled crowd that only faintly resembles God's dream for His church or for your ministry.[12]

"'Packaging' the gospel so that unbelievers can understand it may lead to compromising the message," says Paul Basden about current worship practices. "The overt use of entertainment features in order to attract non-Christians may result in the commercialization of the church, the marketing of the gospel, the watering-down of Christian worship, and the manipulation of evangelism."[13]

The core concern of writers such as these is that they don't want the gospel to be watered down or redefined. They know what has happened in previous generations. Each of these writers affirms the importance of evangelism and discipleship. But each perceives some churches today are yielding to less-than-pure motives or less-than-healthy methodologies in order to reach these goals. Os Guinness aptly adapts a quote from sociologist Peter Berger: "They who sup with the devil of modernity had better have long spoons."[14]

These writers remind us not to get off track in what the gospel is all about as we carry the Bible in one hand and a cup of cold water in the other.

Know the Boundaries of Your Faith

In bringing the "two-prong" issue to the trends of today, the question of boundaries is being applied to many different arenas:

- How far into the study of secular leadership can the church go to determine biblical church leadership? (the John Maxwell leadership question)
- How far into secular marketing studies can the church go to determine methods of communicating the church message? (the George Barna marketing question)
- How far can the church go in stretching its Sunday gathering to accommodate an unsaved clientele? (the Bill Hybels seeker question)
- How far can the church go in heeding intuitive authority apart from biblical revelation? (the C. Peter Wagner "new apostolic" question)
- How far can the church go in encouraging certain unusual emotions as a form of worship and ministry? (the Toronto Airport and Pensacola Revival question)
- How far can the church go in accepting critical theories of history to reinterpret the biblical record? (the liberal–conservative question)

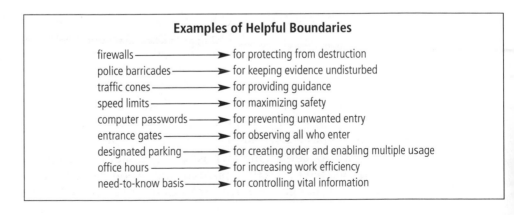

Examples of Helpful Boundaries

firewalls	→ for protecting from destruction
police barricades	→ for keeping evidence undisturbed
traffic cones	→ for providing guidance
speed limits	→ for maximizing safety
computer passwords	→ for preventing unwanted entry
entrance gates	→ for observing all who enter
designated parking	→ for creating order and enabling multiple usage
office hours	→ for increasing work efficiency
need-to-know basis	→ for controlling vital information

Such questions are not unique to our era. In the nineteenth century, for example, John Wesley was ridiculed for his new "methods" and was sarcastically labeled a "Methodist." Jonathan Edwards struggled with emotional expressions of revivalism in the First Great Awakening, and Charles Finney was criticized for embracing "the right use of appropriate means" in the Second Great Awakening.

The Nature of Christianity Demands Limits

Elmer Towns addressed boundary issues at a late-1998 gathering of the American Society for Church Growth.[15] He pointed out that the dictionary defines a boundary as "something that indicates or fixes a limit." In other words, it is a separating line, such as the points of differences between Christianity and non-Christianity.

The dictionary defines a boundary as "something that indicates or fixes a limit."

"The nature of Christianity would demand limits," he concluded. For example, somewhere in the journey from Christianity (1 Tim. 3:16) to heresy (1 Tim. 1:19–20) there is a point of no return, a boundary. Somewhere in a journey from holiness (1 Peter 1:16) to ungodliness (2 Peter 2:21–22) there is a line beyond which God would not have us step. Somewhere between biblical principles of church growth (Matt. 28:19–20) and human efforts (Matt. 7:26–27) there are methods that should not be used. There is also a dividing line between an authentic church (Matt. 16:18) and a group that uses the title "church" but has lost the essential properties of a church (Rev. 2:12–29). There is a boundary between the true manifestation of the Holy Spirit (Acts 2:1–4) and a false desire for spiritual things (Acts 8:19–23) or a false attempt to manipulate the Holy Spirit (Acts 19:13–16).

The study of boundaries is not a new challenge. Nor is it an unusual reaction whenever the gospel becomes dressed in a new set of clothes. Boundary questions arose even during the age when the Scriptures were being penned:

John commanded, "Dear friends, do not believe every spirit, but test the spirits to see whether they are from God, because many false prophets have gone out into the world" (1 John 4:1).

Jude observed, "For certain men whose condemnation was written about long ago have secretly slipped in among you. They are godless men, who change the grace of our God into a license for immorality and deny Jesus Christ our only Sovereign and Lord" (Jude 1:4).

Peter warned: "But there were also false prophets among the people, just as there will be false teachers among you. They will secretly introduce destructive heresies, even denying the sovereign Lord who bought them—bringing swift destruction on themselves. Many will follow their shameful ways and will bring the way of truth into disrepute" (2 Peter 2:1–2).

And Paul affirmed: "The Spirit clearly says that in later times some will abandon the faith and follow deceiving spirits and things taught by demons" (1 Tim. 4:1).

The Jesus Boundary

Christianity centers on the Lord Jesus Christ, including the belief that those who come to God must do so through the Son (John 14:6). Jesus is the revelation to the world of God the Father. To become a Christian we must receive him (John 1:12) and those who teach Christianity must preach him (Acts 4:12). Essential Christianity recognizes the biblical person of the Lord Jesus Christ as the core for its belief and practice.

Ministry crosses the Jesus boundary when what is said about Jesus is inconsistent with what Scripture says about his person and work.

What happens when someone teaches about Jesus from the Koran or the Book of Mormon? Or what about an off-Broadway play that casts Jesus as a homosexual? Has a boundary been crossed by Hollywood movies that present a Jesus who is mistaken about his mission or sinful in his lifestyle? Is there enough gospel in these sources to save any who believe?

Some argue that these are instances like those the apostle Paul describes in Philippians 1:15, 17–18:

> It is true that some preach Christ out of envy and rivalry, but others out of goodwill. . . . The former preach Christ out of selfish ambition, not sincerely, supposing that they can stir up trouble for me while I am in chains. But what does it matter? The important thing is that in every way, whether from false motives or true, Christ is preached. And because of this I rejoice.

But this isn't the case if the barrier has been broken. Ministry crosses the Jesus boundary when what is said about Jesus is inconsistent with what Scripture says about his person and work. Boundary-defining descriptions of Jesus may be found in such passages as Luke 22:67–71,

John 1:1–12, Acts 4:12, Galatians 5:19–26, Philippians 2:5–11, 1 John 2:18–23, and in such early summaries of Scripture as the *Apostles' Creed:*

> I believe in God the Father Almighty, maker of heaven and earth: and in Jesus Christ His only Son, our Lord; who was conceived by the Holy Spirit, born of the Virgin Mary, suffered under Pontius Pilate, was crucified, dead, and buried; He descended into Hades; the third day He rose again from the dead; He ascended into heaven, and sitteth on the right hand of God, the Father Almighty; from thence He shall come to judge the quick and the dead.

The Gospel Boundary

Essential Christianity recognizes that salvation comes through the person of Jesus as accomplished in his death, burial, and resurrection.

The essence of Christianity is the gospel message—the good news of how to come into right relationship with God through Jesus Christ. This message is objectively written as events to be understood and believed, as Paul affirmed in 1 Corinthians 15:3–4: "that Christ died for our sins according to the Scriptures, that he was buried, that he was raised on the third day according to the Scriptures."

But the gospel is more than truth stated as fact. It is also a relationship with a person—the Lord Jesus Christ. In this sense, the gospel is also to be experienced, as Paul continues: "and that he appeared to Peter, and then to the Twelve . . . to more than five hundred . . . to James, then to all the apostles, and last of all he appeared to me" (1 Cor. 15:5–8).

The gospel boundary is crossed in ministry when anything other than belief in the death, burial, and resurrection of Jesus is added as a condition for salvation or when an alternate understanding of salvation is offered.

The gospel message begins with the death, burial, and resurrection of the Lord Jesus Christ. Those who deny the reality of these truths deny the essence of Christianity.

Yet mere mental agreement to a propositional statement is not enough for a person to experience God's salvation. An individual's Christian conversion involves more than giving mental assent to the facts of the death, burial, and resurrection of Jesus. The gospel enters our lives when Jesus Christ enters our hearts: "But as many as received Him [Christ], to them He gave the right to become children of God, *even* to those who believe in His name" (John 1:12 NKJV).

How much about Jesus must a person know and accept to become a child of God? His sinless life? His miracles? His deity? His humanity? His death as a substitution for me? Besides being complete, how accurate must the presentation be?

And when is the gospel *not* the gospel of Jesus Christ, but instead the "other gospel" Paul describes in Galatians? How much correct doctrinal implication must be poured into the message of the gospel? Some think Jesus died as our substitute, others as our example, and others as simply a mystical idea with no basis in history.

These questions about the gospel message are really questions about boundaries. At what point does the gospel of Scripture no longer remain the gospel? When have we not preached Christ? Before drawing a boundary, though, think about a brief Bible story from Luke 9. There Jesus demonstrates that it's not our perception but his that matters:

> "Master . . . we saw a man driving out demons in your name and we tried to stop him, because he is not one of us."
> "Do not stop him," Jesus said, "for whoever is not against you is for you."
>
> verses 49–50

The gospel boundary is crossed in ministry when anything other than belief in the death, burial, and resurrection of Jesus is added as a condition for salvation or when an alternate understanding of salvation is offered, such as a denial of the substitutionary nature of Jesus' death.

The Core-Teachings Barrier

Certain vital truths form the core teaching for those who follow Christ. Like equipment essential to the operation of an automobile, these truths in our doctrinal core are essential to Christianity. A car cannot be operated without tires, steering wheel, fuel pump, or carburetor. Without these, the car is inoperative. Likewise, without certain essential truths, Christianity is inoperative.

The core teachings boundary is crossed in ministry when the essential beliefs of Christianity are not presented, are denied, or are met with an opposing belief.

So which core doctrines are essential to Christianity? What about those who say that Shirley MacLaine's writings are just as much God's Word as is the Bible? What are the implications for those who say the Holy Spirit is unnecessary? What about the idea that Jesus is only *a* god—and that you and I can also become a god? Or that Jesus sinned? Or that angels have more power than Jesus? Each century of church history has been filled with debates over Christian teaching. At the beginning of the twentieth century the following core teachings were regarded as essential:

- the authority, inspiration, and inerrancy of Scripture as the revelation of God's person and plan
- the deity of Jesus Christ as God who became fully man, and man who is fully God, as reflected in the virgin birth
- Jesus' shedding of blood on the cross as a substitutionary atonement for sins
- the physical resurrection of Jesus Christ from death to give us new life
- the bodily return of Jesus Christ to take his children to live with him and to judge those who have rejected his loving offer of salvation

Essential Christianity recognizes the authority of Scriptures, the deity of Jesus, the substitutionary death of Jesus for the forgiveness of sins, Jesus' physical resurrection to give new life, and Jesus' bodily return for the consummation of his program on earth. The core teachings boundary, therefore, is crossed in ministry when the essential beliefs of Christianity are not presented, are denied, or are met with an opposing belief.

The Christian Experience Boundary

Essential Christianity recognizes that the experience of saving faith will produce forgiveness, cleansing from guilt, and assurance of one's relationship with God. The experience of continued faith will, through the indwelling Christ, produce the positive fruit of the Spirit and a desire to serve.

The Christian experience boundary is crossed in ministry when the empirical results that should follow salvation are denied, or when the opposite is taught by those offering salvation.

The child of God has unique spiritual experiences that are not shared with other religions or with the various cults that departed from historic Christianity. The Christian walk begins when men, women, and children believe the gospel (propositional truth) and receive Jesus (relationship truth). Those acts of faith result in an ongoing exchanged life "in Christ" (Gal. 2:20). Individuals experience God's love, God's grace, and God's peace. They give evidence of the fruit of the Spirit (Gal. 5:22–23), and they receive confidence in their relationship to God (1 John 5:11–13).

There are many ways to test the boundaries of Christian experience. When a person claims to be a Christian but cannot identify any manifestations of the fruit of the Holy Spirit or other signs of being "transformed" (Rom. 12:1–2), that person's experience should be questioned. The same lens can be applied to question the validity of an entire ministry. When ministry makes claims that produce the opposite of Christian experience, or when it denies the essential nature of biblical experience, the credibility of that ministry can be questioned.

The Christian experience boundary is crossed in ministry when the empirical results that should follow salvation are denied, or when the opposite is taught by those offering salvation.

The "Blessability" Boundary

God's blessing is evident in his power to transform, motivate, deliver, and give abundant life to his followers. "Blessability" is what happens when God's presence is evident through a ministry that unquestionably serves the Lord by exercising hope in God, faith in his ability to do what he promised, and loving compassion toward those to whom ministry is given.

The blessing of God is similar in definition to an atmosphere of worship or revival, such as when God fulfills the promise, "I will pour out my Spirit" (Joel 2:29). Revival is also described as "times of refreshing [that] come from the presence of the Lord" (Acts 3:19 NASB).

The blessability boundary is crossed in ministry when the presence of God as reflected in Scriptures is denied, or when the opposite is taught by those claiming God's presence.

The blessing of God is not necessarily represented by bigger crowds, large responses at the altar, spectacular healings, or growth in membership, offerings, and baptisms. The blessing of God is an intangible experience of God working in the hearts of listeners as the gospel is at work. It is experiential Christianity that is based on the objective truth of Jesus, the gospel, essential doctrine, and Christian experiences.

Many problems may be associated with using the blessability of God as a criteria for the boundary of Christianity. First, Scripture contains illustrations of ungodly people that God used to his glory (e.g., Pharaoh [Rom. 9:17] and Cyrus [Isa. 45:1]). Second, God may sometimes use unsaved persons to communicate truth about Jesus. He may even use a person who is anti-God, such as Nebuchadnezzar, to accomplish his purpose. Being used by God, therefore, does not guarantee that someone has the blessing of God.

When God blesses a person, we must ask what he is blessing. Is God blessing the person's Bible message or spiritual gifts, prayer ministry or preparation, or his or her spirituality?

Because our emotions and feelings are both fleeting and misleading, John tells us to "test the spirits" (1 John 4:1). We can deceive ourselves and deceive others. We must test our feelings—and the blessing of God—by objective truth (1 John 4:2–3). Paul tells us to get the big picture, "Test all things; hold fast what is good" (1 Thess. 5:21 NKJV).

The blessability boundary is crossed in ministry when the presence of God as reflected in Scriptures is denied, or when the opposite is taught by those claiming God's presence.

Marking Boundaries

"In essentials, unity. In non-essentials, tolerance. In all things, love." We have many earnest Christian friends who disagree in nonessentials with us, who have different standards from us for Christian living and practices of holiness. Most Christians do.

But what happens when we fear that someone we're working with has crossed the line? On three different occasions, Elmer Towns has been asked to speak to a group on the other side of Christian boundaries. On all three occasions he has done the following: politely pointed out the difference; asked, "Do you think I am going to heaven?"; and commented, "I wouldn't want to help a group build churches if they thought I wasn't going to heaven." On all three occasions, the invitation was rescinded.

Situations such as these aren't occasions for pride. Our ongoing hope and prayer is that each group who claims the name of Christ could believe the same simple message: "For it is by grace you have been saved, through faith—and this not from yourselves, it is the gift of God—not by works, so that no one can boast" (Eph. 2:8–9).

Become Known for Your Good Works

"What is a real Christian like?" many ask. The answer to this question, even from those only casually familiar with the Christian faith, usually boils down to one basic concept: someone who lives like Jesus.

In most people's thinking, if I'm a follower of Jesus Christ, then I help people in need, I'm honest even when no one's looking, I care deeply about the concerns that matter most to God, and I've left all of my selfish attachments to follow Jesus. Indeed, a study of Jesus' teachings will produce many of these same conclusions. A quick tally of Jesus' many "follow me" commands (e.g., Luke 9:23–24) does the same. We are not saved by good works, but the Mother Teresas of this world do fulfill Jesus' mandate more than most: "In the same way, let your light shine before men, that they may see your good deeds and praise your Father in heaven" (Matt. 5:16).

In a world that loves to spot hypocrisy in everyone from television evangelists to church-going soccer moms, deeds of compassion make a loud statement about the love and power of God. Find encouragement in the following example:

In a world that loves to spot hypocrisy in everyone from television evangelists to church-going soccer moms, deeds of compassion make a loud statement about the love and power of God.

Donna, a widow at New Hope Community Church in Portland, Oregon, had raised her son by herself. She belonged to one of the ladies' small groups at the church. In 1987, one of the members of that group noted, "Donna, you look yellow. Have you been to a doctor?" Donna replied that she couldn't afford insurance to do so.

What does a loving church family do in an instance like this? Donna's group took up an offering, gave her the money, and instructed her to go to the doctor.

A medical examination found a serious problem with Donna's liver. Without a liver transplant in the next six weeks, physicians said, she would die.

Doctors told Donna that specialists at Baylor University, Waco, Texas, could do the operation for $140,000. The situation looked impossible.

Soon the women in Donna's small group made an appointment with the church's pastor, Dale Galloway, to ask if the church could do something for Donna. Galloway was troubled. The church was just finishing up a building campaign, and was still $400,000 from meeting the budget. Galloway was convinced everyone was financially tapped out and feared he would be pegged as the pastor who over-saddled the church with discouraging debt.

With that in mind, he had determined not to get involved in Donna's financial crises. But as he prayed, the Holy Spirit prompted his inner conscience: "Help her." Galloway listened, and immediately decided to call the initiative, "Save My Mom." Lay leader Tom Peterson, whose business was widely known across the city, agreed to be honorary chair. Another friend agreed to give six weeks of his life to organize people.

Galloway laid the need before the people, and in response, they gave $60,000 in cash. Galloway hadn't imagined they would have that kind of money!

The day after the offering was received, Galloway was invited to testify with Donna before the Oregon legislature. The legislature was dealing with the issue of people who couldn't afford insurance. The largest newspaper in the state took a photo, put it on the front page, and labeled it "Save My Mom."

People started bringing jars of money from bars. Little kids brought allowances. Local TV stations joined the publicity, and together they raised $220,000 in seven days.

Donna, check in hand, went to Baylor. There she was cared for by a small group that God had already prepared for her. The church put the excess money in a trust fund that generates funds for her medications. Now, more than a decade later, you'll find Donna singing in the New Hope choir on Sundays.

For years, when people looked to the large cross atop a building on the hill, they'd say, "You're the church who cares about the widow." They don't comment on the lovely new facility, they didn't care how the leadership sweated over building payments, and they'll never know how the people sacrificed and stretched. But the Holy Spirit used the church's relationship with Donna to multiply the ministry to lots of people who were needy for Christ. What a joy to love people in Jesus' name!

No one could ever buy that kind of publicity. Something greater than any human plan was at work. "Greater is he that is in you, than he that is in the world," says 1 John 4:4 (KJV). That same Holy Spirit can take your church to new pinnacles of health.

? APPLICATION QUESTIONS
FOR INDIVIDUAL RESPONSE OR GROUP DISCUSSION

1. Which portions of this chapter do you feel were so obvious that they perhaps did not need to be written? Why? Which portions are you glad you read?
2. In what ways has your church balanced the Bible in one hand with a "cup of cold water" in the other? What could you do to help your church become even more balanced in these areas?
3. What story from God's work through your church is closest to Dale Galloway's "Donna" story at the end of this chapter? What has the impact been on the unchurched of your community?

Arn on Social Concern

I'm writing this response from Ohio, where I have just been the guest of Grove City Church of the Nazarene, just outside Columbus. This congregation is doing a fantastic job of identifying and meeting human needs. Its people run many programs and activities that make the community a better place.

I'm also impressed with Grove City Church's commitment to evangelism. These days, effective evangelism begins with addressing and meeting the needs of people.

This effective evangelistic church represents a definite trend that this chapter identifies: growing churches—particularly those who are emphasizing conversion growth—are focusing on finding needs and filling them.

The congregation's social concern, an outgrowth of how "God has poured out his love into our hearts by the Holy Spirit" (Rom. 5:5, see also 1 Cor. 9:19–22, James 1:27, and Matt. 5:16) is a means to an end. The end is making disciples and responsible church members.

This healthy approach is in contrast to an older paradigm, where churches saw social concern as an end in itself. I have not seen this kind of good-works-without-evangelistic-concern produce growth. Social concern alone certainly has no correlation to evangelism or church growth.

W. Charles Arn
president, Church Growth Inc., Monrovia, California
author, *The Master's Plan for Making Disciples* (Baker, revised 1998)

PASTORS   4. Think through your teaching or preaching themes from the last year. If you've not preached on social compassion, pray about developing such an emphasis, using such passages as Proverbs 19:17 ("He who is kind to the poor lends to the Lord"), Matthew 25:31–46 ("I needed clothes . . . I was in prison"), or James 1:27 ("to look after orphans and widows in their distress").

Part 2

Churches Move toward Relational Communication

Enter the World of *Cheers*, *Friends*, and *Seinfeld*

People today typically learn best and are reached best through multisensory and relational frameworks.

Learn the Language That Connects with Postmoderns

People today show interest in the truth of the gospel only after they've seen the relevance of the church and the credibility of Christians.

three

Enter the World of *Cheers, Friends,* and *Seinfeld*

*Trend #3: People today typically learn best
and are reached best through multisensory
and relational frameworks.*

☙

Prison Fellowship's Chuck Colson will long remember having dinner with a certain media personality and trying to talk with him about faith in Jesus Christ. "I don't believe in God," the man told him straight out. "But tell me why you believe." So Colson started in—not realizing he was about to learn a hard lesson in what evangelism means for a new millennium.

As Colson began his testimony, his friend cut him off. "I've heard all that before," he said, and went on to tell him about someone he knew whose life had been turned around by New Age spirituality.

"Crystals, channeling—it worked for her," the friend said. "Just like your Jesus."

Colson tried to explain the difference but got nowhere with his argument that Jesus is a historical person. His friend shrugged it off. "My friend's guru is a real person, too," he said.

Colson then argued for the historical validity of the Bible, but his friend did not believe in heaven or hell, did not believe in the Bible or any other spiritual authority, and was not particularly bothered by the prospect of dying.

Servant Evangelism Shows God's Love with No Strings Attached

Vineyard Community Church

Denomination:	Vineyard
Location:	Cincinnati, Ohio
Senior pastor:	Steve Sjogren (since 1983)
Recent goal:	To keep focusing on meeting people's needs as we transition from our 576-seat auditorium to a new 2,500-seat facility.
Church vision:	To create a contemporary church environment that models what Jesus lived and taught.
Year founded:	1985
Attendance:	5500 (now)
	3000 (5 years ago)
	500 (10 years ago)
Internet address:	www.cincyvineyard.com

"Could we clean your toilets as a practical way of showing you God's love?" When Steve Sjogren voices this request at a gas station or convenience store, two responses are common. Sometimes the clerk is confused and asks, "Say that again?" Other vendors drop their jaw and tilt their head. "Why would you do something for free?" they ask.

Sjogren's spiritual gifts include both serving and evangelism. "We desire to show God's love in practical ways to people all over the city," he explains. "We do this by handing out free items like sodas, candy, and stamps, and by doing simple acts of service like packing grocery bags and cleaning restrooms absolutely free because God's love is free."

This relational approach to evangelism has caused Vineyard Community Church, where Sjogren is pastor, to have meaningful contact with thousands of pre-Christians each year throughout greater Cincinnati. Whether through free car washes or free gift wrapping at the mall, each servant-evangelism team from the church inevitably has opportunity to build a relationship and strike up a personal conversation. "My hope is that with each pre-Christian we touch, God is using us to nudge someone forward toward Christ," says Sjogren.

The Cincinnati community has responded very positively to this outward-focused congregation. "Our first job is to be enthusiastic seed sowers," says Sjogren. "God created the human heart to thrive on love, acceptance, and unconditional forgiveness. We want to convey that kind of atmosphere to show love, with no strings attached, that's real."

With so many pre-Christians being nudged toward Christ, the visitor-friendly, outward-focused worship services receive a steady stream of first-time guests. A high percentage of the congregation are adult converts to Christianity.

"God is strongly at work," says Sjogren. "We believe 'small things done with great love will change the world'®," so we make a habit of performing everyday services for people throughout our city."

Finally, as Colson fumbled with his fork, an idea popped into his mind. "Have you seen Woody Allen's movie, *Crimes and Misdemeanors*?" he asked.

The friend became thoughtful. Yes, he'd loved it, in fact. The movie introduces a successful doctor who is haunted by guilt after hiring a killer to murder his mistress. His Jewish father had taught him that an all-seeing God always brings justice to bear. In the end the doctor suppresses his guilt, convincing himself that life is nothing more than the survival of the fittest.

The Christian's task, with the apostle Paul of old, is to utilize contemporary culture as a tool to meaningfully introduce the message of salvation.

Colson asked his friend, "Is that our only choice—to be tormented by guilt or else to kill our conscience?"

Colson followed that question with examples from Tolstoy and C. S. Lewis regarding the reality of moral law. His friend was listening intently.

Finally Colson cited the Book of Romans, which teaches that, try as we may, we cannot run from the voice of conscience. His friend wasn't ready to make a decision, but he did listen carefully to the message of what Jesus Christ did on the cross to reconcile God and humanity.

Although the friend did not become a Christian, Colson was pleased he had finally found a common frame of reference to replace old evangelistic approaches.

Colson's conclusion?

> We can take a lesson from the early church, which developed different evangelistic approaches to Jews and Greeks. The Jews knew the Scriptures, so the apostles could begin directly with the message of Christ as the long-awaited Messiah.
>
>   But the Greeks had no prior knowledge of Scripture, so the apostles had to find a starting point familiar to them. The classic example is Paul's speech on Mars Hill in Athens (see Acts 17:16–33). As his springboard Paul uses a religious site in the city: an altar to an unknown god. Later in the same presentation he quotes a Greek poet. He appeals to the Athenians' own experience in order to create a common ground before presenting the gospel.

North America today may at one time have been like Jerusalem—an environment where most people worshiped the same God (or at least claimed that they did), shared a common knowledge of Scripture, and held a similar worldview.

Today North America is becoming increasingly like Athens. The Christian's task, with the apostle Paul of old, is to utilize contemporary culture as a tool to meaningfully introduce the message of salvation. The challenge is how to enter the language of today to engage the "Athens" in which we live with the life-changing good news of Jesus Christ.[1]

People today typically learn best through multisensory and relational frameworks. "Electronic culture doesn't create a culture of couch potatoes, it creates a culture of experiencers, participators, and interactors," says futurist theologian Len Sweet.[2] In response, churches are developing new structures and communication styles to match. Here are ways you can communicate the unchanging message of Christ in a rapidly-changing culture:

Use the Classics as Bridges to the Gospel

Imagine that the police knocked on your door, accompanied by a scruffy ex-convict whom only yesterday you befriended. As thanks for your generosity, the ex-con had stolen most of your silverware, and the police were now ready to cart him away at your word. What would you do? How could you best show Christ's love and forgiveness?

One of the many significant dramatic moments of Victor Hugo's *Les Miserables* portrays precisely this scenario. The convict's name is Jean Valjean, and the man he has stolen from is a bishop. This is no ordinary bishop, though. He's a radical believer who takes the words of Jesus literally. The bishop informs the startled police that the silver, originally given for the poor, was a gift to Valjean. Following Jesus' teaching in the Sermon on the Mount, the bishop turns the other cheek by giving Valjean a pair of silver candlesticks as well, then setting him free.

Valjean's background includes nineteen years in prison for merely stealing a loaf of bread in order to help a starving relative, an injustice that left him deeply embittered. The bishop's act of generosity and grace breaks the cycle of anger and sin.

This is Valjean's first taste of grace, and it transforms him. The ex-convict later shows the same extraordinary forgiveness and grace to an avenging police officer. The drama is compelling, exuding a powerful Christian message.

This magnificent Hugo novel has found wide acceptance in both movie format and as a popular Broadway play. In any form it offers a stunning illustration of the way truly great art incorporates rich biblical themes.

Why exactly is this story with a thoroughly biblical story line so compelling? What makes it appeal to non-Christians just as much as it does to Christians, especially since it was composed in another century, in another language, and on another continent?

According to Chuck Colson, a longtime advocate of using the classics in evangelism, teaching, and preaching, any story that deals with biblical themes also addresses the universal themes that are at the very core of human existence—themes that are inherently interesting. "It's

---

Preaching and Teaching to Different Kinds of Learners

Everyone has a preferred way of learning—a style that helps each person learn faster and with more enjoyment. Learning involves the senses, or modalities. Marlene LeFever, author of *Learning Styles: Reaching Everyone God Gave You to Teach* (Cook), says 40 percent are tactile kinesthetic learners (by movement of hands or body), 40 percent are visual learners (by pictures or printed word), and 20 percent of adult learners are auditory learners (by verbal words or sound). "Most pastors are tied to auditory teaching, so they're only reaching about 20 percent of their congregation," she says. LeFever has suggestions for changing that:

Reaching Kinesthetic Learners: Try using hand motions as you sing. Or put something in people's hands. For example, if your focus is on Jesus' crucifixion, give each adult a nail to hold as you speak. "Research shows that many people learn best when they stand," LeFever says. Ask the congregation to stand during an important part of your teaching and explain why you want them to

do so. "They may think it's weird, but it's not so weird that people won't do it," she says.

Reaching Visual Learners: Expecting visual learners to sit for thirty to forty minutes and listen to someone talking is like asking them to read a Chinese novel when they don't know the language. Use video clips to illustrate key points, or PowerPoint to project Scripture references and a teaching outline.

Reaching Auditory Learners: Talking and listening are important to auditory learners. Ask people to interact with others for two minutes during your sermon by discussing a question. This also helps kinesthetic learners as they move to talk with people.

LeFever says that these ideas don't have to scare people or turn your sermon into a circus. Instead, they focus listeners on what you're trying to say.

Adapted from *Vital Ministry,* September/October 1998, 14.

no accident," says Colson, "that the account of Jesus' own life has been called 'The Greatest Story Ever Told.'"[3]

As Gene Edward Veith writes in his book, *State of the Arts*, "What can send the imagination reeling like the doctrine of the Incarnation, the infinite concealed in the finite, or the Atonement, the tragedy of sacrifice and the comedy of resurrection and the forgiveness of sin?"[4]

Colson likes to quote literary giant Dorothy Sayers who says, "The dogma is the drama." To Colson this means "the story of salvation is, indeed, the story of all stories, the one that fascinates like no other."[5] Whether through verbal storytelling, media clips, drama, slideshows, or other creative means, you will enter today's mind, heart, and soul, as you use great stories of old to point to the greatest story ever told. According to one content analysis of Scripture, 75 percent of the entire Bible is story narrative, 15 percent is poetry, and only 10 percent is composed in a thought-organized format. Our presentation of the gospel should likewise use story-rich formats.

Emphasize the Role of Friendships

Why is it that in the mid-1990s the most popular and most copied television program was *Friends*? In the late 1990s the highest-paid syndication rights went to *Seinfeld*. Dozens of other shows have tried to use the same concept—a group of friends trying together to make sense of life. In both shows, the friends have become a community of people who care for each other. They have become the family they all lacked growing up.

"In the postmodern era the tribal group or community, not the autonomous self, is the essence of existence."

How do those two shows differ from the dominant television shows of the 1950s—*Father Knows Best, Ozzie and Harriet,* and *Leave It to Beaver*? Today the themes of many shows center around friends more often than around blood-related family.

Generation X (generally defined as those born between 1965 and 1985) has helped form a new sense of extended American family. Close friends, stepparents, adopted siblings, half-siblings, spouses, and even live-in lovers are found within this new sense of "tribalism." Xers are turning more and more to their friends as a new family.

Those who work with today's twentysomethings and younger warn against misinterpreting this trend. "This generation's legacy to our culture may be a return to community," says Jimmy Long, longtime campus minister with InterVarsity Christian Fellowship and author of *Generating Hope: A Strategy for Reaching the Postmodern Generation.* "In the postmodern era the tribal group or community, not the autonomous self, is the essence of existence."[6]

The idea of community is not limited to younger generations, however. Think about the Boston bar depicted in the hit television sitcom *Cheers.* As the theme song says, people long for a place "where everybody knows your name." Years ago, the writer of *Megatrends* predicted that the more high-tech the world becomes, the more "high touch" it will need to be as people seek out personal connections and a sense of community.[7] This value has significant implications for the role of church fellowship. For example, in the 1960s and 70s the nurture component or Bible study was the essence of most small groups, often to the neglect of emphasis on community building. Many members understood their small group as a place to come and study the Bible with other people so they could better understand the Christian faith. As was the case during the Enlightenment, rational understanding was the supreme focus.[8]

"As we minister among Generation X and this emerging postmodern culture, we need to emphasize different truths of Scripture for the changing times," says Long. "Those of us in the baby-boomer generation must not fall into the trap of ministering to our own needs rather than the needs of others."[9] For example, just because you once struggled with a legalistic view of Christianity, don't assume that your children or the young people your church is reaching also struggle with the same issue. In fact, the issues in the forefront of the hearts and minds of the younger generations have radically changed from those of years ago. Says Long, "Relational issues are crucial to Xers, who come from dysfunctional families and are moving away from an autonomous self to a community orientation."[10]

Most of the books that coach churches on how to reach today's younger and media-shaped generations underscore the need to em-

---

Life Today Is Different

DAILY: Where once Americans depended on the vagaries of the post office to communicate in personalized, written messages, now we send 2.2 billion e-mail messages a day, compared with just 293 million pieces of first-class mail.[*]

ANNUALLY: According to eMarketer Inc., more than 3.4 trillion e-mail messages crossed the Internet in the United States in 1998. That compares with a mere 107 billion pieces of first-class mail delivered in 1998 by the U.S. Postal Service.[**] In December 1999, the number of U.S. adults who use the Internet (90 million) exceeded the number who do not use the Internet (83.5 milliion).[***]

[*]Sara Sklaroff, "E-mail Nation," *US News & World Report,* 22 March 1999, 54.

[**]"News and Views," *USA Weekend,* 26–28 March 1999, 8.

[***]See http://ZonaResearch.com

phasize friendships and relationships—a "new foundation that is centered on community, adoption and hope."[11]

Use Multisensory Communication in Worship and Teaching

Tex Sample grew up in an oral culture. He learned about life from proverbs such as "Don't squat with your spurs on, buddy" and "Don't let your makeup write a check your body won't cash."

Today Sample is a professor of church and society at a seminary and he says it concerns him greatly "that my children and grandchildren find church 'boring' and not relevant to their lives."[12] His newest book, *The Spectacle of Worship in a Wired World,* says that a chasm separates the generations born since 1945 and those who came before that time.

At the heart of the difference between these generations, he argues, is electronic culture, a framework that involves fundamentally different ways of experiencing and knowing the world. "If we are to reach the generations that have grown up with television and other electronic media as daily parts of their lives," he says, "we must understand that for those steeped in this 'wired' culture, [meaning arises

---

Ten Strategies for Preaching in a Multimedia Culture

Tom Troeger, a theology professor, surveys how evolving forms of communications over the centuries have shaped the public presentation of the gospel. He then suggests ten strategies for creating sermons that effectively deliver the Word at church in an age of mass media and computerization:

1. Assume there is more to the story—name the character in the text that you're most like and explain why.
2. Create a parable—introduce the Bible text with an if-it-happened-today drama.
3. Play with an image—create a stage prop such as a wall, cross, or beacon of light based on your text.
4. Write the sermon as a movie script—and also use a movie clip to draw parallels to Scripture.

5. Use a flashback—pretend you were there witnessing what happened in the past.
6. Reframe a sacrament—tell the story of how baptism, or another ordinance, got started.
7. Let a little child lead you—with kids present, deliver your message as a children's sermon.
8. Play a game—engage the congregation in guessing the right option or suggesting ideas.
9. Listen to the muffled voices—"argue" on behalf of someone hurt in the story.
10. Compare translations—build your message from several acceptable Bible translations.

From Thomas Troeger, *Ten Strategies for Preaching in a Multimedia Culture* (Nashville: Abingdon Press, 1996), 22–116.

from] the convergence of image, sound, and visualization, rather than from any one of them individually."[13]

A number of churches are doing just that with their worship and training. Teachers and preachers are putting just as much energy and creativity into the delivery as into the content. "Talking head" monologues are being replaced by team presentations, dramatic illustrations, and other multimedia enhancements. Or they're at least being supplemented by creative visual support, such as colorful overheads or Power-Point-style video projection.

Churches that reach high percentages of the unchurched or the younger generations almost without exception are very intentional about maintaining high standards of excellence and cultural relevance in communication. There are many ways to increase a church's effectiveness in these areas. The only requirement is a biblically motivated passion to show that God cannot be limited to yesteryear. Jesus is the same yesterday, today, tomorrow, and forever (Heb. 13:8)!

Expert speech communication theorist Albert Mehrabian has shown that 55 percent of all meaning communicated in a face-to-face setting is communicated by the body, 38 percent by the tone of voice, and only 7 percent by the actual spoken words.[14] These statistics illustrate what any good communicator already knows: "If a speaker's verbal and nonverbal communications contradict each other, it is the nonverbal that will be believed."[15] As communications expert Suzette Haden Elgin says, "When the words and the body language don't match, believe the *body*."[16]

Your church can't afford not to capitalize on the opportunities today to increase your communication effectiveness by using multisensory, multimedia tools.

Multimedia Basics for Welcoming Today's Mindset into Worship

Use understandable language to introduce the preaching or teaching themes.

Show how the sacred impacts and interfaces with the secular.

Provide written and verbal instructions to explain everything expected of the worshiper (when to sit, stand, sing, speak, etc.).

Offer multiple means of communication, both verbal and visual—such as using overhead projectors, video projection, artwork in the bulletin, physical gestures in music, etc.

Design the worship service or teaching session to creatively incorporate several senses.

Stimulate participants visually, musically, physically, mentally, and emotionally as you deal with spiritual issues.

Model warmth, welcome, and friendliness through greeters, ushers, and worship leadership.

Create an environment where people know that it is possible to slip out during the worship service or class if they need to do so.

Offer tasty food and a friendly reception time prior to or following the worship experience.

From Mary Scifres, *Searching for Seekers* (Nashville: Abingdon Press, 1998), 63, 67.

Talk Unashamedly about the Spiritual Side of Faith

Ever since the Enlightenment and throughout the modern age, says Gene Edward Veith in a chapter called "Spirituality without Truth," scholars have expected the Christian faith to die out. The twentieth century opened with a theological battle between the so-called modernists and the fundamentalists. After the Scopes Evolution "Monkey" Trial of 1925, the media caricatured fundamentalists' faith, and the intellectual elite ridiculed most core values of historic Christianity. Modernist viewpoints seized the denominational structures of most mainline churches, including the seminaries, and emerged triumphant. Leading theologians and pastors stripped the Bible of its role as the written Word of God. They assumed that "modern man" is so oriented to the scientific method and to the triumph of the "secular city" that no one should be asked to believe in miracles, divine revelation, and a God unseen.[17]

The whole idea behind Jesus' incarnation is the "Emmanuel factor." God is with us.

By contrast, today's *Touched by an Angel* era almost expects God to be involved with the nitty gritty of everyday human life. Ten years ago, if you had begun a conversation with, "Can I tell you about an unusual answer to prayer that we just experienced?" most of your unchurched neighbors or work associates would have tuned you out. But now they are far more likely to be interested in your story of God doing something supernatural in your day-to-day life.

Church services have made a similar shift in apologetics. A sermon titled "Our God Is a God of Miracles" a decade ago, designed to prove that God is all-powerful and active, might be cast today as "Will You Trust God to Do Miracles?" God's supernatural activity is assumed, and the question shifts to my willingness to be part of what God is doing.

Some Christians have voiced concern that this God-and-me emphasis will water down the awesomeness and dignity of the Creator of the universe. It doesn't have to do so. The whole idea behind Jesus' incarnation is the "Emmanuel factor." God is with us.

Likewise, phrases similar to Veith's "spirituality without truth" warn of a make-up-your-own-God view of the supernatural. Michael Slaughter, a pastor in Ohio, found this idea on

---

What Seekers Look For

Community

Spiritual nourishment

Theological challenge

Safe places to explore questions and doubts

A relevant message about the Good News (gospel)

A reason and hope for turning to Christ

From Mary Scifres, *Searching for Seekers* (Nashville: Abingdon Press, 1998), 28.

Kageler on Winning Postmodernists

In reading this chapter, I thought about a popular evangelistic tract from the 1960s, in which the reader sees a picture of a train with a locomotive, coal car, and caboose bearing the labels "Fact," "Faith," and "Feelings." The idea is this: the gospel facts are compelling, so put your faith in them and the good feelings will follow.

To win postmodernists, the "fact . . . faith . . . feeling" sequence needs to be completely reversed. People are drawn by the warm, relationship-framed *feelings* of community and transcendence experienced in authentic worship. They put their *faith* in the community that provides those feelings. Then the believing community finally helps the new one understand the *facts* upon which the faith ultimately rests.

A major television network in the United Kingdom documented this change. In asking why so many normally empty cathedrals are now full of youth and young adults, they visited four of the new-style churches. They observed that church leadership had aimed worship at producing feelings of wonder, majesty, and mystery. Newcomers, attracted by the wonder and the authentic Christian community, asked, "What did I feel in there? What was that all about?" In response, the church invites them to join a Christian small group where many soon commit to Christ and eventually learn the facts of their new faith.

Leonard M. Kageler
professor, Nyack College, Nyack, New York
author, *How To Expand Your Youth Ministry* (Zondervan, 1996)

---

the newsstand. In his book, *Real Followers*, he says, "I picked up an issue of the July-August, 1998 *Utne Reader* with a feature article called 'Designer God.' The subtitle reads, 'In a mix-and-match world, why not create your own religion?' Here's the rub: the author is serious! His core idea is that we can have a god our way without any of the risks or costs. Yet at the same time, we can structure our god to appear on the outside like we're the real deal."[18]

This is a danger. More and more, people are shunning labels and exercising the personal right to draw from several seemingly contradictory belief systems. In *God Is Relevant,* evangelist Luis Palau writes, "Pick-and-choose religion is all the rage, even if it doesn't always make sense."[19] As theologian R. C. Sproul writes: "We are inconsistent and confused because we fail to understand where Christianity ends and paganism begins. We do not know where the boundary lines are."[20]

"We have a generation that is less interested in cerebral arguments, linear thinking, theological systems," observes Leith Anderson, a pastor in Minnesota and author of such books as *Dying for Change*. Instead they are "more interested in encountering the supernatural," he says.[21]

Christians, however, do not need to compromise their faith to meaningfully engage the thought currents of the day. By being alert to the changes, we can find new opportunities for deeper spirituality. "The old paradigm taught that if you have the right teaching, you will experience God," comments Anderson. "The new paradigm says that if you experience God, you will have the right teaching."[22]

New Reception Points for a New Century

The twentieth century began with a *New York Times* editorial (January 1, 1901) that proclaimed itself "optimistic enough to believe that the twentieth century will meet and overcome all perils and prove to be the best this steadily improving planet has ever seen."[23]

Certainly the editorialist did not foresee that this century would include two world wars, a worldwide depression, Nazism, fascism, communism, the Holocaust, and the threat of nuclear destruction for most of the second half of the century. According to Jimmy Long, "The optimism in which the century began has turned to despair and pessimism at the conclusion of the century. We now live in a culture of distrust."[24]

What are the most important ways your church can build the kind of trust needed to connect with the dominant mindset of today? Emphasize relationships and communicate with the savvy of multimedia and multisensory impact.

?

APPLICATION QUESTIONS
FOR INDIVIDUAL RESPONSE OR GROUP DISCUSSION

1. What example of success have you seen personally or at your church from the use of multisensory, multimedia communication tools? How does that motivate you to experiment further?
2. Which idea in this chapter made you most uncomfortable? Why?
3. Which idea in this chapter made most sense to you? Why? What will you do about it?

PASTORS
4. How many stories do you typically use in your preaching or teaching? Ask someone who is highly supportive of your ministry to help keep count for you. See what happens when you try to increase the number of illustrative stories you use by 20 percent.

four

Learn the Language That Connects with Postmoderns

Trend #4: People today show interest in the truth of the gospel only after they've seen the relevance of the church and the credibility of Christians.

✐

The word *postmodern* in this chapter title can conjure up a world of futuristic communication—talking e-mail or technological wizardry taken from *Star Trek* or *Star Wars*. That's not what postmodernism is all about, though.

In the postmodern world, there is a story for every occasion. The following two word pictures describe the concepts behind postmodernism.

Story #1: Best Ribs

The story is told of a Dallas restaurant that features delicious ribs. After years of being complimented for their tasty ribs, the owner put a sign outside the building: "Best Ribs in Dallas."

As the town continued to grow, more restaurants sprang up on the same street. Soon one of the newer eateries just down the road, which also boasted scrumptious ribs, made its own marquis claim: "Best Ribs in Texas."

A year or two later still another new restaurant on that road made an even broader claim: "Best Ribs in the United States."

Church Finds "Language" that Speaks to MTV Generation

Ginghamsburg Church

Denomination:	United Methodist
Location:	Tipp City, Ohio (just north of Dayton)
Senior pastor:	Michael Slaughter (since 1979)
Recent goal:	To impact the youth culture of the greater Dayton area.
Church vision:	Win the lost, set the captive free.
Year founded:	1863
Attendance:	3500 (now)
	1200 (5 years ago)
	400 (10 years ago)
Internet address:	www.ginghamsburg.org

"Postmoderns are not looking for *information about God*," says Michael Slaughter, senior pastor. "Instead, today's generation is looking for an *experience of God*." As a result, Ginghamsburg Church has pioneered a much-studied model of multisensory worship. Using video projection, drama, metaphor, and story, Ginghamsburg wants seekers and worshipers to encounter God in the sight-and-sound language of today.

According to Slaughter, "Whoever controls the media in effect controls the values and direction of today's culture, where children kill other children over a pair of 125-dollar Michael Jordan gym shoes and where teens learn their sexual values from *Baywatch*."

"Church bores people because the mystery has been removed," Slaughter says. "Cathedrals once were filled with incense. They provided wonderful paintings and murals to capture our senses. There were stained-glass sculptures and carvings," he said. Today's equivalent, multisensory worship, likewise has as its goal to "connect people with God," says Slaughter. "I want my senses, the whole of me, to be aware of God's presence."

Underneath all the technology and visuals is a powerful, uncompromising call to costly discipleship. "Jesus didn't die for bazaars and 'country club' church meetings," says Slaughter. "He died and rose from the grave so that the captives could be set free." Every week, the people of Ginghamsburg are pushed to rediscover the radical, counter-culture mission of Jesus and to move out on the edge as a result.

According to Slaughter's book, *Out on the Edge*, "The new motto for doing business in the postmodern world is 'Fix it before it breaks.'"* Such passion has led Ginghamsburg to become a breakthrough church for God's kingdom.

*Michael Slaughter, *Out on the Edge* (Nashville: Abingdon Press, 1997), 118.
An earlier version of this case study appeared in "Leadership on the Edge," catalogue 11, January 1999, and is used by permission from The International Centre for Leadership Development and Evangelism, Winfield, BC, http://www.GrowingLeadership.com, 800-804-0777.

Not to be outdone, the next newcomer made the most extravagant claim yet: "World's Best Ribs."

All the locals were curious as construction began on the newest rib house on this now-full, mile-long section of places to eat. What would its claim be? "Best ribs *on this strip.*"

All of the grand claims had become relativized. In the postmodern world, the best sign says the least.

In a postmodern era, the "truth" value in a statement is not interpreted to reflect an absolute, global reality. The postmodern mindset sees truth as relative to who said it, and in what circumstances. For example, when television personality Ellen DeGeneres went public about her sexual lifestyle, she explained in media interviews, "That was truth for me."

> *In the postmodern world, the best sign says the least.*

Story #2: Three Umpires

Walter Truett Anderson's book with the intriguing title, *Reality Isn't What It Used to Be*, illustrates current developments in the area of worldview—the set of assumptions, often unconsciously made, that frame how people view themselves and the world around them. In North America, modernism is still in force, but it is waning. Postmodernism is gaining ground as a dominant worldview.

"That's True for You but Not for Me"

In a world of relativism, no fact is true at all times and in all places. When everyone's point of view is different, the implications for evangelism are significant. Here are the kinds of postmodern perspectives, highlighted in Paul Copan's book, *True for You, but Not for Me*, that often leave Christians speechless:

To persuade is to proselytize. "Your evangelism is nothing short of cramming your religion down someone's throat."

To be exclusive is to be arrogant. "You say there's only one way to God through Jesus? That's another Western example of bigotry and narrow-mindedness, imposing your ideas on unknowing or unwilling hearers."

To challenge someone's views is to be intolerant. "I thought Christians were supposed to be open and accepting of others. When you tell me I'm wrong, you're being terribly intolerant."

As Gene Edward Veith Jr. concludes in *Postmodern Times*, in the postmodernist eyes, the cardinal sins are being judgmental, being narrow-minded, thinking that you have the only truth, and trying to enforce your values on anyone else.

From Paul Copan, *True for You, but Not for Me* (Minneapolis: Bethany House, 1998), 21–22, and Gene Edward Veith, *Postmodern Times* (Wheaton: Crossway, 1994), 196.

Anderson illustrates the contrast in worldviews by an imagined conversation between three baseball umpires who are having a drink together after a game.[1] They're talking about what they do each time a batter is ready and the pitcher throws the ball toward the catcher's mitt. Each umpire's assertion reflects a different worldview. Each begins with the statement: "There's balls and there's strikes and . . .":

Premodern—". . . I call them as they are." This umpire's world deals with objective, right-and-wrong absolute truth.

Modern—". . . I call them as I see them." This umpire's world is shaped by relativism. Truth depends on the stance of the observer.

Postmodern—". . . they ain't nothing until I call them." This umpire's world contains no truth except what he makes up. How does he know, after all, if there is anything "real" beyond his judgments? His perspective is all there is, or at least all that matters.

Two Christians edited a book designed to respond to postmodern outlook. Playing off Anderson's title, they called it *Truth Is Stranger Than It Used to Be.*

According to their analysis of Anderson's story, philosophers would label the first umpire's view as naive realism—things are exactly what they appear to be on the surface. He represents the autonomous self of the Enlightenment era, "believing that human knowing is a matter of seeking direct correspondence between the external world and epistemological judgments."

The second umpire admits that his view of the strike zone will vary from day to day, depending on how he is feeling. A relativist, he "recognizes that the way he sees the world is always mediated by the perspective of the knower."

The third ump's "radical perspectivism epitomizes the postmodern shift." For this umpire, there is no truth or falsehood, only choices.[2] Postmodernism invites people to rethink the notions of self, society, community, reason, values, and history that dominate modernity.[3]

Engaging the Postmodern World

What's the overall issue at stake for your church? Today's world is increasingly postmodern. By being aware of these new ways of viewing reality, churches can learn to speak with fresh relevance.

Our society is changing the meaning of words such as *values, truth,* and *character*. This concern is one of Allan Bloom's central points in *The Closing of the American Mind*. "There is one thing a professor can be absolutely sure of: almost every student entering the university believes, or says he believes, that truth is relative."[4]

Truth, in today's mind, is that which is meaningful and helpful to me. There is no eternal or transcendent perspective on truth. Values, similarly, are things that are valuable or helpful to me. People tend not to see values as eternal or permanent. The same can be said about character. People assume that character is becoming who I am. The focus is more on becoming authentic than on aspiring to universally held goals or standards.

What steps can you help your congregation take to understand and communicate with the postmodern personality? Eugene Peterson's *The Message* renders 1 Corinthians 9:21 this way: "I didn't take on their

---

Five Core Values of Postmodernism

Michael Crichton's sequel to *Jurassic Park* was called *The Lost World*. In *Jurassic Park*, the modern dream collapsed and decayed. In *The Lost World*, the postmodern view is seen as the survivor.

In *The Lost World*'s last paragraphs, a boatful of survivors speed away from the terror and disaster. Various people, including a scientist, try to explain what went wrong.

Doc Thorne then frames the future by saying: "I wouldn't take any of it too seriously. It's just theories, . . . just fantasies. They're not real. . . . A hundred years from now, people will look back at us and laugh. They'll say, 'You know what people used to believe? They believed in protons and electrons. Can you imagine anything so silly?' They'll have a good laugh, because by then there will be newer and better fantasies."

Thorne continues. "And meanwhile, you feel the way the boat moves? That's the sea. That's real. You smell the salt in the air? You feel the sunlight on your skin? That's all real. You see all of us together? That's real. Life is wonderful. It's a gift to

be alive, to see the sun and breathe the air. And there isn't really anything else."

Brian McLaren, in *Reinventing Your Church,* says this story illustrates five core values of postmodernism:

1. Postmodernism is skeptical of certainty— "It's just theories, just fantasies."
2. Postmodernism is sensitive to changes in context—"A hundred years from now there will be newer and better fantasies."
3. Postmodernism leans toward the humorous—"Can you imagine anything so silly?"
4. Postmodernism highly values subjective experience—"You feel the way the boat moves? That's the sea. That's real."
5. For postmoderns, togetherness is a rare, precious, and elusive experience—"You see all of us together? That's real. Life is wonderful."

From Brian McLaren, *Reinventing Your Church* (Grand Rapids: Zondervan, 1998), 167–72. Dialogue is from Michael Crichton, *The Lost World* (New York: Ballantine, 1995), 391.

way of life. I kept my bearings in Christ—but I entered their world and tried to experience things from their point of view." In that spirit, Brian McLaren's *Reinventing Your Church* suggests the following "opportunity maximizers" that churches can use to enter and engage the postmodern world.[5] Which of them could you agree with and work toward?

Acknowledge Your Culture-Encoded Version of Christianity

Regularly acknowledge that there's a difference between genuine Christianity and your culture-encoded version of it. This distinction can remove huge barriers. Postmodernists are often sensitive to overstatements that come across more as dogmatism than as someone still in the process of learning and growing.

Jesus is the living truth, but nowhere has his church reached the unity and maturity of faith and knowledge that Paul describes in Ephesians 4. Instead, Christians are weighed down with extra baggage and are marred by impurities, biases, misconceptions, and gaps.

The Bible is indeed God's Word, but not even the best church interprets it perfectly. As prayerfully and eagerly as we may try "rightly dividing the word of truth" (2 Tim. 2:15 KJV), incompleteness and error are part of what it means to be human.

Affirm Truth and Goodness

Affirm truth and goodness even when they exist in postmodernism. Postmodernism tends to chasten the know-it-all arrogance of a modern world. Postmodernists are skeptical of the idea that science will eventually be able to discover solutions to all life's unknowns. Christians can agree with this attitude of humility.

People today are asking "does it work?" or "is it real?" more than "is it true?"

People today are asking "does it work?" or "is it real?" more than "is it true?" Postmodernists typically want to experience spirituality, and that's often all the evidence needed to conclude that spirituality is real and worthy of exploration. Christians can affirm this experience-before-knowledge sequence as one that shows up even in the ministry of Jesus (see John 9).

Christians can even agree with some of the relativism that postmodernists are quick to notice. Without compromising on the absolute,

---

Five New Themes for Apologetics Today

1. *We don't just offer answers, we offer mysteries.*
Instead of offering an easy, quick solution, we point instead to where answers can be explored.

2. *We don't debate minutiae; we focus on essentials.*
If we have to choose between helping someone get the "facts right" versus getting the "relationship with God right," we focus on the latter first.

3. *We don't push credibility alone; we also stress plausibility.*
We don't want people to agree with the sensibility of our logic (credibility), only to say, "but it doesn't appeal to me—I have no interest in becoming like you" (plausibility).

4. *We don't condemn competitors; we dialog together with winsome gentleness and respect.*
We don't persuade people by caricatures ("all Muslims are . . ."), worst examples ("your faith produces people like Saddam Hussein"), or name-calling ("you're really a pantheist").

5. *We don't rush people; we help them at a healthy pace.*
Just as the human birth event is the culmination of a sometimes-painful, nine-month process, so the new spiritual birth is often the high point in a much longer journey.

From Brian McLaren, *Reinventing Your Church* (Grand Rapids: Zondervan, 1998), 77–85.

---

without-exception claims of Scripture, we can acknowledge the places where God's plan changes over time or shows ambiguities. For instance, is it absolutely wrong to worship in an idol's temple? (Naaman was given permission to do so.) Is it always wrong for a man to become friendly with a prostitute? (Hosea was commanded to do so.) Is it wrong under all circumstances to hold slaves? (Then why does the Bible regulate rather than categorically forbid slavery?)

These examples, though perhaps extreme, remind Christians to be a bit more thoughtful before we use an "always" or "without exception" statement about God.

Magnify the Importance of Faith Perspectives

The idea of faith used to be an embarrassment in the modern world. Today in most scientific quarters, however, the era of dogmatic, scientific certainty is gone. In keeping with today's postmodern turn, the world of science increasingly realizes that all conclusions involve a degree of faith.

Christians have known this all along. As Augustine said, "I believe in order to understand." In other words, there is no certainty apart from faith, and the only kind of understanding possible for us humans grows in the environment of faith.

Bend Over Backwards to Be Fair

Jesus' splinter-and-beam principle (see Matt. 7:3–5) has special relevance for today. The desire to be fair—to treat others no more harshly than one treats oneself or wants to be treated—is precious to postmodernists.

Postmodernists can spot hypocrisy a mile away. If Christians want to win a hearing with an unbelieving postmodernist, we must be very careful in how we treat those with whom we disagree.

Learn to Listen to Postmodern Stories

Learn to listen to the postmodernist's stories—and learn to tell your own. Brian McLaren tells a story from his graduate school days. One of his friends was a true postmodernist, doing his doctorate in deconstructionist literary criticism. He had a brilliant mind and a sensitive spirit.

One day as Brian and his friend stood together in a checkout line in a store, the friend said, out of the blue and with great sincerity, "Brian, it must be nice to have faith."

In response, Brian said, "Yeah, but it's not easy sometimes."

His friend replied, "Not having faith isn't so easy either."

As Brian walked away he thought, *There were stories behind those words. I wish I would have listened to more.*

Our doubts, failures, fears, problems, embarrassments, and confessions have tremendous apologetic and pastoral value in a postmodern world.

In the postmodern world, we need to tell our own stories: unsanitized, rough and lumpy, not squeezed into a formula. Our doubts, failures, fears, problems, embarrassments, and confessions have tremendous apologetic and pastoral value in a postmodern world. They illustrate truth in its postmodern form of honesty, authenticity, and transparency.

Do you know how to be authentic by expressing honest feelings and unhyped experiences? Many Christians have a hard time talking about what God is doing in their life without their story seeming plastic, put on, or inflated. Some of us can't admit weakness. Some of us have to preach whenever we talk.

Likewise, in our churches we must rely more than ever on art, music, literature, and drama to communicate our message. Jesus was the master storyteller. Everywhere he went, Scripture says, he told a parable. He engaged the senses as well as the mind.

God also worked through stories in the Old Testament. For instance, according to 2 Samuel 12, Nathan the prophet won King David's interest by telling a story that began, in effect, "There was once a rich man who misused his power." Once David's emotions were fully engaged, Nathan drove the point home by saying, "You are that man!"

> **A Postmodern Conversion Process**
>
> Jimmy Long's *Generating Hope: A Strategy for Reaching the Postmodern Generation* suggests that the postmodern conversion process will involve six steps. "These steps are not necessarily sequential, nor does everyone go through all of them. The purpose is to help guide both the Christian and the one seeking Christ along the journey to faith," he says.
>
> 1. Discontentment with life
> 2. Confusion over meaning
> 3. Contact with Christians
> 4. Conversion to community
> 5. Commitment to Christ
> 6. Calling to heavenly vision— an understanding of God's purpose from creation to second coming
>
> From Jimmy Long, *Generating Hope: A Strategy for Reaching the Postmodern Generation* (Downers Grove, Ill.: InterVarsity Press, 1997), 206–9.

Deal with the Issues and Language of Postmodernists

Deal with the issues and language that meet postmodernists where they are. Brian McLaren tells a story about meeting some visiting Chinese scholars. One asked this question, "Sir, I have been trying to read the Bible. But I find it very difficult, and I think it is driving me farther from God, not closer. Maybe you can help me. I read that God told the Jewish people to kill all non-Jewish people in a certain area. I realize that if I had lived in that area, God would have told them to kill me, since I am Asian, not Jewish. This makes me feel more alienated . . . like he hates me and is prejudiced against me. How am I to respond to this problem?"

There is no easy answer. This Chinese scholar was a seeker. He needed help. He probably wouldn't have responded positively to a cliché or to coercion. He needed to know that God (or God's representatives here on earth) took his question seriously.

If "turn or burn" was the connection point for seekers reached by the revivals of the nineteenth century, the language that makes sense with twenty-first-century people is closer to: "What step can you take next?" or "Where do you see yourself in this process?" For both centuries, the end goal is the same: developing fully committed disciples of Jesus Christ.

Remember that the same Holy Spirit, who came to your help in the hour of darkness, is at hand waiting to enter and illumine their hearts also.

Reassert the Value of Community

Reassert the value of community and rekindle the experience of it. The greatest apologetic for the gospel is and always has been a community that actually lives by the gospel. As a British missionary to India, Lesslie Newbigin wrote, "Jesus . . . did not write a book, but formed a community."[6] Newbigin is simply reaffirming Jesus' own promise: Our love for one another, our visible demonstration of living community, will prove both our legitimacy and his.

Are You Ready?

In the spirit of 1 Corinthians 9:22, this chapter challenges you to become "all things to all men" without forsaking the absolutes of God's law. For Paul the idea meant that when he was in Rome, he tried to relate to the Romans in as many ways as possible. This is what missionaries overseas do every day. This is also what churches need to do—being "in the world" of the postmodernist, but not necessarily "of the world."

God used the Egyptians to educate his servant Moses so that Moses could proclaim the wonders of God in the language and culture that Pharaoh could understand. Likewise, as postmodernism moves toward becoming the dominant mindset, it is important to learn this new language in order to show the relevance of Christ to their world. As they see the relevance of the church and the credibility of Christians, don't be surprised when they show interest in the truth of the gospel.

APPLICATION QUESTIONS
FOR INDIVIDUAL RESPONSE OR GROUP DISCUSSION

1. Practice telling your story. Imagine you are talking with a postmodernist. Using story format, describe how and why

Martin on Postmodern Communication

This chapter clearly explains what so many pastors and lay leaders have been trying to understand for years. It verified many of my assumptions, opening the door to our church for greater ministry in a postmodern world.

The sidebar entitled "Five Core Values of Postmodernism" (see page 71) is critical for all who are burdened to reach this next generation to understand. As a conference speaker traveling across North America, I see many churches failing to grasp the difference between the modern and postmodern mind. We are living in a cross-cultural age and, therefore, must become missiologists who learn the culture in order to best penetrate it.

In light of the suspicious, skeptical, and highly sensitive age of postmodernity, I have had to learn a new language and new paradigm of ministry while maintaining a commitment to the Word of God. This is what this chapter reminds us.

I see in these pages not only what the church of the twenty-first century will look like, but I also find a picture of the pastor in the twenty-first century.

Glen S. Martin
pastor, Community Baptist Church, Manhattan Beach, California
author, *God's Top Ten List: Guidelines for Living* (Moody, 1999)

you came to faith in Jesus Christ. Give a specific example of how he has changed your life as a result. (Checkpoint: Did you have more "I learned" statements than "you ought" statements?)

2. Do you feel like you'd compromise the clarity of the Christian faith if you used more stories to illustrate and convey God's truth? Why? What biblical examples would be for and against communication through storytelling?

3. Which idea in this chapter made most sense to you? Why? What will you do about it?

PASTORS 4. If you have a teaching or preaching role, have you ever tried telling an illustrative story first, then explaining the truth you're wanting to convey? Talk about the pros and cons of such an approach in this increasingly postmodern world.

Part 3

Churches Move toward Targeted Outreach

Turn On Your Daytime Running Lights

Congregations of all sizes are learning that it's better to do a few things well, rather than try to be "everything" to "everybody." As a result they are more intentionally targeted in how they position themselves.

Set Benchmarks for Reaching the Unchurched

One of the most distinctive marks of certain churches today is their ability to find and reach unchurched people. As a result, an increasing number of churches are identifying new benchmarks for measuring evangelistic success.

five

Turn On Your Daytime Running Lights

Trend #5: Congregations of all sizes are learning that it's better to do a few things well, rather than try to be "everything" to "everybody." As a result they are more intentionally targeted in how they position themselves.

⁓

As you went to church this past weekend, how many of the following scenarios were true?

You passed stores open for business with people shopping.

You saw people playing basketball, soccer, golf, or some other group sport.

You observed people exercising, on a bicycle or at a health center.

You passed restaurants where people were having a leisurely meal together.

You noted that your local hospital hosts Sunday morning support and recovery groups.

You glimpsed students heading to the library or working on laptops.

You heard or saw people having a party or simply hanging out with each other.

You're aware of friends who regularly tune in to certain Sunday morning talk shows, one of the sports channels, or some other favorite television fare.

Relocation Perseverance Turns Tragedies into Triumphs

Skyline Wesleyan Church

Denomination:	Wesleyan
Location:	Lemon Grove, California (metro San Diego)
Senior pastor:	Jim Garlow (since 1995)
Recent goals:	To develop the spiritual infrastructure of our church with discipleship, accountability groups, home groups, and Sunday school classes being reinstated and focused on in a profound way for the purpose of preparing us for the great harvest of 2000.
	To relocate the church to its new six-building campus.
Church vision:	To help people feel God's love, know God's ways, be God's person, and do God's work, for the purpose of reaching San Diego and beyond.
Year founded:	1954
Attendance:	3200 (now)
	2950 (5 years ago)
	2900 (10 years ago)
Internet address:	www.skylinechurch.org

For sixteen long years, Skyline Wesleyan Church has tried to relocate from its current "unsafe" location and inefficient facilities. "The congregation has had so many disappointments; it must number in the hundreds," says Jim Garlow, who became senior pastor in 1995.

The delays have been tedious and costly—almost comical from an outsider's point of view. A vein of blue granite catapulted their blasting contract to more than twenty times over budget. Nearly 7 million dollars was spent simply trying to get permission to build; the parking-lot infrastructure has cost nearly 9 million. And all of that before the first construction was started in March 1999.

The discovery of a blackened hearth stone saddled the church with underwriting a $120,000 archaeological dig. They were even forbidden to go onto their new property during the annual six-month breeding season of a single pair of California black-tailed gnat catchers, an endangered species of birds. In short, "state officials have been brutal on us," summarizes Garlow.

For Garlow himself, "I've learned how to release and relinquish things into God's hands." And the twelve-person church board? "I marvel how unshaken they are," he says.

During this prolonged relocation effort, emotions in the congregation have ranged from fatigue and cynicism to perseverance and faith. "I'm extremely impressed with their resilience," says Garlow. "I am proud of them; they've kept at the basics. This church is strong in discipleship, home groups, and other values essential to a healthy future. They're doing well spiritually."

In fact, Garlow, author of *Partners in Ministry* and long an advocate of lay ministry, believes God has used the long ordeal to cement into Skyline's culture the idea that every believer is truly called to ministry. "They have been able to maintain focus on doing what needed to be done," he says. "What other evidence could we ask for?" *

*James Garlow, *Partners in Ministry* (Kansas City: Beacon Hill Press, 1981).
An earlier version of this case study appeared in "Leadership on the Edge," catalogue 11, January 1999, and is used by permission from The International Centre for Leadership Development and Evangelism, Winfield, BC, http://www.Growing Leadership.com, 800-804-0777.

You noticed shades drawn or some other indicator that folks were snoozing.

You listened to radio announcements, saw billboards, or read newspaper ads giving you even more ideas of what you could be doing besides worshiping!

Chances are that you could check off many of those items as true. Long gone are the days when worship was the sole Sunday morning activity. No longer is church a person's primary option for socializing. And almost completely absent nowadays are the social expectations or pressures on a person to be seen at church.

What social competition has emerged! Today is the era of "mega-choices," as John Naisbitt predicted two decades ago.[1] Many alternatives not only knock at everyone's door, they all but turn the knob to come in.

These actively promoted alternative activities have deeply impacted how people view church. First, Christianity is not the only organized faith in town. On the way to your church you may pass Jewish, Muslim, Hindu, and Buddhist places of worship, not to mention worship sites for various cults. No doubt several of these groups sport appealing, impressive facilities.

Image, reputation, affinity, distinctives, and first impressions make a huge difference.

You also might pass five, ten, or even fifteen church facilities before stopping at the church you actually attend. At one, you saw a church marquis promoting its singles group. Another church building boasted a huge banner-like invitation for an upcoming concert. Yet another church's facility waved banners and flags that proclaimed, "Kids Central."

If you were new to a city, looking for a church home, would you find all this imaging to be a help or a distraction? In your church search, suppose you saw a run-down church building with nothing winsome about it. Would you conclude, "It may look shoddy, but I bet the Spirit of God is just as active here as with the group down the street whose properties just ooze with excitement and new life"? Not likely.

Your opinions are part of something people have acknowledged for years—that image, reputation, affinity, distinctives, and first impressions make a huge difference. The more recent development, known as marketing, occurs when a church tries to increase its "responsiveness to those myriad groups whose needs must be satisfied if the organization is to be successful in its ministry endeavors."[2] This chapter will help you sort through how and why churches are becoming more intentionally targeted in how they position themselves.

State Clearly What Your Church Does Best

During the 1990s, organizations from airlines to zoos carefully analyzed why they exist. An organization would then formulate a clear, compelling, concise, mission statement designed to summarize its distinctives. The next step was to teach the mission statement to all employees and to evaluate all priorities in light of that statement. If you enter a hotel, car dealership, high school, civic organization, or bank, you're likely to find a helpful mission statement posted in a central location.

The "rifle method" . . . involves targeting a specific group or groups of people, as did Paul, who targeted Gentiles, and Peter, who targeted Jews.

Thousands of churches and parachurch organizations have done the same thing. Pastors have led their congregations to prayerfully seek God, study Scripture, sit at a table together, and sift through exactly what God is calling them to do and become. After the leadership team signs off on a final version, they teach it at all levels of the church and evaluate all ministries in light of it.

One of the leading Christian writers in this field is Aubrey Malphurs, a professor at Dallas Theological Seminary and author of such books as *Values-Driven Leadership, Strategy 2000*, and *Developing a Vision for Ministry in the Twenty-first Century*. After working with hundreds of churches to develop mission statements, he observed:

> In trying to preach the gospel most churches attempt a broad unfocused approach, or what I call the "shotgun method." They hope to reach anybody and everybody. While that is a noble goal, the reality is that they will not and cannot attain it. Instead, most who attempt the shotgun method end up reaching no one in particular. That is why it takes all kinds of churches to reach all kinds of people. Therefore, it is strategic to take a more focused approach or what I call the "rifle method." This involves targeting a specific group or groups of people, as did Paul, who targeted Gentiles, and Peter, who targeted Jews.[3]

Mark Galli, an associate editor of *Leadership* journal, reached the same conclusion. He reported that his search for common methodologies among successful churches resulted in a baffling variety. The only clear principle he found was this: "Each church I examined has decided that it cannot be all things to all people. In one way or another, each has decided its unique identity as well as whom it is able to reach."[4]

As George Barna has pointed out, "God's vision for your ministry is like a fingerprint: there is no other one exactly like it."[5] According to Barna, "Vision for ministry is a clear mental image of a preferable future, imparted by God to his chosen servants, based upon an accurate understanding of God, self, and circumstances."[6]

Nothing can substitute for clarifying your church's unique God-given mission and vision. Once you've done so, you will be more able to state clearly the few things you can do best, rather than try to be "everything" to "everybody."

Notice How Many Ways You Advertise

As you read the following church-based conversations, note all the positive benefits that can come from advertising.

"Hey everyone, did you see the newspaper story on our church's ministry to compulsive gamblers? I don't think any of us knew they were writing it. What a positive statement it makes about God's work through us! Let's pray that the article will help us become known as a safe place for people to come with their problems."

"Before we begin our study of God's Word, could I ask everyone to prayerfully help the elders by taking a quick survey? We're designing a new outdoor sign and want to ask you which three

---

In Whatever You Do, Keep Focusing Outward

According to George Gallup, North America is the only continent where Christianity is not growing.

According to George Barna, approximately 70 to 80 percent of church "growth" can be attributed to the movement of Christians from one church to another.

According to the American Society of Church Growth, half the churches in America typically end each year without adding one single new member through conversion growth.

According to a Fuller Theological Seminary study, it takes three people to lead one person to Christ in a church one to three years old, seven people to win one person in a church four to seven years old, and eighty-five people to lead one person to Christ in a church more than ten years old.

The estimated unreached American population is now 190 million souls. There are plenty of sheep left in the pasture and the field continues to be "white unto harvest." Let's go for it. Don't ever give up.

From H. B. London Jr., "The Pastor's Weekly Briefing," *Focus on the Family*, vol. 7, no. 27, 2 July 1999.

Ads "Sell" God to Television Audience

Christians who work in television and radio are running an aggressive evangelistic campaign to reach millions of people in the Philadelphia area.

Forty professionals from almost every media outlet in Philadelphia, including NBC, ABC, CBS, and cable, have donated their time and expertise to produce and air top-quality Christian ads for television, radio, billboards, and the Internet.

The group, which calls itself Mission Media: Delaware Valley, is under the auspices of the Urban Family Council, an educational and research organization. A similar ad campaign already is occurring in Boise, Idaho, and organizers there have provided ideas and inspiration for the Delaware Valley outreach.

The greater-Philadelphia target area includes 6 million people and is the fifth-largest media market in the United States. It includes southeast Pennsylvania, central and south New Jersey, and northern Delaware.

The ads will run "from now until Jesus returns," says Bob Jacobus, twenty-nine-year-old former assignment editor at WCUA-TV, an NBC affiliate. Jacobus works full time as director of the project,

which began in the fall of 1997. Over one hundred evangelical Protestant churches are currently donating money to the project monthly, and more are joining, he said. Churches are being asked to make a long-term commitment to the campaign, whose goal is to raise $100,000 per month to blanket the area with the gospel. Those who respond to the ads by calling a toll-free number are introduced to a local church.

"It's the same marketing style as the milk-growers have used," said Jacobus, referring to the advertising campaign they chipped in to fund. Their *Got Milk?* ad campaign has produced a 34 percent increase in the sale of milk.

Jacobus said he has a "burning desire" to reach everyone in the area, especially young people, with the gospel. "About 98 percent of people in the region have access to television," he said.

The television ad campaign includes four phases. The first is meant to show that "the church loves you," Jacobus said. It portrays the church as a relevant place, the cornerstone of society, the best place to raise children. The second phase

(continued) ⟶

---

qualities would best touch the hearts of your unchurched neighbors: "Co-op City Community Church is known for its . . ."

People's perception of your church is very important. If they don't know about it, they can't be part of what God is doing. Every congregation is continually doing things that shape its public identity, whether it means to or not.

Does your church "Sing to the LORD, praise his name; proclaim his salvation day after day. Declare his glory among the nations, his marvelous deeds among all peoples" (Ps. 96:2–3)? If so, you are advertising in many ways. Like a car that attracts attention by keeping its headlights active at all times, you are turning on your daytime running lights.

Ads "Sell" God to Television Audience (continued)

shows that there is a God. It is "more intellectually aggressive," discussing evidences for the existence of God in the complexity and design of nature, from the stars to DNA. The third and fourth phases discuss fulfilled biblical prophecies to show that Jesus is God and that the Bible was inspired by God.

The ads, which run for thirty seconds each, are intended to capture the interest of a wide spectrum of individuals, including "those with the Northeast intellectual mindset as well as Joe six-pack," Jacobus said. The campaign aims to take the meaning of life directly to those who would never otherwise visit a local church.

"It is not for a lack of strength or accuracy that the Christian faith wanes in the United States," Jacobus said. "The fault lies in our failure to communicate the essential evidence and implications of the gospel. The result is an entire generation of young people who fail to find the meaning of life.

"Shamefully, as a whole, the church of Jesus Christ has remained on the cutting edge of the 1940s in these areas. We are failing to proclaim the reasons we believe or even the fact of our existence. Nor do we articulate our importance in maintaining a civil society. Yet we live in a world faced with imminent demise, now culturally, and in the future spiritually, the lost [people in society] facing a Christless eternity in conscious torment."

"Television is the modern Mars Hill and we have virtually no voice," Jacobus said, alluding to the ancient Athens forum. "We have to do more than just have a Christian TV subculture. We can't build a tower and loathe everyone else. We have to go out with a loving, compassionate voice and speak in the venues where people go listening— whether it's easy or not."

Adapted from *Religion Today*, 9 September 1998 (web access at http://www.ReligionToday.com) and updated by correspondence with Bob Jacobus.

Focus on Marketing Rather Than Advertising

Bill Hybels and three colleagues conducted door-to-door interviews before they launched a new church in the Willow Creek Theatre in Palatine, Illinois, a western suburb of Chicago. At each house they asked, "Do you actively attend a local church?" If the person said yes, they replied, "Good, keep it up. Have a nice day." If the person said no, they asked, "Why not? What is there about church that makes it difficult for you to attend?" The five most-cited reasons could be summarized as follows:

1. It is irrelevant to my life. They use words I don't understand. The church and the Bible have no practical application in my everyday life.
2. It is boring. Everything they do is a dull, predictable routine. I'm turned off by their liturgy and symbolism.

3. All they want is my money. They don't care about me. All they care about is what they can get out of me.
4. I always leave feeling depressed or guilty.
5. They invade my privacy and embarrass me. They want me to stand up or sign a book or wear a tag.

To conclude, the interviewer would ask, "If a church existed that was not like this, would you be interested in attending? If we start such a church, may we call you?" Then Hybels and his friends resolved that the gospel would not be compromised if a new church would address those concerns.[7]

Their first service was October 12, 1975. Today they're the largest-attended congregation in North America, still being characterized by these values, which correspond to the five needs discovered in their door-to-door interviews:

1. Present the message with a high sensitivity to how it applies to personal life.
2. Demonstrate excellence and creativity in programming. Explain the meaning of any symbols used.

Does Your Congregation Welcome or Push Away?

The following checklist, adapted from Mary Scifres, *Searching for Seekers*, will help you catch yourself on communication habits that may not be helpful to newcomers:

Do you avoid the use of unexplained abbreviations in your bulletin, newcomer letter, or churchwide announcements? (examples: use "leader and congregation" instead of "L & C" in responsive readings, "fellowship hall" instead of "FH," "Southern Baptist Convention" instead of "SBC" or other denominational identifiers)

Are symbols or codes explained? (example: "The congregation will read aloud the words in bold.")

Are worship tools clearly identified? (example: "As we say the Lord's Prayer in unison, you will find it printed inside the back cover of the blue prayerbook.")

Do you clarify where rooms are? (example: "Everyone, especially our guests today, is invited for coffee in the church parlor, which is just outside the door underneath our 'Alleluia' banner.")

Do you identify the worship leaders? (example: "Isaiah and Thelma Johnson, who head our neighborhood prayer ministry, will read today's Scripture for us.")

Do you avoid words such as "you are dismissed" that confuse church with a public school? (example: "As we conclude our worship together, may a spirit of praise and worship accompany everything you do this week.")

Adapted from Mary Scifres, *Searching for Seekers* (Nashville: Abingdon Press, 1998), 111, 114.

3. When offerings are taken (and they weren't for years on Sundays), the leader asks nonmembers not to give because they are there as guests.
4. Offer opportunities for spiritual response, but avoid pressure on a person to decide anything until he or she feels ready.
5. Provide anonymity, so that the person is not singled out or embarrassed.

Willow Creek's founders understood what marketing is all about. Not primarily selling, not primarily advertising, but doing the kinds of needs assessment that leads to an exchange between two parties. In this case, unchurched Harry or Mary might give up a day at the lake to find answers to some of their problems. Later on, perhaps Harry or Mary will give God control of their lives, in return gaining peace of mind and eternal life with God. As a *Harvard Business Review* case study concluded, the staff of Willow Creek "attribute much of their success to the simple concept of knowing their customers and meeting their needs."[8] Thus, contrary to most people's perceptions, the essential component of marketing is not selling. As Peter Drucker, one of the world's leading management theorists, says, "The aim of marketing is to make selling superfluous."[9]

Instead, "Marketing is the analysis, planning, implementation, and control of carefully formulated programs to bring about voluntary exchanges with specifically targeted groups for the purpose of achieving the organization's missional objectives. In other words, marketing can help a religious organization accomplish its desired ends through its interactions with various groups."[10]

How do we identify and listen to the needs of people to learn how best to market to them? Many inexpensive means are available. Options include surveys (mail, telephone, congregational), focus groups (eight to ten people with a trained facilitator asking questions), one-on-one personal interviews, suggestion boxes, and "phone us today" or "write to us" campaigns.

As you market, be careful never to sacrifice the core content of your message in order to fill more seats, increase your cash flow, become

> **Summary of the Seven-Step Marketing Process**
>
> 1. Collect information on your ministry context—the people to be reached.
> 2. Capture God's vision for your ministry.
> 3. Identify your ministry resources and ministry opportunities.
> 4. Create a marketing plan that reflects steps one through three.
> 5. Implement the marketing plan.
> 6. Get feedback on what happened.
> 7. Revise the plan and reimplement it with improvements.
>
> From George Barna, *A Step-by-Step Guide to Marketing the Church* (Ventura, Calif.: Regal Books, 1992), 30–32.

more highly regarded in your community, or even to reach more people for Christ. The gospel never changes, but people's needs continually change. Many of the issues and problems they face today, such as fear surrounding dictators with nuclear bombs or high-school shootings, are markedly different from what they were dealing with one year ago, ten years ago, or thirty years ago. Yet the same timeless truths of Scripture apply to whatever concern is foremost in their mind and emotions.

It is possible that a focus on people's needs might lead you to compromise the gospel itself, as this writer warns: "A distortion of the gospel . . . necessarily results from a fixation with the audience's felt needs. Marketing makes the audience sovereign as it shapes or creates products to satisfy the audience's felt needs and desires. . . . The methods have tended to warp the content of the Christian gospel."[11] Pastor and teacher John MacArthur is even more blunt: "The simple reality is that one cannot follow a market-driven strategy and remain faithful to Scripture."[12]

However, this needn't be the case any more than the idea that cooking someone's favorite meal requires abandonment of the laws of nutrition. As George Barna says, "Without compromising one iota of the gospel, we are challenged to serve God by cultivating our ministry fields for a full spiritual harvest. Marketing is simply one of the tools we can employ to maximize the harvest that God has prepared."[13]

Prayerfully Target Specific Population Segments

In order to target your ministry, a church must first segment the population into distinct, identifiable groups who have different wants

⌐○○ Ficken on Intentional Change

This chapter deals with taking the initiative to bring about intentional change. The Christian church in America is in desperate need of leadership that can guide it through change. Otherwise we run the danger of drifting downstream and over the waterfalls of irrelevance. We will drift farther and farther away from the shores of engaging our world with the gospel of Jesus Christ.

The good news is that we can choose our response. This chapter gives several examples of how we can seize the challenge, confronting the forces of inertia in stable, positive approaches. Church by church, we can make the choice to seek to be more healthy.

I have served a 140-year-old congregation since 1983. During that time, under God's leadership, we introduced significant changes in this once struggling congregation in the heart of our town. This has also happened in other congregations as I met with them and together we made important choices about future planning.

Each congregation represented by the readers of this book has been commissioned for kingdom work by God himself. You have the promise of God that not even the gates of hell will prevail against his church. Dare to take the risk to change.

Jock Ficken
pastor, St. Paul's Lutheran Church, Aurora, Illinois
author, *Change: Learning to Lead It and Living to Tell About It* (Fairway Press, 1999)

and needs. For example, how would you target the following representative people groups? Would you use the same strategy for each?

A. Joe, age forty, doesn't believe church attendance is essential to his faith. According to a Gallup survey, three out of four Americans say, with Joe, to the effect of, "I feel I can be a good Christian without attending church."[14]
B. Jeannie, age seventy-five, is a die-hard Southern Baptist who has recently moved to your area. "If it doesn't have Baptist in its name and doesn't support the denomination's Cooperative Program, then I don't even want to visit it," she says.
C. Rebecca, age eighteen, has never heard the gospel. She's hungry for spiritual help, but she's full of unanswered concerns. She's peppered her friends with heavy questions such as, "If God exists, how could he have allowed the Jewish holocaust?" and "If I'm not just a random-chance product of evolution, then how can I find out my purpose and meaning in this world?"

If you concluded that a different ministry (or even church) might be required to reach Joe, Jeannie, or Rebecca, you wouldn't be alone. "You can't be all things to all people," summarize John Pearson and Robert Hisrich in *Marketing Your Ministry: Ten Critical Principles*. "Today's effective ministries have a select and well-defined market."[15]

Churches are becoming more intentionally targeted in how they position themselves. In most cases, the greatest and most durable spiritual fruit shows up in those congregations, big and small, who have discerned their distinctive calling and are prayerfully, consistently, and persistently improving their effectiveness at communicating with those whom God is calling them to reach.

? APPLICATION QUESTIONS
FOR INDIVIDUAL RESPONSE OR GROUP DISCUSSION

1. How does advertising differ from marketing, according to this chapter? Does your church do more advertising or marketing? Which direction would you like to see your church move? How can you help?
2. What are some of the dangers associated with intentional marketing? How could they be avoided in your setting?
3. What kind of people does your church do the best job of reaching and ministering to? How does your answer square with your church's stated vision or mission?

PASTORS 4. Have you led your church through a process of defining a specific vision for its ministry? If ten people were randomly selected from the congregation, and each were asked, "What is the distinctive purpose of this church that sets it apart from other congregations in this city?" what would they say? Consider devoting an upcoming preaching or teaching series to the idea of your church's mission. Check the focus or purpose of each ministry or group in your church to see that the mission is being fulfilled.

six

Set Benchmarks for Reaching the Unchurched

Trend #6: One of the most distinctive marks of certain churches today is their ability to find and reach unchurched people. As a result, an increasing number of churches are identifying new benchmarks for measuring evangelistic success.

∾

The following invitation makes almost incredible claims:

> In nearly every region of the world, they are the fastest-growing segment of Christianity. They are adopting new names, new methods, and new worship expressions, yet are steeped in the fundamentals of the faith. They are held together by the glue of biblical methods, not their particular doctrinal distinctives nor their traditions. Discover why hundreds of thousands are becoming part of this powerful, new . . . grassroots phenomenon.[1]

That is the bold claim church growth researcher C. Peter Wagner makes for what he calls the New Apostolic Reformation. In his book on the subject, Wagner declares: "The more I have studied during the past few years, the more convinced I have become that we have a major

From One Church to a Movement of Churches

Redeemer Presbyterian Church

Denomination:	Presbyterian Church of America (PCA)
Location:	New York, New York
Senior pastor:	Tim Keller (since 1989)
Recent goal:	Successfully launch a third service
Church vision:	To change New York City in every way—spiritually, culturally, socially—with a movement of the gospel.
Year founded:	September, 1989
Attendance:	3000 (now)
	1000 (5 years ago)
	90 (10 years ago)
Internet address:	www.redeemer.com

It started with nothing more than an audacious dream: to launch a movement of churches from the heart of the nation's largest and most influential city. More than a decade later, that goal remains at the forefront of every long-range planning discussion held by Redeemer Presbyterian Church on the island of Manhattan.

Under the leadership of Tim Keller, the church reaches professionals of all ages. The worshiping congregation is about 80 percent young, single adults, reflecting the demographics of Manhattan. It has expanded from one to two and now three different services, each with a distinctive style. One is noted for classical music, another for the use of jazz.

"The next phase of our vision is for the mother church itself to become a multi-site church of four worshiping congregations in different locations," says Keller. "We are already worshiping at three permanent locations and are looking for a fourth, to give us East Side A.M., West Side A.M., East Side P.M., West Side P.M. That is the 'multi-site' model we are aiming for, in direct challenge to the megachurch model."

Redeemer Presbyterian has also begun to ring metro New York City with daughter congregations: two in 1994, one in 1995, one in 1999. All share a highly positive view of the city as the strategic center for ministry. Churches in the "Redeemer movement" share the distinctives of intelligent teaching, thoughtful engagement with culture, excellence in music, worship that draws on a variety of both traditional and contemporary sources, a non-condemning evangelistic heart for those who don't believe, and a balanced concern for ministry both in word and deed. "The implications of the gospel must be recognized and lived out in every area of life, whether private or public," says Keller.

Every evidence suggests that Redeemer will remain focused on greatly accelerating the planting of new churches, and in the process reaching people for Christ. Says Keller: "We have just begun to start new churches. We are currently approaching foundations to raise money for the Urban Development Center, which will train people to plant and grow gospel-driven churches in cities worldwide."

transformation of Christianity on our hands. . . . I believe we are witnessing a reinventing of world Christianity."[2]

"New Wineskins" Shape the Church for the Twenty-first Century

According to Peter Wagner, "Every time Jesus began building his church in a new way throughout history, he provided new wineskins. While he was still on earth, he said that such a thing would be necessary: 'Neither do men pour new wine into old wineskins. If they do, the skins will burst, the wine will run out and the wineskins will be ruined. No, they pour new wine into new wineskins, and both are preserved' (Matt 9:17). The growth of the church through the ages is, in part, a story of new wineskins." Here are the new wineskins that Wagner identifies:

1. *A New Name.* In virtually every region of the world, the churches Wagner has described as "new apostolic" constitute the fastest-growing segment of Christianity.

2. *New Authority Structure.* This is the most radical of the nine changes because it deals with the amount of spiritual authority delegated by the Holy Spirit to individuals. He sees a transition from bureaucratic authority to personal authority, from legal structure to relational structure, from control to coordination, and from rational leadership to charismatic leadership.

3. *New Leadership Training.* Although new apostolic pastors are fervently dedicated to leading their churches, they are equally dedicated to releasing the people of their congregations to do the ministry of the church.

4. *New Ministry Focus.* Instead of being heritage driven (returning to what we were), new apostolic Christianity is vision driven (starting with the present and focusing on the future).

5. *New Worship Styles.* With only a few exceptions, new apostolic churches employ the language, music, and so on of the people they are called to reach. Worship leaders typically replace music directors. Their goal is to help every person in the congregation become an active participant in worship.

6. *New Prayer Forms.* Prayer in new apostolic churches has taken forms rarely seen in previous years. Concerts of prayer, prayer songs, prayer walks, prayer mapping, or prayer journeys become a standard part of congregational life and ministry.

7. *New Financing.* Finances are often abundant because generous giving is expected. Joyful tithing is taught without apology. Tithes and offerings are regarded as seeds that will produce fruit of like kind for the giver.

8. *New Outreach.* Aggressively reaching out to the lost and hurting of the community and the world is part of the new apostolic DNA. Planting new churches is usually an assumed part of what a local congregation does. Compassion for the poor, the outcast, the homeless, and the disadvantaged is also a strong characteristic.

9. *New Power Orientation.* The new apostolic reformation seems to combine the technical and spiritual principles of church growth better than any other grouping of churches. The majority of new apostolic churches not only believe in the work of the Holy Spirit, but they also regularly invite him to come into their midst to bring supernatural power.

Based on C. Peter Wagner, ed., *The New Apostolic Churches: Rediscovering the New Testament Model of Leadership and Why It Is God's Desire for the Church Today* (Ventura, Calif.: Regal Books, 1998), 15, 18–25.

His book, *The New Apostolic Churches,* contains the accounts of eighteen church leaders, each of whom have played an "apostolic" role by raising up, shaping, and multiplying a network of churches. The structural models differ, some appearing as new denominations, some working within existing denominations. All, however, are borne from evangelistic passion to find new paths for reaching an increasingly needy world.

Wagner's book symbolizes the source of the most influential voices shaping tomorrow's church. The marching orders no longer come from seminary professors or denominational mandates. They aren't voices that necessarily hold a "we've-always-done-it-that-way" respect for past methodologies. The voices usually are not those of wealthy business leaders. Nor are they former superstars from Hollywood or the sports arenas.

Instead they are entrepreneurial pastors, high on vision and passion, convinced that God, if taken at his Word, still delights to do the impossible in building his kingdom today. In their creative, prayerful efforts to follow God's commands, they are identifying new benchmarks for measuring evangelistic success. This chapter presents several of the "new" standards they are establishing.

Set Outwardly-Focused, Measurable, and Relationship-Based Growth Goals

Perhaps the first recent book to uncover new "apostolic" ways for a congregation to live out the gospel was George "Chuck" Hunter's *Church for the Unchurched,* published in 1996. "To be sure, today's apostolic churches are not all alike, any more than the churches of the New Testament period were all alike," Hunter says. "What makes these churches different is not a single feature like prayer, small groups, a guitar in the sanctuary, or seven-day-a-week scheduling, but a combination of multiple features that function synergistically."[3]

While no church, no matter how apostolic its orientation or obsession, reaches unchurched pre-Christian people exclusively, this new generation of churches is "reaching significant numbers of the unchurched, non-Christian, secular people in America's mission fields," says Hunter. "Indeed, that is their main business."[4]

This new generation of churches is "reaching significant numbers of the unchurched, non-Christian, secular people in America's mission fields."

For example, New Song Church, West Covina, California, was founded in 1986, as a church to target unreached Baby Busters. According to Hunter's research, the church teaches that if its people are fulfilling the vision to which God has called the congregation, five vital signs of growth will be evident. The saints can say the following:

1. *I am growing in my intimacy with God and faithfulness to his Word.* This vital sign is demonstrated in my life by spending time with God through prayer, worship, listening to him, reading the Bible, and actively living out his principles in my life.
2. *I am growing in real relationships with others in a small group.* This vital sign is demonstrated in my life by gathering with others to actively use my spiritual gifts, to build them up in Christ, and to be involved in disciple making.
3. *I am growing in my service to God and others.* This vital sign is demonstrated by discovering my unique God-given gifts, passions, and personality, selflessly and effectively to serve my family, my church, and my community so that God's kingdom and work can be furthered.
4. *I am growing in reaching my pre-Christian relationships for Christ.* This vital sign is demonstrated by my growing compassion and ability to build friendships with pre-Christians that will lead to an opportunity to introduce them to Jesus.
5. *I am growing in my sensitivity toward the training of leaders and planting of groups and churches.* This vital sign is demonstrated by my enthusiasm to support God's heart to develop individuals and teams to strategically extend God's kingdom nearby and far away.[5]

Another example of outwardly-focused, measurable, and relationship-based goals comes from the "purpose-driven" model of Rick Warren and Saddleback Community Church (see pages 29–31). Warren identifies different levels of commitment and spiritual maturity, which he illustrates by concentric circles (see next page).

Each circle is measurable. On any given week, Saddleback can identify how many people are at each specific level. Using a baseball diamond analogy, Rick Warren continually asks people whether they're ready to move to first base (a commitment to membership), to second (a commitment to maturity), to third (a commitment to ministry) or to home plate (a commitment to missions).[6]

For example, consider the Congregation stage. "At Saddleback, only those who have received Christ, been baptized, taken our member-

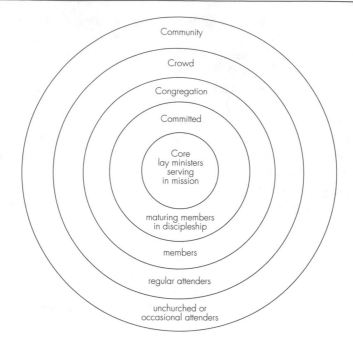

ship class, and signed the membership covenant are considered a part of the congregation," says Warren.

To move to the next group, the Committed, a person must take a certain class and sign a "maturity covenant card" that indicates a commitment to three spiritual habits: (1) having a daily quiet time, (2) tithing 10 percent of your income, and (3) being active in a small group. "We consider these three habits essential for spiritual growth," says Warren.

Finally the Core are dedicated to ministering to others. They are people who lead and serve in the various ministries of the church. Saddleback has a very intentional process for helping people find their best niche for service. It uses the acronym S.H.A.P.E. to describe the ministry discovery and placement process. When asked, "How has God shaped me for ministry?" people look to their *s*piritual gifts, *h*eart, *a*bilities, *p*ersonality, and *e*xperience.

From there a believer goes through an interview process with the help of a lay ministry guide. The purpose is to identify three or four possible ministry settings. Then the individual meets with the staff who supervise the ministries being considered. Finally the person begins the ministry and also attends monthly meetings called S.A.L.T.

Characteristics of Growing and Expanding Ministries

1. They know why they're in business.
2. They're person-oriented rather than program-centered.
3. They involve their members in developing and carrying out their ministries.
4. If large, their congregation is able to maintain an intimacy by being honeycombed with small groups dedicated to serving the differing needs of the members and those segments of the community they have chosen to target in their outreach ministries.

From Norman Shawchuck, et. al., *Marketing for Congregations: Choosing to Serve People More Effectively* (Nashville: Abingdon Press, 1992), 37–38.

(Staff and Leader Training), two-hour training rallies designed for core members of the church.

"What happens when people finally get to the core?" asks Warren. "We move them back out into the community for ministry."[7] "A church's health is measured by its *sending* capacity, not its *seating* capacity," he summarizes.[8]

Set Higher Standards for "Membership"

While Warren Bird was an elder in a highly respected evangelical church, a member of the church sued the pastor and church for 3 million dollars for defamation. The man's real estate company had been hired to do a research report, and the pastor, in a counseling setting, had allegedly commented negatively about this man's business ethics.

The man's legal documents opened with a claim that he was a member "in good standing." The elders quickly discovered, however, that he only sporadically attended morning worship, never attended other services, was not a donor of record, and held no ministry responsibility. In prior months he had refused to meet with the elders about another matter, claiming that he was too busy.

That man certainly displayed a lack of understanding of membership by any biblical standard! Yet such examples are common.

In too many churches, if you show up regularly and put money in the offering plate, you qualify for membership. If you dress appropriately and regularly shake hands with the right people, you could be elected to church office.

The churches mentioned earlier in this chapter, New Song and Saddleback, as well as Willow Creek (see sidebar on next page) raise a far higher standard for membership than pew warming or philanthropy. The criteria Peter Wagner highlights for a new apostolic church also imply a high level of ongoing commitment to church community and personal spiritual growth.

Place Renewed Emphasis on Evangelistic Prayer

Many of yesteryear's outlines for spiritual growth were linked to all-church gatherings held on church properties. Congregational leaders have often used this popular adage: "If you love *church,* you show up on Sunday mornings. If you love the *pastor,* and want to show your support to him, you show up for the Sunday evening service. And if you love *Jesus,* you come out to Wednesday night prayer meeting." This three-to-thrive thermometer of spiritual temperature is measurable, but it links prayer ministry to one particular format, in this case an on-premises, all-church, single-weeknight time slot.

Today's churches seem to be experimenting not only with new styles of prayer, but also with the whole idea of prayer as a window for better partnering with God in evangelism.

Willow Creek's "Seven-Step Strategy" from Evangelism to Membership

"The story of Willow Creek Community Church is essentially a story of evangelism," says Bill Hybels. "When we began Willow, our hearts were overwhelmed with the need to reach unchurched people. Today our heartbeat remains the same." *

To that end, here is Willow Creek's strategy for bringing an irreligious person toward becoming a fully committed follower of Christ.

1. A friendship develops between unchurched Harry or Mary, and a Willow Creek attender.
2. The attender shares a verbal witness with Harry or Mary.
3. Harry or Mary visits a Willow Creek weekend meeting designed for unchurched individuals.
4. Harry or Mary begins attending "New Community," a midweek worship and teaching meeting.

5. Harry or Mary joins a small group.
6. Harry or Mary uses his or her gifts in serving.
7. Harry or Mary becomes a good steward of his or her finances.

These steps are also summarized by the "Five Gs" that are fundamental requirements for membership at Willow Creek: grace, (personal) growth, (small) group, (spiritual) gifts, and (financial) good stewardship.**

*Bill Hybels in a Willow Creek Association promotional document dated May 1998.

**Church Leaders Handbook, 4th ed., (South Barrington, Ill.: Willow Creek Association, 1997), 62. See also www.willowcreek.org.

Henry Blackaby's popular *Experiencing God* series uses cooperation with God as its final principle. Blackaby says: "God takes the initiative to involve his people with him in his work. When he opens your spiritual eyes to see where he is at work, that revelation is your invitation to join him."[9] Rick Warren's *Purpose-Driven Church* suggests the same idea in its opening pages, explaining it with a surfboard analogy. Surfers can take classes on how to choose the right equipment, how to use it properly, how to recognize a "surfable" wave, how to catch a wave and ride it as long as possible, and how to get off a wave without wiping out. But surfers will never find a course that teaches how to build a wave.[10]

> "*The power behind the message is still birthed through the timelessness of prayer.*"

The spiritual translation is that growth cannot be produced by human effort; only God makes the church grow, as 1 Corinthians 3:6 affirms. "Our job as church leaders, like experienced surfers, is to recognize a wave of God's Spirit and ride it. It is not our responsibility to *make* waves, but to recognize how God is working in the world and to join him in the endeavor," Warren says.

"The problem with many churches is that they begin with the wrong question," says Warren. They ask, "What will make our church grow?" That's like asking, "How can we build a wave?" Instead, says Warren, the questions church leaders need to ask are, "What is keeping our church from growing? What barriers are blocking the waves God wants to send our way?"[11]

"Lack of focused prayer" is how an increasing number of leaders today answer those questions. T. D. Jakes pastors one of North America's fastest-growing churches during 1998–99, the Potter's House in Dallas. Speaking for many, he observes, "Jesus' disciples asked how to pray—not how to preach." His point is this: Should prayer be our *first* priority or a *secondary* priority in evangelism? Jakes concludes, "In my own ministry, I have used the media, making shrewd business deals to propagate the gospel message through all available avenues. But despite the success, I am very conscious that while the mode may be different than a few years ago and the audience vaster, the power behind the message is still birthed through the timelessness of prayer."[12]

This valuing of focused prayer has led to great innovation in intercession. For example, in recent years researchers have identified almost one billion people who have never heard the gospel and have noted that most of these people groups lie within a geographical location known as the 10/40 Window. This area, south of the equator, stretches across Africa and Asia.

In response to that research, a global prayer movement has exploded as the Spirit of God has fallen on the nations, compelling God's people to pray. Prayer initiatives such as "Praying through the Window" have mobilized millions of believers to pray for the lost. As a result of unified prayer, barriers to the gospel are coming down, and thousands are coming to Christ in areas resistant to the gospel.

Another initiative, the World Prayer Center, is a communications hub, serving the church throughout the world by linking prayer requests, practical needs, and reporting evangelistic breakthroughs. It collects and compiles requests from every continent as national prayer centers report what God is doing and how his people ought to pray.

The physical facility, located in Colorado Springs, Colorado, has already been built. Eventually it will include the latest telecommunications system, interactive touch screen monitors, prayer rooms, a spiritual mapping repository, classrooms, a large auditorium, and a bookstore containing the world's largest collection of prayer and spiritual warfare material.

The World Prayer Center is a transdenominational effort spearheaded by two key Christian leaders: Dr. C. Peter Wagner, president of Global Harvest Ministries, and Pastor Ted Haggard of New Life Church, both based in Colorado Springs, Colorado. According to Wagner, "We see our task as getting people in touch with one another to form interactive, human web networks that are properly equipped to wage effective spiritual warfare."[13] The World Prayer Center networks prayer ministries, denominations, churches, and cell groups. "This creates a united prayer front that will end Satan's attempt to divide and isolate believers, and to blind so many to the gospel of Jesus Christ," says Haggard.[14]

The idea is to pray five blessings on five neighbors, starting at five minutes a day, five days a week, for five weeks.

Another initiative called Lighthouse of Prayer is intercession at its most basic and essential element: individual intercessors, families, home prayer groups, and other cell groups praying for breakthroughs in their local community.

"Now is the time to build a canopy of prayer that will change the spiritual climate over the nation through prayer evangelism . . . city by city, block by block, and house by house," says Ed Silvoso, author of *That None Should Perish.*[15] Silvoso is currently at the forefront of strategizing ways to pray for the lost at the community level. The World Prayer Center is partnering with Silvoso to help Lighthouses of Prayer get their prayer needs out to others and provide them with strategic information and tools to help them reach their city.

> ### Clegg on Reaching the Unchurched
>
> The big problem today is not that the gospel isn't being told, but that it's not being heard.
>
> My research and experience confirm the assumptions of this chapter about learning to speak the *lingua franca* of the people who must be embraced if we are to be engaged in the re-missionization of the United States as the largest post-Christian nation in all the world.
>
> The idealism that hallmarked America in previous decades has been replaced by what some call a clinical narcissism. This shift requires fresh approaches to a culture inclined to interpret the gospel solely in terms of personal benefits.
>
> Christians have historically assumed that people struggle with guilt and a conscious sense of sin. Instead, people today wrestle more with anxiety, low self-esteem, lack of meaning, hopelessness, and a need to belong.
>
> This chapter, as a heralding wake-up call to the church, equips us to be heard by the people we say we're in business to reach.
>
> Tom Clegg
> consultant, Church Resource Ministries, Des Moines, Iowa
> coauthor, *Releasing Your Church's Potential* (ChurchSmart, 1998)

Yet another recent prayer evangelism initiative is called Houses of Prayer Everywhere.[16] Executive Director Alvin Vander Griend offers a "five-and-five prayer challenge." The idea is to pray five blessings on five neighbors, starting at five minutes a day, five days a week, for five weeks. One person who accepted the challenge was a pastor in Walnut Creek, California, named Johnny Jones, who pastors a church of 150. Jones reported that within a month, one neighbor came to the pastor and said, "I've always wondered what it means to have a personal relationship with Jesus Christ." Jones saw her come to faith in Christ. Another neighbor came to Johnny, admitting an involvement in drugs and asking for help. A Buddhist Vietnamese neighbor asked to go to church with him. A Roman Catholic couple asked him to start a Bible study.

As God's people rally in prayer, they are discovering a whole new pathway to evangelistic effectiveness.

Keep the End Result in Mind

When DisneyWorld opened in Orlando, Florida, Walter Cronkite commented to Mrs. Disney about her late husband's absence at the celebration. "It's too bad that Mr. Disney is not here to see this," he said. Her reply? "If he had not seen it first, we would not be seeing it today."

Readers may not agree with all the forecasts or affirmations offered by the authors cited in this chapter. We can't wholeheartedly support every facet of every development either. But we can affirm with George Hunter that, "The Christian movement now faces its greatest opportunity in the Western world in the last three centuries."[17] We must stay focused on the mission Christ gave to his followers—to make disciples of all nations.

With Donald McGavran, the founder of the modern church growth movement, we rejoice in anyone who shares this passion: "The heart of Christian Mission is evangelization. Its supreme task is to proclaim Jesus Christ as God and only Savior and encourage men and women to become responsible members of his church. Evangelism is the greatest and holiest work of the church."[18]

Isn't it time for your church to step out in faith and set new benchmarks for reaching the unchurched in your community, region, and world?

? APPLICATION QUESTIONS
FOR INDIVIDUAL RESPONSE OR GROUP DISCUSSION

1. In the material drawn from Peter Wagner, *The New Apostolic Churches*, which qualities are most like the church you serve? Would you have drawn up the same list of qualities? Which would you add or delete? Can you think of a better term than "new apostolic"?

2. Pick one of the churches described in this chapter. How does its approach to measuring growth compare to your church's? Does your congregation's pathway to spiritual maturity seem more clear or less clear? How can you use what you learned from the churches featured?

3. How did you feel about the role and methods of prayer described in this chapter? What can you do at your church to develop a greater partnership with God through prayer?

PASTORS 4. What value would there be in going to a conference featuring one of the churches or people described in this chapter? Could you take a couple of key lay leaders with you for help in assessing and applying the insights you glean?

Part 4

Churches Move toward New Forms for Faith Transfer

Make More Room for Truth

Today's generation is the first to grow up with virtually no "public square" connection to its Judeo-Christian roots, and the next generation will be raised in North America's most secularized culture since the Pilgrims landed.

Go Confidently to Mars Hill

Today's church is birthing a new generation of apologists, intellectuals, and scientists who are both rigorously academic and unabashedly Christian.

seven

Make More Room for Truth

Trend #7: Today's generation is the first to grow up with virtually no "public square" connection to its Judeo-Christian roots, and the next generation will be raised in North America's most secularized culture since the Pilgrims landed.

∽

One of the most dramatic moments of the Second World War occurred when the British army was stranded helplessly on the beaches of France. In June 1940, the British Expeditionary Force, sent to stem the Nazi advance into Belgium and France, was pushed steadily back to the sea at Dunkirk. A dark covering fell over England. Hitler's armies seemed poised to destroy the cornered Allied army. As the British people waited anxiously, a besieged army at Dunkirk transmitted a three-word message: "But if not."

England's citizens instantly recognized what the message meant: Even if we are not rescued from Hitler's army, we will stand strong and unbowed. "But if not" came from Daniel 3:18, where Shadrach, Meshach, and Abednego defied the evil Nebuchadnezzar by saying they would not bow to the king's idol. They were trusting God to deliver them, "but if not," they were willing to die.

That message galvanized the British people. Thousands of private boats of all sizes set out across the English Channel in a gallant bid to

Truth Bites for a Prodigal Generation

McLean Bible Church

Denomination: nondenominational

Location: Tysons Corner, Virginia (suburb of Washington, D.C.)

Senior pastor: Lon Solomon (since 1980)

Recent goal: Begin relocating ministries to the new property in Tysons Corner.

Church vision: To impact lives through the life-changing message of Jesus Christ.

Year founded: 1961

Attendance: 6500 (now)
                  2000 (5 years ago)
                  1200 (10 years ago)

Internet address: www.mbcva.org or www.front line.to (registered in Tonga)

What can a fairly traditional church do to reach an unchurched, younger generation? For McLean Bible Church, based in suburban Washington D.C., the answer was to launch a church within a church.

Frontline, the ministry of McLean Bible Church for eighteen- to thirty-five-year-olds, began in 1994. Within five years it had exploded to fifteen hundred young adults worshiping in two packed-out services on Sunday evenings. All week long even more targeted small-group community meetings take place for in-depth and interactive teaching in a more informal, casual atmosphere. These include thirties and early forties, ages eighteen to twenty-five, young marrieds, and older single parents.

The "host" church of four thousand attendance holds its corporate worship services on Saturday evenings and Sunday mornings. It likewise sponsors numerous programs during the week.

According to Lon Solomon, senior pastor at McLean Bible Church, and an occasional speaker at the Frontline gatherings, a common thread ties together all the ministries of the church. "Our values and our vision illustrate that we are all about relationships: experiencing a growing relationship with Jesus, enjoying the care and encouragement of close friends, and developing a personal vision to touch lives with the love of God."

Frontline's particular niche is to create an environment designed to draw in unbelievers, as churched young adults bring their unchurched friends. "The strategic idea was to create a unique feel that people might not have experienced before," says Ken Baugh, Frontline pastor.

For Baugh, the approach parallels his own return to faith. "My real passion is to reach prodigals because I was a prodigal," he explains. "I received Christ at age twelve. In high school I fell away from the Lord, and came back at age twenty-one when reality hit me hard. Frontline's target is young adults who had an experience with Christ or walked with Christ at one time but ditched him. They want somehow to come back but don't know how. Or maybe they're afraid God won't take them back."

Baugh and other leaders at McLean Bible Church are keenly aware that the response they've seen to date represents only the tip of an iceberg. Baugh coauthored a book that describes what is needed to win today's young adult population for Christ. Baugh and his coauthor do not insist the church-within-a-church idea as the only strategy. Instead they affirm, "Not every church needs a separate program to reach young adults, but any church can have an effective ministry with them."*

* Ken Baugh and Rich Hurst, *Getting Real: An Interactive Guide to Relational Ministry* (Colorado Springs: NavPress, 2000), 4.

rescue their army. They succeeded marvelously. Nearly 350,000 British and Allied soldiers were saved from the advancing Nazis.[1]

Today, more than fifty years later, would the average person in Great Britain or any other Western country grasp the meaning of such a cryptic biblical allusion? How many people today would be steeped enough in Christian understanding to be moved by the message "But if not"?

Obviously a major shift has occurred in Western culture. Public awareness of biblical themes is at an all-time low. Christians can no longer depend on society's help to nurture people in their faith.

This chapter will look at new forms of faith transfer that are teaching truth and inspiring the kind of hope that cannot be explained apart from Christ. Today's generation may be the first to grow up with virtually no "public square" connection to its Judeo-Christian roots. But even in such a secularized culture, believers are still asked, "Why is your life different?" and "How can my life become more like yours?"

Six Historical Traditions of Discipleship

1. *Contemplative:* "a life of loving attention to God" by which we are reminded that "the Christian life comes not by gritting our teeth but by falling in love" with God. We practice it by using solitude and silence to develop "a personal history with God."

2. *Holiness:* by which "we are enabled to live whole, functional lives in a dysfunctional world." The goal is "not to get us into heaven, but to get heaven into us." This tradition "focuses upon the inward reformation of the heart and the development of 'holy habits.'"

3. *Charismatic:* "a life immersed in, empowered by, and under the direction of the Spirit of God." We ask for and embrace the supernatural working of God in our lives and our communities, resulting in the experience of God's presence and the building up of the body of Christ. "We are empowered by God to do his work and to evidence his life upon the earth."

4. *Social Justice:* which is "a life committed to compassion and justice for all peoples." As we practice this tradition, "God develops in us the compassion to love our neighbor freely and develops in our world a place where justice and righteousness prevail."

5. *Evangelical:* which is "a life founded upon the living Word of God, the written Word of God, and the proclaimed Word of God," through which "we experience the knowledge of God that grounds our lives and enables us to give a reason for the hope that is in us."

6. *Incarnational.* which offers us "a life that makes present and visible the realm of the invisible Spirit." Through this tradition God calls us to "find God in the details [of daily living] and serve God through these same details." We "learn to do our work as Jesus would do our work if he were in our place."

Summarized from Richard Foster's *Streams of Living Waters* (San Francisco: Harper SanFrancisco, 1998), 23–272.

Don't Anticipate a Quick Fix for Biblical Illiteracy

Tonight Show host Jay Leno periodically does on-the-street interviews. During national Bible week in 1998, he went to a Los Angeles nightclub and asked questions about the Bible.

"Can you name one of the Ten Commandments?" he asked two college-age women. One replied, "Freedom of speech?" Leno then asked the other student to complete this sentence: "Let him who is without sin . . ." Her response was "have a good time." Leno finally turned to a young man and asked, "Who, according to the Bible, was eaten by a whale?" The man's confident answer was "Pinocchio."[2]

According to pollster George Barna, a significant number of North Americans would demonstrate the same woeful lack of basic Bible understanding. Most wouldn't have a clue what "but if not" means.

Recent surveys indicate that only a fraction of Americans can name all of the Ten Commandments, and only 42 percent can identify who preached the Sermon on the Mount. Most people think the preacher was someone mounted on horseback, or they attribute the sermon to Billy Graham. Few guess that Jesus was the source.[3]

According to another poll, biblical illiteracy is such that 12 percent of the American people think Noah was married to Joan of Arc.[4] Perhaps more alarming is another trend: Americans are abandoning the belief that absolute truth even exists. As early as 1991 Barna found that 67 percent of those questioned answered "no" when asked: "Is there any such thing as absolute truth?" Two years later the percentage had risen to 72 percent. Further, Barna observes that 44 percent of Americans believe Jesus sinned, only 31 percent read their Bible regularly, and 84 percent don't even know the meaning of the Great Commission.[5]

For the follower of Jesus, understanding the Bible-based foundations of one's faith is essential. Not only is it important for personal spiritual growth, but it is also vital for helping other people become Christians and for making an impact on the world around us. Author and apologist Chuck Colson affirms, "Society cannot survive without Christian truth."[6] Professor Alister McGrath of Oxford University explains, "In an increasingly secular culture . . . fewer and fewer people outside the Christian community have any real understanding of what Christians believe. Half-truths, misconceptions, and caricatures abound."[7] As the apostle Peter reminded Jesus' followers, "Be prepared to give an answer . . . for the hope that you have" (1 Peter 3:15).

Americans are abandoning the belief that absolute truth even exists.

1,000th Commitment to Christ via Web Site!

Ron Hutchcraft Ministries, based in Arkansas, developed a seeker-friendly web site designed to present life's most important relationship: knowing Jesus Christ. In non-religious language, cyberspace visitors are presented with practical help for everyday issues. Ultimately, these felt-need issues address the difference a relationship with Jesus Christ can make. Hutchcraft's online gospel presentation, "Yours for Life: How to Have Life's Most Important Relationship" (http://www.gospelcom.net/rhm/yours/yours4a .htm), has been read by many thousands of Internet guests.

In the web site's first thousand days online, more than a thousand people indicated that they had prayed to receive Christ.

Web visitors are encouraged to sign a commitment page after they pray to begin a relationship with Christ. Commitments have come from most states and numerous countries worldwide, including the People's Republic of China, Romania, Indonesia, Singapore, South Korea, Malaysia, Taiwan, the Philippines, Ecuador, Botswana, Nigeria, New Zealand, Austria, Kuwait, and the United Arab Emirates.

Ron Hutchcraft Ministries (http://www.hutchcraft.com) has been online since February 1, 1996, and is a member of the Gospel Communications Network (www.gospelcom.net), the world's largest coalition of Christian cyberspace ministries.

Discern How Culture Has Shifted from Judeo-Christian Values

Mahatma Gandhi, known as the father of India, studied the teachings of Jesus and once said: "You Christians look after a document containing enough dynamite to blow all civilization to pieces, turn the world upside down and bring peace to a battle-torn planet. But you treat it as though it is nothing more than a piece of good literature."[8]

Indeed, lack of Bible knowledge has contributed to a clear lack of identity on the part of many Christians. Os Guinness described one implication in a curious book title: *Fit Bodies, Fat Minds: Why Evangelicals Don't Think and What to Do about It.* "Failing to think Christianly, evangelicals have been forced into the role of cultural imitators and adapters rather than originators," he wrote. "In biblical terms, it is to be worldly and conformist, not decisively Christian."[9]

Sociologist of religion Christian Smith notes that whenever American evangelicals feel at home in their culture, they tend to quit reaching out and growing. They thrive when they feel embattled with culture; they fail to shape culture when they feel successful and prosperous, as the evangelical movement does today.[10]

The prevailing culture is clearly changing. Many, though not all, of its shifts are away from Judeo-Christian values. Only with a strong

North America's Changing Absolutes

Christian journalist William Watkins wrote *The New Absolutes: How They Are Being Imposed on Us, How They Are Eroding Our Moral Landscape* to demonstrate the world of ideas in collision over values and lifestyles. His point is to show that those who claim tolerance and decry moral absolutes are at the same time imposing new absolutes on society.

1. Religious Freedom

Old: Religion is the backbone of American culture, providing the moral and spiritual light needed for public and private life.

New: Religion is the bane of public life, so for the public good it should be banned from the public square.

2. Sanctity of Life

Old: Human life from conception to natural death is sacred and worthy of protection.

New: Human life, which begins and ends when certain individuals or groups decide it does, is valuable as long as it is wanted.

3. Marriage

Old: The institution of marriage is God-ordained and occurs between a man and a woman until death severs the bond.

New: Marriage is a human contract made between any two people, and either party can terminate it for any reason.

4. Family

Old: The normative family is a married father and mother who raise one or more children.

New: Family is any grouping of two or more people, with or without children.

5. Sex and Marriage

Old: Sexual intercourse should be reserved for marriage.

New: Sexual intercourse is permissible regardless of marital status.

6. Sex and Partners

Old: Same-sex and bisexual intercourse are immoral.

New: All forms and combinations of sexual activity are moral as long as they occur between consenting parties.

7. Women

Old: Women should be protected and nurtured but not granted social equality.

New: Women are oppressed by men and must liberate themselves by controlling their own bodies and therefore their destinies.

8. Race

Old: All white people are created equal and should be treated with dignity and respect.

New: All human beings are created equal and should be treated with dignity and respect, but people of color should receive preferential treatment.

9. Western Culture

Old: Western civilization and its heritage should be studied and valued above others.

New: Non-Western societies and other oppressed peoples and their heritage should be studied and valued above Western civilization.

10. Political Correctness

Old: Different perspectives should be heard and tolerated, but only the true and right ones should prevail.

New: Only those viewpoints deemed politically correct should be tolerated and encouraged to prevail.

From William Watkins, *The New Absolutes: How They Are Being Imposed on Us, How They Are Eroding Our Moral Landscape* (Minneapolis: Bethany House, 1996).

foundation in Scripture will Christians be able to discern which trends are harmful and which are healthy.

Look for New Forms of Christian Education

In May 1943, *Coronet* magazine observed, "If you're inclined to wager that America's largest radio audiences tune in to Charlie McCarthy or Bob Hope, ignore your hunch and save your money."

Why? The article continued: "A couple of preachers operating on shoestring budgets are giving them a run for their money . . . They are Walter A. Maier of St. Louis . . . and Charles E. Fuller of Los Angeles. . . . Fuller is the founding father of the 'Old Fashioned Revival Hour,' which has so many outlets there probably isn't a radio set anywhere in the United States which can't pick up his hymn singing and sermons on Sunday nights."[11]

Many senior-age saints today credit radio sermons and printed books of sermons as a significant venue in which they learned the content of their faith. Those who grew up in mainline denominations also experienced the catechisms as a major vehicle of faith transfer.

Likewise the Sunday school movement, which reached its peak in the 1950s for most congregations, made Sunday school the primary forum for assimilation, conversion, and discipleship. In many churches

---

Christian Partners for Internet Evangelism

The number of people who use the Internet doubles every eighty days. Christians are at the forefront of this new technology. It is being harnessed for kingdom usage from missionaries who use e-mail to seminaries that offer online training. At one time, *Christianity Today*'s web site and chat room drew more hits than the site sponsored by the *New York Times*!

In addition to communication and training, other Christians want to use the Internet evangelistically. In 1999, Billy Graham's organization cosponsored a conference on how to use the Internet to reach people for Jesus Christ. The largest-known coalition of Christian web sites, GospelCom.net, reports a steady stream of conversions to Christianity, based on 414 million hits in 1998 from Internet users in 193 countries and territories around the world.

Is the Internet the next wave of evangelism? Leading researcher David B. Barrett has compiled some statistics about global missions using the Internet. He writes, "The vast majority of Christian web pages are visited only by Christians. Additionally, only 2 percent of the world's 4 billion non-Christians have any chance of ever accessing the Internet [in the near future]."*

*From *International Bulletin of Missionary Research*, vol. 23, no. 1, January 1999.

Did Somebody Say, "Give Me a Sign, Lord"?

Since September 1998, billboards and signs bearing the messages below have appeared on roads in all fifty U.S. states and even overseas. In their first year alone they appeared in ten thousand places, representing a commitment of $15 million in ad space, most of which was donated as a public service.

The non-denominational campaign was originally commissioned by a Florida resident who insisted on anonymity. He paid an advertising agency in Fort Lauderdale $150,000 to produce a spiritual campaign "that people could relate to in a 90s kind of way," said the agency's president, Andrew Smith, according to *The New York Times*.* Ads such as the following have appeared in many places, including the inside and outside of buses.

"Let's Meet at My House Sunday before the Game."—God

"C'mon Over and Bring the Kids."—God

"We Need to Talk."—God

"Loved the Wedding. Invite Me to the Marriage."—God

"That 'Love Thy Neighbor' Thing, I Meant It."—God

"I Love You . . . I Love You . . . I Love You . . ."—God

"Will the Road You're On Get You to My Place?"—God

"Follow Me."—God

"Big Bang Theory—You've Got to Be Kidding."—God

"Need Directions?"—God

"Tell the Kids I Love Them."—God

"Need a Marriage Counselor? I'm Available."—God

"Have You Read My #1 Best-Seller? There Will Be a Test."—God

*Tom Kuntz, "Word for Word/Billboards from God," *New York Times,* Week in Review section, p. 7. See also www.godspeaks.net.

---

today Sunday school and church-based lay Bible institutes continue to be at the epicenter of Christian education, according to Thom Rainer's research.[12]

A revolution has occurred, however, that is rapidly transforming the appearance of Christian education. Consider these statistics:

It took thirty-eight years for radio to attract 50 million listeners.

It took thirteen years for television to attract 50 million viewers.

It took only four years for the Internet to attract 50 million users.

And traffic on the Internet is doubling in a time period of less than every eighty days. By November 1999, researchers were claiming that 100 million Americans were using the Internet, up from 65 million just over a year earlier.[13]

Have you noticed the continual presence of Internet influences in this book? Although *Into the Future* is a print medium, the primary research for this book occurred through the electronic pulses of cy-

Shelley on Teaching Truth

In this chapter, Towns and Bird make a persuasive case for the reintroduction of truth and the life of the mind into the church's overall disciple-making task.

Yesterday I had a conversation with a Christian man who discovered that his eighteen-year-old daughter, raised in a seeker-sensitive church, was not able to recite the Lord's Prayer, name the Ten Commandments, or list even five of Jesus' Beatitudes. The man and his wife were crushed, asking whether or not they had failed their family by not making sure that, while being raised in a church, their daughter received a biblical education that was up to code.

The challenge for our churches is to combine cultural relevancy with clear communication of the truth. As this chapter affirms, "A major shift has occurred in Western culture. Public awareness of biblical themes is at an all-time low. Christians can no longer depend on society's help in nurturing people along in their faith."

Marshall Shelley
executive editor, *Leadership*, Carol Stream, Illinois
author, *Well-Intentioned Dragons: Dealing with Problem People in the Church* (Bethany House, 1994)

berspace. We also designed the callout quotes, abundant sidebars, and end-of-chapter discussion questions to engage today's visual, interactive imagination.

How will the coming generation learn about Christianity? New forms of communication are emerging and gaining popularity. Most have relational and story-driven components.

Hollywood cinema is "at the vanguard of the technology-based art forms that came to dominate entertainment and leisure in twentieth-century America," says Calvin College professor William Romanowski in *Pop Culture Wars: Religion and the Role of Entertainment in American Life*.[14] However, today's "most viewed film in history" did not come from Hollywood. The "Jesus" video, promoted by a division of Campus Crusade for Christ, is available in 525 languages and seen by 2.9 billion people in 230 countries (on television in 111 countries), with 5.8 million videos in circulation.[15]

Today's "most viewed film in history" did not come from Hollywood.

"A persuasive argument can be made that the contemporary demand by the public to be entertained represents the most significant change in the context for ministry during the last third of the twentieth century," says church observer Lyle Schaller in *Discontinuity and Hope*.[16] One evidence of this is the enormous popularity of Christian fiction. For example, the combined sales of the first five apocalyptic novels by Jerry Jenkins and Tim LaHaye have topped 12 million. The fifth in the series, *Apollyon*, was listed on *The New York Times* fiction bestseller list and remained there for more than six months. It was the first Christian fiction book to jump onto this secular bestsellers list.[17]

It comes as no surprise, then, that perhaps the United States' most popular evangelistic training in the late 1990s has been the Becoming a Contagious Christian series created by Willow Creek Community Church. The series uses videos of dramatic vignettes, interactive discussions, and a relationship-centered theology as its training springboards.

Likewise, the use of Internet chat rooms by Christians enables people to learn relationally and to tell their story in a way that makes them feel heard. The same can be said for the popular concepts of mentoring and team building as a way of doing ministry.[18]

Note that these new forms of faith transfer are just as public and can be just as evangelistic as their counterparts in previous generations. Even highway billboards are having an effect in outreach and Christian education!

Leith Anderson, senior pastor of Wooddale Church just outside Minneapolis, has observed, "My task is to take the Bible and make it *relevant* to those who listen. Yet the Bible was written not only in language different from ours, but in totally different culture and centuries. Translating it into English may be the easiest part; translating it into twentieth-century American culture is far more difficult."[19]

Yet something huge is happening. Overall church attendance may still be flatlined or slightly declining, but the Christian faith is being transferred to the next generation. Indeed, three of four people joining an American church today are young adults between the ages of eighteen and thirty-five.[20] The question is whether that religious interest can be translated by the power of the Holy Spirit into fully committed disciples of Jesus Christ.

A 1980 Gallup Poll on religion reports that, "We are having a revival of feelings but not of the knowledge of God. The church today is more guided by feelings than by convictions. We value enthusiasm more than informed commitment."[21] The task ahead is clear for the church of the next generation—and it begins today.

APPLICATION QUESTIONS
FOR INDIVIDUAL RESPONSE OR GROUP DISCUSSION

1. Does today's general biblical illiteracy trouble you? Why or why not? What has your church done to help train people in the content of their faith?
2. Which new forms of faith transfer are most popular with the people of your church? Why?
3. Do you agree with the concluding Gallup quote? What are the implications for your congregation? Specifically, how can you act on those implications?

PASTORS 4. What experimentation have you recently encouraged with the kinds of Bible training and faith transfer that are best received by people of today (and tomorrow)? Of the ideas mentioned in this chapter, which could you experiment with? When and where?

eight

Go Confidently to Mars Hill

Trend #8: Today's church is birthing a new generation of apologists, intellectuals, and scientists who are both rigorously academic and unabashedly Christian.

⁑

Harvard University, founded to train Puritan ministers and the oldest institution of higher learning in the United States, is now expressing interest in a theology it long ago abandoned. In the spring of 1998, Dr. Mark Noll, professor of Christian thought at Wheaton College, served as Harvard Divinity School's first visiting professor in evangelical theology. Described by *The New York Times* as "an evangelical intellectual who finds a kind of heresy in evangelicalism's neglect of the mind," Dr. Noll is the author and editor of many books and articles, including *The Scandal of the Evangelical Mind; Between Faith and Criticism;* and *Evangelicals, Scholarship, and the Bible in America*.

Unfortunately, people like Mark Noll are so rare that their presence at a major intellectual center rated such unusual coverage in *The New York Times*. According to Noll, "The scandal of the evangelical mind is that there is not much of an evangelical mind. . . . Despite dynamic success at a popular level, modern American evangelicals have failed notably in sustaining serious intellectual life. They have nourished millions of believers in the simple verities of the gospel but have largely abandoned the universities, the arts, and other realms of 'high' culture."[1]

New Slant on Apologetics: Reaching Artists through the Arts

Mosaic (formerly The Church on Brady)

Denomination:	Southern Baptist Convention (SBC)
Location:	Los Angeles, California
Lead pastor:	Erwin McManus (since 1993)
Recent goal:	To produce radical disciples of Jesus Christ; to be a spiritual reference point throughout Los Angeles and a sending base to the ends of the earth.
Church vision:	To live by faith, to be known by love and to be a voice of hope.
Year founded:	1953
Attendance:	1100 (now)
	500 (5 years ago)
	600 (10 years ago)
Internet address:	www.mosaic.org

Mosaic draws arguably the highest concentration of painters, designers, screenwriters, actors, directors, and producers of any Southern California church. The lead pastor, Erwin McManus, is known for focusing on the relationship between spirituality and creativity.

"The church, being connected to the Creator God, ought to become the most creative entity on earth," says McManus. "Creativity is the natural result of spirituality. We believe creativity glorifies God and expresses who he is."

The church meets in two locations—a church building on the east edge of downtown section for three services (Saturday night and Sunday morning), and in the heart of downtown at Club Soho, which is transformed into a church each Sunday night. All four services feature numerous creative expressions of the worship arts, from smells to paintings.

But the idea is not to imitate MTV or the latest Hollywood special effects. "If people are coming here to be entertained, they're going to be shocked. What we're doing is for people who are serious about truth," says McManus, known for his hard-hitting preaching. The church offers serious training for those who would become Jesus' disciples. For several years it sent out more overseas believers than any other Southern Baptist congregation, even those ten times its size. In thirty months they sent thirty-two adults into the 10/40 window.

McManus is also serious about equipping believers for local outreach. "The two major currents of today's postmodern era are urbanization and technology," he explains. "Most of our approaches toward leadership and evangelism are remnants of our rural roots and are both irrelevant and ineffective in the urban challenge."

"The future world is a mosaic," says McManus in linking today's culture to the name of the church. "It is a place where every assumption about truth, God, and reality is questioned, if not challenged. People will move from 'church hopping' to 'god shopping.' Or they will seek guides simply to teach them to make their own gods.

"We're to take Jesus to those who need him," says McManus. "God is enabling us to impact an emerging postmodern culture in a way in which people find the gospel in a life-transforming manner."

That's changing though. An era of "intellectual mediocrity" is slowly transitioning into "a rich harvest of mature Christian scholarship" according to Oxford's Allister McGrath and *Christianity Today* book review editor John Wilson.[2] Just as the apostle Paul confidently took on the intellectual leaders at Athens' Mars Hill with at least two immediate conversions as a result (Acts 17:16–34), so Christians almost two thousand years later are building bridges with the intellectuals who reign over today's Mars Hills. In the process, the church is birthing a new generation of apologists, intellectuals, and scientists who are both rigorously academic and unabashedly Christian.

Reach the Mind through Compelling Stories

Imagine the following scenario:

Charley really doesn't like Sara very much, but one day it hits Charley that the best way to help Sara is to date her. Charley marches up to Sara's door with a book entitled *100 Things Sara Needs to Change in Order to Become a Real Person*. She answers the door and he shoves the book in her face saying, "I've decided it would be best for you if we date. When you finish reading this, I'll be waiting in my truck."[3]

> ### Anti-Intellectualism's Impact on the Church
>
> "The modern understanding of Christianity is neither biblical nor consistent with the bulk of church history," says J. P. Moreland, professor of philosophy at Talbot School of Theology, Biola University, in La Mirada, California. According to his book, *Love Your God with All Your Mind: The Role of Reason in the Life of the Soul*, today's outlook by Christians has led to the following:
>
> 1. A misunderstanding of faith's relationship to reason.
> 2. The separation of the secular and the sacred.
> 3. Weakened world missions.
> 4. The spawning of an irrelevant gospel.
> 5. A loss of boldness in confronting the idea structures in our culture with effective Christian witness.
>
> From J. P. Moreland, *Love Your God with All Your Mind: The Role of Reason in the Life of the Soul* (Colorado Springs: NavPress, 1997), 25–31.

This caricature of an apologist—someone who defends the Christian faith—positions the church as Charley and the surrounding culture as Sara. If you identified with Sara, you'll understand how some people who are not yet Christians view the church as arrogant, uncaring, and irrelevant.

Fortunately, this model is increasingly hard to find among today's passionate apologetic evangelists. More commonly Christian apologists use the platform of storytelling to communicate truth and disarm objections.

For example, San Antonio pastor Max Lucado is one of today's most gifted storytellers. The popularity of his books set publishing records during 1999 when as many as three of his titles appeared on the Christian best-seller list at the same time.

Lucado's communication style makes writing appear simple. He's like the professional golfer who makes the golf swing look easy, the skilled tenor who leads an audience to believe that anyone could hit those high notes, or a NASA scientist who speaks about mathematical equations with the same effortlessness the rest of us display only when rattling off the alphabet.

Some people who are not yet Christians view the church as arrogant, uncaring, and irrelevant.

If Lucado is at the top of his league as a narrative communicator, then who does he look up to as someone who can use stories to present lucid answers to tough questions, all the while making the problems look simple?

"Ravi Zacharias," answers Lucado. "When it comes to wrestling with tough issues of faith and life, I know of no one who does it better."[4] "Tough issues" is an understatement. The Atlanta-based, India-born apologist Ravi Zacharias takes on everything from suffering to despair, to atheism to restoring the soul in a disintegrating culture.[5]

"The whole world loves a story," Zacharias said in a recent conversation with Warren Bird. "Stories are a bridge—sometimes for difficult arguments, sometimes for simple truths." He has addressed the issue of God's existence in numerous major university settings, including Harvard and Oxford. He has lectured in more than fifty countries, and his weekly radio program, *Let My People Think,* is broadcast on more than 850 stations around the world.

"The burden I feel most is to clear the intellectual hurdles in the minds of the resistant and to regain the moral focus so that the cross can be seen for what it is," says Zacharias.[6] His trademark way of doing so is to unpack a complex concept through an engaging series of illustrations.

Zacharias represents a new breed of Christian thinkers who seem to thrive most when met with resistance. His mission is like the experience of a man named Jakob, a Yugoslavian evangelist during World War II, who preached Christ to a skeptic named Cimerman.

"These men of the cloth tortured and killed my own nephew before my eyes," Cimerman explained to Jakob with great emotion. "A few minutes later . . . they ate their supper in the parish house . . . as if nothing had happened."

"My heart suffers with your heart," the evangelist replied. Then Jakob asked Cimerman a series of questions. What if he put on Cimerman's coat and shoes, and then went into town and was seen stealing? Wouldn't the police come and say, "Cimerman, we saw you stealing"? And wouldn't Cimerman reply, "But it wasn't me!"

Cimerman understood Jakob's point about the hypocritical priests, but still he persisted, "I do not believe in the name of your God." And so the evangelist left.

Every week for a year Jakob walked 10 kilometers to Cimerman's cottage to visit him and talk with him about the Lord Jesus Christ.

At length, Cimerman greeted Jakob on one of his visits with these words: "You have convinced me. Your God is real. Your God is God. *You wear the coat well.*"[7]

Ravi Zacharias, commenting on that story, says "We need to be close to those who despise his name so we can give to them the coat of Christ . . . and let God bring about the conversions."[8]

Be Prepared to Deal with a Wide Array of Worldviews

In the polished wooden pews of a white-steepled New England church, the weekend congregation sits with heads reverently bowed. The town of Chelmsford, Massachusetts, is Yankee to the core, and so

The 30 Largest U.S. Religious Groups Include Cults and Non-Christian Religions

1. Roman Catholic	60,300,000	17. Seventh-Day Adventist	790,000
2. Baptist	36,400,000	18. Church of the Nazarene	600,000
3. Pentecostal	10,450,000	19. Islamic	530,000
4. Methodist	8,730,000	20. Reformed Churches	520,000
5. Lutheran	8,200,000	21. Unitarian Universalist	500,000
6. African (and Christian) Method. Episcop.	5,450,000	22. Salvation Army	450,000
		23. Armenian Church	410,000
7. Mormon	4,890,000	24. Buddhist	400,000
8. Eastern Orthodox	4,080,000	25. Christian and Missionary Alliance	310,000
9. Presbyterian	3,940,000		
10. Jews	3,140,000	26. American Orthodox	300,000
11. Churches of Christ	3,130,000	27. Polish National Catholic	280,000
12. Episcopal Church	2,540,000	28. Community Churches	250,000
13. Evangelical Church	2,540,000	29. Evangelical Free Church	240,000
14. Christian Churches	1,070,000	30. Hindu	230,000
15. Jehovah's Witnesses	970,000		
16. Disciples of Christ	930,000		

U.S. Bureau of the Census, statistical abstract, 1997.

are most of its inhabitants. Like the sober, straitlaced Pilgrims three hundred years before them, the worshipers here shun liquor, dress modestly, and feel uplifted when they call out, "God is great!"

Unlike their Puritan predecessors, however, those gathered here address their Maker in Arabic: "Allah-u Akhbar!" they chant, in a call offered five times each day by Muslims from Maine to Alaska. The hands-down winner for the number one spot of the largest faith group in the United States is Christianity. The number two spot for decades has been Judaism. However, that second-largest entity is being replaced.

Islam, not Christianity, will be the world's fastest growing religion of the twenty-first century.

Many demographers say Islam (the Muslim faith) has overtaken Judaism as the country's second-most commonly practiced religion. Others say that at 5 to 6 million strong, it is in the passing lane. Muslims make up one of the fastest-growing religious groups in America, largely because of immigration.[9]

Islam, not Christianity, will be the world's fastest growing religion of the twenty-first century. "While Western Christianity accounted for 27% of the world's population in 1900, and peaked at about 30% in 1980, the Muslim population increased from 12% in 1900 to as much as 18% in 1980 with well over 1 billion adherents in the 1990s . . . while Christianity has declined," says futurist Leonard Sweet.[10]

Attack Strategies of the Cults

Tactic #1: You can't trust your church.

Your church has misled you, they say. Some say it went totally apostate, others say it's merely been infected by thinking that leads you away from the real truth that can be found only with them.

Tactic #2: You need a better, higher authority than you can get from the Bible.

Your church is not enough, they charge, along with its pastors, elders, and deacons. You need their final word on what the Bible really means.

Tactic #3: You need our NEW discovery—an improvement on what Christians have always taught.

You need the whopper insight that the rest of Christendom somehow missed for two thousand years.

Tactic #4: You need to join us because we're really cool, neat folks.

They often do many nice things. They're sincere about their faith. Perhaps their enthusiasm and idealism is contagious. Their people sacrifice time and money to further their cause.

From Kevin Johnson and James White, *What's with the Dudes at the Door?* (Minneapolis: Bethany House, 1998), 43–46.

The implication is that more and more neighborhoods and work-places will look like a United Nations tea party of religious beliefs and practices. Recent book titles designed to help people reach their neigh-bors of other faiths include *The World at Your Door: Reaching Interna-tional Students in Your Home, Church, and School; Neighboring Faiths: A Christian Introduction to World Religions; Reaching Muslims for Christ;* and *The Universe Next Door: A Basic Worldview Catalog.*[11]

Likewise, many cults are larger, stronger, and faster-growing than groups committed to the historic gospel. A spate of Christ-centered resources are available for understanding and reaching out to those whose thinking has been deceived.[12]

The academic disciplines are also being invaded by Christians who apply the rigors of intellectual scrutiny to every subject imaginable, from challenges to atheistic evolution to issues of social morality and bioethics. Even with the headline-making resurgence of the high-cal-iber Christian university, young believers continue to invade the sec-ular campus as students, although sometimes armed with such books as *How to Stay Christian in College: An Interactive Guide to Keeping the Faith.*[13]

The social acceptability of being a religious seeker has also given rise to sensitive, no-nonsense books directed to seekers. *A Search for the Spiritual: Exploring Real Christianity* by James Emery White is one such book. It starts by exploring the benefits of becoming a seeker (chapter 1), deals with what's-in-it-for-me issues such as why the life of Jesus matters (chapter 5), and covers commonly voiced concerns such as why there is so much suffering (chapter 9) and belief that there can't be only one way (chapter 10). The book even deals with today's pragmatic question, "but will it work?" (chap-ter 12).[14]

Christians are learning how to genuinely accept others in love and compassion without necessarily approving of their worldview or behaviors.

And despite the public outcry for tolerance—de-fined today not as respect for other views, but as an acceptance that every individual's beliefs, values, lifestyles, and perception of truth claims are equal[15]—Christians are learning how to genuinely accept others in love and compassion without necessarily approving of their worldview or behaviors.

The net result in today's apologetic evangelism is a slow shift away from defense ("How Sciences Are Undermining a Christian World-view") to more of an offensive tactic ("Scientists Who Believe" and "Darwin on Trial"). In fact, in light of today's X-Files, popular-level fascination with the paranormal, books such as *The Dark Side of the Su-pernatural* are being written to help Christians recognize the difference

Spiritual Turnaround Beginning in Canada Also

Christians in Canada are struggling to reverse their country's long-term church decline. An estimated 24 million of Canada's 27 million people are unchurched.

Many Canadians have left Christianity—or they simply ignore it as irrelevant. According to government census figures, 82 percent of Canadians in 1991 identified in some way with the Catholic (12.3 million), Protestant (9.3 million), or Orthodox (0.4 million) faiths. By 1996 identification in some fashion with Christianity had fallen to 68 percent. In 1999 the percentage seemed to slip even lower in this vast and culturally diverse country.

Most Canadians who still identify with Christianity seem to possess only a nominal faith. Among Canadians who say they believe in Christ, only 21 percent participate in worship services at least twice a month or read the Bible regularly. Among Canada's estimated 3.4 million people who call themselves evangelicals, about half don't attend church.

Canada's largest Protestant church, the 1.8-million-member United Church, is in turmoil over its core teachings. "I don't believe Jesus was God," the *Ottawa Citizen* quoted the denomination's moderator Bill Phipps as saying. Asked about heaven and hell, Phipps said, "I have no idea if there is a hell. I don't think Jesus was that concerned about hell. He was concerned about life here on earth. . . . Is heaven a place? I have no idea." Phipps also said, "I don't believe Jesus is the only way to God. I don't believe he rose from the dead as scientific fact. I don't know whether those things happened. It's an irrelevant question."

Even though Phipps's comments are "at the liberal fringe" of Canadian Christianity, they are "pretty mainstream" in the larger Canadian society, according to Doug Keep, editor of *Christian Week,* a national biweekly newspaper based in Winnipeg, Manitoba. Large-scale rejection of Christianity has resulted in enormous cultural change as Christian values have faded in government, education, and the media, according to a report prepared in 1997 for evangelical Protestant leaders. Canadian society is "denying the reality or possibility of absolute truth," said Murray Moerman, coordinator of Church Planting Canada, who co-sponsored the report.

To counteract these trends, Renewal Fellowship, Church Alive, and Community of Concern are active as renewal movements within the United Church. Evangelical denominations are cooperating to plant new churches across the country. Church Planting Canada has set a goal of mobilizing Canadians to plant ten thousand new churches by the year 2015. This would ensure that there is a culturally relevant, biblically orthodox church for every two thousand persons. Campus Crusade for Christ and other parachurch ministries are likewise working hard to increase their presence and influence.

High-visibility congregations, such as Trinity Baptist Church and Centre Street Evangelical Missionary Church (profiled on pages 132 and 164 of this book), are unashamedly evangelistic. "Leading people to passionately follow Jesus" is the mission statement at Northview Community Church, Abbotsford, British Columbia, the largest-attendance congregation in the country. One of the church's nine core values is that "each person actively introduces their network of friends to Christ."

The turnaround may be hard, but numerous Christian groups show no signs of letting up on their efforts.

Significantly adapted from Current Feature Story, December 8, 1997, www.religionroday.com.

ᓕ⬤⬤⬤ McNeal on Asking Tough Questions

This chapter highlights evidences of a new generation of apologists, intellectuals, and scientists who are both rigorously academic and unabashedly Christian. Another example would be major organizations that are beginning to give serious attention to Christian writers. For instance, the respected publisher Jossey-Bass has partnered with Leadership Network to produce a Religion in Practice line of books, the first of which was released in 1999. Their aim is to give thoughtful treatment to challenging trends that churches must face.

If I were to formulate my own list of present-futures being faced by the North American church, I might suggest two possible responses to each—a wrong question and a tough question.

For example, if we talk about a second Reformation that returns the work of God to the people of God, a wrong question would be, How can we *employ* more laity as church workers? The tougher question is, How can we deploy God's priests to impact their world for Christ? Or if we think about the development of missional partnerships and alliances between denominations, a wrong question would be, How do we beat our church competitors? The tougher question is, How do we pray, strategize, and work with all believers toward establishing the body of Christ in our communities?

I find it encouraging that Christians are not opting for the easier answer to such issues.

Reggie McNeal
director, Leadership Development Department, South Carolina Convention, Columbia, South Carolina
author, *Revolution in Leadership* (1998, Abingdon)

---

between what is fraud, what is a supernatural counterfeit, and what is truly of God.[16]

Yet through all the new thinking that has emerged, the evangelist's central message remains unchanged. The invitation is to relationship— a wholehearted commitment to God, with an accompanying dramatically changed heart and altered lifestyle.

For example, more than 112,000 people attended an evangelistic crusade in Anaheim, California, July 23–25, 1999, that featured preaching by evangelist Greg Laurie, Christian rock music, and fireworks. Laurie is pastor of Harvest Christian Fellowship in Riverside, California. The crusade was broadcast on Laurie's Internet site (www.harvest.org), where it drew another 23,000 people from around the world. A total of 10,880 people made decisions to become a Christian or rededicate their lives to Christ, the ministry said.

"What is the meaning of life?" Laurie had asked the audience. He urged the young people in attendance to seek fulfillment in a relationship with God instead of in alcohol, sex, and violence. "You think you have all the time in the world, but John F. Kennedy Jr. is an example that our lives could end at any time. If you give your life to Christ, you won't regret it," he said.[17]

The timeless message remains the same, but the culteral forms of illustrating it and transferring it are ever changing.

? APPLICATION QUESTIONS
FOR INDIVIDUAL RESPONSE OR GROUP DISCUSSION

1. What apologist or evangelist has been of greatest help to you in learning the "why" answers to your faith? How have you been assisted by this person? How would your Christian life be different without that help?

2. What offensive tactics has your church taken in dealing with competing values or competing worldviews? What could you do to help that training become more "story-based" and "offense-based"?

3. Of the statistics cited in this chapter, which was the greatest surprise to you? Why? What are the implications for how your church might train the people of God? When and where can you apply one of these implications?

PASTORS 4. What are your dominant spiritual gifts? More pastors confess to being teachers (52 percent) than to any other spiritual gift. If gifts of apologetic evangelism aren't high on your gift mix, with whom could you partner or bring in to provide apologetic, evangelistic training to your congregation?

Part 5

Churches Move toward Greater Appreciation of Worship

Maximize the Strong Points of Your Worship Service

Worship styles in the future will be more diverse, with broader acceptance of the idea that one worship style doesn't have to fit all congregations.

Cash In on Two Millennia of Good Ideas

Christians increasingly want to partici- pate in worship as an experience. Many appreciate feeling connected to the two- thousand-year stream of church history by the use of liturgical worship elements.

nine

Maximize the Strong Points of Your Worship Service

Trend #9: Worship styles in the future will be more diverse, with broader acceptance of the idea that one worship style doesn't have to fit all congregations.

∽

True worship results in life change. Each time we encounter God afresh, he changes us. Worship never allows us to remain the same person because it impacts us in several ways:

Heart Response. Worship is not legitimate unless it comes from the heart. In worship we give God the "worthship" he is due.

Transformed Life. When we worship in the presence of God, we repent of sin. We deepen our relationship with God. Our faith, hope, and love become more radiant and more certain.

Raised Ante. Genuine worship regularly calls for a greater sacrifice from the worshiper. When worshipers feel God's presence and hear his voice, they follow his call to go deeper in Christ than they have previously experienced.

Changed Environment. In worship, dull and nonproductive elements receive new meaning or are replaced with new forms and new

Four Worship Styles Are the Result, Not the Starting Point

Centre Street Evangelical Missionary Church

Denomination:	Evangelical Missionary Church (EMC)
Location:	Calgary, Alberta
Senior pastor:	Henry Schorr (since 1987, associate pastor 5 years previous)
Recent goals:	To see 365 decisions for Christ and that they will be discipled. To develop 100 new cell leaders, and 20 more coaches (50% are in cells now)
Church vision:	To be a biblically functioning community of fully devoted followers of Christ committed to accomplishing God's redemptive purposes in the world.
Year founded:	1958
Attendance:	3800 (now) 1100 (5 years ago) 400 (10 years ago)
Internet address:	www.centrestreetchurch.ab.ca

"What we've seen has been profound because it's such a God thing," says Henry Schorr, senior pastor of Centre Street Church in Calgary, Alberta, Canada. An explosive growth has led to four worship services, each with a different personality and style.

Since Centre Street was the first Protestant church in Canada to launch a Saturday evening service (1990), many observers assumed that the eightfold growth in size over the last decade started with experimentation over worship style. "Technique itself won't do it," insists Schorr. "The additional services and styles were required because of our growth. Our primary goal in worship

is to lead people to the throne of grace. If they don't meet and hear from God, we've failed."

The church's leadership became strategic about worship style when Sunday morning growth required a spillover into Saturdays. "We want all our people involved in fulfilling our mission," says Schorr, "and we recognize that people are led into worship differently. If they're uncomfortable with the worship style, they won't invite their friends."

The pastoral leadership works hard not to segment worshipers by age. "We don't so much target a different audience, as provide a different form of worship," says Kervin Raugust, executive pastor. So while the one-thousand-person group that enjoys worship with the Sunday evening praise band tends to be of collegiate age, a surprising percentage of other young adults are interested in traditional worship on Sunday morning.

The worship-centered attitude has influenced the entire congregation, as a sizable percentage of the membership regularly bring friends and family to services. In 1998, the church saw 235 people make a first-time decision for Christ.

An earlier version of this case study appeared in "Leadership on the Edge," catalogue 11, January 1999, and is used by permission from The International Centre for Leadership Development and Evangelism, Winfield, BC, http://www.GrowingLeadership.com, 800-804-0777.

People Attend Church Services, but Don't Worship

VENTURA, Calif. (EP)—Other than watching television, the most popular activity on weekends is not watching NFL football games, or making a long-distance call to distant family or friends. According to the Barna Research Group, on a typical Sunday more than 75 million adults attend worship services at Christian churches. That is more than triple the number of adults who will tune in to football games on a typical Sunday during the regular season.

But according to researcher George Barna, what's really amazing is people continually return to churches, week after week, in spite of their failure to accomplish the most important reason for coming: to connect with God. Barna says new research shows a majority of people who attend worship services at Christian churches *leave the church without feeling that they experienced God's presence.*

In a nationwide survey among people who attend Christian churches, Barna discovered that in a typical weekend, less than one-third of the adults who attend church services say they feel as if they truly interacted with God. In fact, Barna's survey data reveal that one-third of the adults who regularly attend Christian church services say that they have never experienced God's presence at any time during their life.

Evangelical Press News Service, September 6, 1998.

---

methods. As the old adage says, "Methods are many, principles are few; methods may change, but principles never do."[1]

Worship is responding from the heart to God for who he is and what he has done. Worship is not an elective for a Christian who has enrolled in the school of Christ; it is a required course.

Most churches place a central focus on worshiping God and will continue to do so into the future. This fact does not guarantee, however, that people are really worshiping, nor does it suggest that all worship will look and feel the same.

According to renowned musician and hymnologist Donald P. Hustad, "Worship is one of the most divisive issues in churches today." In fact, he says, virtually all communions except the Orthodox "are arguing bitterly" about worship's form and style. "The current worship revolution," he concludes, "has been the source of some creative growth and much bruising conflict in today's church."[2]

What shape will worship take in twenty-first-century North America? Tomorrow's healthy churches will embrace at least six different traditions of worship as valid, acceptable, and perhaps even desirable. Church leaders will also have the confidence that each of these expressions can represent a healthy New Testament church.

This chapter explains how your church can end any fighting that you might be experiencing over worship styles, and then how, after making peace with competing worship traditions, you can maximize the strong points of the worship styles God leads your congregation to utilize. It proposes four action steps drawn from various experts in the field. Each is designed to help you know what the church of the future will look like—and how you can prepare your church for it.

Remember That Most Christians Register Strong Emotions and Definite Opinions about Worship

True worship can indeed lead to controversy. The first murder in human history seems to have taken place between brothers in a disagreement over worship. What was the issue between Cain and Abel? The jealousy arose because Cain's vegetable sacrifice to God wasn't received as his brother's blood sacrifice had been (Gen. 4:1–16).

While few church people today come to actual blows over the worship services in their congregation, many voice strong feelings about corporate worship. The youth group can do a goofy new thing in the name of Christ, and a church-sponsored outreach event can experiment with something innovative for the sake of advancing the kingdom of God. But try tampering with the worship service, and suddenly everyone has an opinion—and sometimes an "I'll just go elsewhere" threat.

The Ultimate Controversy

Probably the most emotional discussions concern musical style used in worship. For example, in discussing some of the newer music used in churches, one prominent American pastor remarked:

> There are several reasons for opposing it. One, it's too new. Two, it's often worldly, even blasphemous. The new Christian music is not as pleasant as the more established style because there are so many new songs, you can't learn them all. It also puts too much emphasis on instrumental music rather than on Godly lyrics. This new music creates disturbances, making people act indecently and disorderly. The preceding generation got along without it.[3]

Those words were voiced in 1723. They were a critique of Isaac Watts, who produced the first hymnbook in the English language, and

Six Areas of Tension in Worship

1. *Seeker Sensitivity v. Edified Christians.* Is your congregation using its worship services to value lost people and help them find Christ? If so, you might be hearing accusations such as this: "Our worship has accommodated the unsaved at the cost of violating biblical values." Some churches make their time of worship so evangelistic that they rename the gathering as a "seeker" event. When that happens, long-time church members sometimes feel that biblical mandates about worship are being compromised. Other long-time church members rejoice at the outreach.

2. *Human-Centered v. God-Centered.* Many churches today work hard to show how relevant God is to day-to-day life. What happens when increased emphasis is placed on God's concern for "my" cares and concerns? A shift can occur. If we center too much attention on people's felt needs rather than on God, then believers sometime question, "What did *God* get out of the service?"

3. *Dumbing Down v. Shaping Up.* When worship focuses so heavily on solving the problems of life, we may fail to lift people up to God's level. Marva Dawn, in *Reaching Out without Dumbing Down*, points out how American educational institutions have made tests easier so more students can pass. In the same way, she asks, "Do we accommodate the worst in popular culture, lowering standards to meet people where they are at the expense of lifting people to where they should be?"

4. *Conforming to the World v. Transforming the World.* Christians face a constant tension between Scripture's call not to "let the world around you squeeze you into its own mold" (Romans 12:2 PHILLIPS) and the mandate to be culture-transforming "salt of the earth" and "light of the world" (Matthew 5:13–16). Should Veterans Day or Mother's Day come into the church year? To what extent should current movies, television shows, or hit songs be referenced or used in worship? Behind each of these efforts at cultural relevance lies the issue of conforming to the world versus transforming it.

5. *Egotism v. Community.* A significant 1990s trend is illustrated when one person raises hands in worship, another claps, another stands, and another sits. Is this kind of individualism healthy for a church? Sometimes concerned Christians will maintain that a church should build a sense of community in worship. They believe we please God most when we sing together, pray the Lord's Prayer together, read Scriptures together, affirm the Creed together, and break bread together.

6. *Institutional Event v. Individual Event.* Is worship a group event or does it take people individually to God? In some churches it seems that all you hear about is God and you. It almost doesn't matter that other people are present. In other churches, the emphasis is highly relational and affective. As one veteran saint observed, "It bends my Builder-generation buddies out of shape that we are not focusing on the kind of solid, cognitive truth evident in the hymns of Charles Wesley and Reginald Heber."

Adapted from Elmer Towns, *Putting an End to Worship Wars* (Nashville: Broadman & Holman, 1997), 54–61.

wrote such traditional favorites as "Jesus Shall Reign" (based on Psalm 72), "O God, Our Help in Ages Past" (based on Psalm 90), and "When I Survey the Wondrous Cross."

Watts (1674–1748) lived in a day when some felt that the words of the Psalms had been put in a pattern of rhyme that was dreary. "Those metrical Psalms, they're so dull, and they're too repetitive," Isaac Watts argued with his father after they came home from morning church services.

"Well," his father replied, "if you want anything better, then you must write it yourself."[4]

That's just what Watts did—he gave Christians the English hymn as we now know it.

Worship Has Always Been Controversial

Most innovations in worship that are widely accepted in churches today were quite controversial as they were introduced. The following list, including imagined dialog, recounts the various frictions that have surrounded worship practices over the centuries:

"Honey wake up. It's almost midnight. We've got to get to church!"

100s A.D.: Many churches had daily worship services. One early practice was for Christians to rise and pray at midnight. Morning and evening prayer in church became customary through the fourth century, especially at centers of pilgrimage such as Jerusalem.[5]

"Get rid of that flute at church. Trash that trumpet, too. What do you think we are, pagans?"

200s A.D.: Instrumental music was almost universally shunned because of its association with debauchery and immorality. Lyre playing, for example, was associated with prostitution.[6]

"Hymns to God with rhythm and marching? How worldly can we get?"

300s A.D.: Ambrose of Milan (339–397), an influential bishop often called the father of hymnody in the Western church, was the first to introduce community hymn-singing in the church.[7] These hymns were composed in metrical stanzas, quite unlike biblical poetry. They did not rhyme but they were sometimes sung while marching.[8] Many of these hymns took songs written by heretics, using the same meter but rewriting the words.[9]

"The congregation sings too much. Soon the cantor will be out of a job!"

500s A.D.: Congregations often sang psalms in a way that "everyone responds." This probably involved the traditional Jewish practice of cantor and congregation singing alternate verses.[10]

"Musical solos by ordinary people? I come to worship God, not man!"

600s A.D.: The monasteries, referencing "Seven times a day I praise you" (Ps. 119:164), developed a seven-times-daily order of prayer. The services varied in content, but included a certain amount of singing, mainly by a soloist, with the congregation repeating a refrain at intervals.[11] The services were linked together by their common basis in the biblical psalms in such a way that the whole cycle of 150 psalms was sung every week.[12]

"Boring, you say? Someday the whole world will be listening to monks sing these chants."

800s A.D.: Almost all singing was done in chant, based on scales that used only the white keys on today's piano. The monastery was the setting above all others where Christian music was sustained and developed through the Dark Ages.[13]

"How arrogant for musicians to think their new songs are better than what we've sung for generations."

900s A.D.: Music began to be widely notated for the first time, enabling choirs to sing from music. Thus new types of music could be created which would have been quite out of the reach of traditions where music was passed on by ear.

"Hymns that use rhyme and accent? Surely worship should sound different than a schoolyard ditty!"

1100s A.D.: The perfection of new forms of Latin verse using rhyme and accent led to new mystical meditations on the joys of heaven, the vanity of life, and the suffering of Christ.[14]

"This complicated, chaotic confusion is ruining the church!"

1200s A.D.: Starting in France, musicians began to discover the idea of harmony. The startling effect of the choir suddenly changing from the lone and sinuous melody of the chant to two-, three-, or even four-part music did not please everyone. One critic commented how harmony "sullies" worship by introducing a "lewdness" into church.[15]

"Don't try that hymn at home; leave it to the professionals at church."

1300s A.D.: Worship in the great Gothic-era cathedrals and abbeys used choirs of paid professionals, "a church within a church," sealed off by screens from the greater building. Ordinary people generally had no place in the spiritual life of these great buildings, except perhaps in the giving of their finances.[16]

"It's too loud, and the music drowns out the words."

1400s A.D.: Music became increasingly complex (Gothic sounds for Gothic buildings), prompting criticisms that only the choir was allowed to sing. As reformer John Wycliffe had complained, "No one can hear the words, and all the others are dumb and watch them like fools."[17]

"They want us to sing in today's language. Shouldn't God-talk be more special than that?"

1500s A.D.: The new prayerbook, pushed by King Henry VIII of England decreed that all services would be in English, with only one syllable to each note.[18]

"Now they're putting spiritual words to theater songs that everyone knows."

1500s A.D.: Martin Luther set about reforming public worship by freeing the mass from what he believed to be rigid forms. One way he did this was by putting stress on congregational singing.[19] "Although Luther led the revolt against the abuses of the Roman Catholic church, he continued to make use of its texts and tunes. He modified Roman Catholic tunes and texts to fit his new theology. As a result, people recognized familiar hymns and chants and felt at home in the new church. He used music which was already familiar to the majority of the people in Germany."[20] As one writer quipped: "The Catholic, in church, listens without singing; the Calvinist sings without listening; the Lutheran both listens and sings—simultaneously!"[21]

"Okay, men on verse 2, ladies on verse 3, and the organ on verse 4."

1600s A.D.: The organ played an important part in Lutheranism, Anglicanism, and Roman Catholicism, while in the Reformed churches there was much opposition to it.[22] Initially the organ was not used to accompany congregational singing, but had its own voice, often substituting for a sung part of the service. As a result, the organist would often play a verse on the congregation's behalf.[23]

"Our children will grow up confused, not respecting the Bible as an inspired book."

1700s A.D.: Isaac Watts gave a great boost to the controversial idea of a congregation singing "man-made" hymns, which he created by freely paraphrasing Scripture. Charles Wesley paraphrased the Prayer Book, and versified Christian doctrine and experience. Wesley's songs "had at least as great an effect as his sermons."[24]

"Their leader is just asking for trouble when he says, 'Why should the devil have all the best music?'"

1800s A.D.: William Booth, founder of the Salvation Army, used rousing melodies with a martial flavor to set the tone for his Army. He is credited with popularizing the "why should the devil" question cited above.[25]

"These Christian radio quartets are on a slippery slope. Don't they realize that the airwaves are the domain of Satan, 'ruler of the kingdom of the air'?"

1900s A.D.: When radio was in its infancy, a handful of Christian pioneers such as Donald Grey Barnhouse and Charles E. Fuller began featuring gospel music and evangelistic teaching over the airwaves. Many Christians initially showed skepticism.

Identify and Understand the Areas of Tension

In *Putting an End to Worship Wars*, Elmer Towns points out that almost every church across North America can identify itself with one of six worship traditions (see sidebar below).

If your church is experiencing tension over worship styles, the conflict might be traced to differences in "personality." Sometimes friction

---

Most Churches Reveal a Distinct Personality in Worship

1. The *evangelistic* church makes sure many people get saved.
   Danger point: New converts sometimes don't stay long enough to be discipled or assimilated.
2. The *Bible expositional* church effectively teaches people the Word of God.
   Danger point: Christians can spend more time learning new truths than in applying and experiencing what they already know.
3. The *renewal* church motivates people toward holiness and obedience.
   Danger point: Christians can be so focused on experiencing the latest trend in spiritual passion that they remain shallow in other crucial areas.
4. The *body life* church helps people develop close relationships as they learn one-another ministry.

   Danger point: Christians can so value their know-everyone environment that they miss the festival-like electricity and power that can come from larger worship settings.
5. The *liturgical* church values historic traditions that help worshipers truly minister to God.
   Danger point: Congregations can so appreciate the importance of their worship that they become ingrown and lacking in fervor for conversion-based growth.
6. The *congregational* church encourages many people to take ministry roles in the worship service.
   Danger point: Christians can miss the importance of pastoral leadership, overriding vision, and gift-motivated ministry. As a result, quality can decline and lack of leadership can keep the church from growing.

emerges when a church transitions from one model to another, such as when the senior pastor or key lay leadership changes. Sometimes a second or third model tries to emerge as a "sub-vision" for your church, such as when new ministry opportunities find a positive and growing response.

Each model has implications for worship, and tension points might arise with each (see sidebar page 135).

Preventing such tensions from erupting into a worship war requires that a church understand the different perspectives present within the congregation, identify points of agreement, make peace among warring factions, and then facilitate congregational healing.

Four tough action steps will reduce feelings of "worship wars" in your congregation:

1. *Embrace diversity.* Search out the biblical basis for each worship paradigm evidenced at your church. Do you understand how other people look at the issues? Have you reviewed the scriptural basis they would use for explaining their particular style of worship?
2. *Strive for balance.* Acknowledge that your favorite worship style has weaknesses too. Can you honestly identify areas where your worship could be improved?
3. *Recognize your biases.* Realize the enduring influence of the church where you found Christ or first grew in the faith. If you became a Christian in a small group, you'll probably develop a life-long passion for small groups. If you responded to a Billy Graham–style public invitation, you may not understand why every church doesn't do altar calls.
4. *Identify dominant spiritual gifts.* Discover your spiritual gifts and your church's dominant gift, such as teaching, evangelism, or serving. Worship will look different, depending on which of these strengths are most emphasized. What if a church's dominant spiritual gift is different from yours? You might not feel as comfortable there. Understanding why will help you make the best of it.[26]

Develop Worship Styles Appropriate for Each Targeted Group

The majority of Protestant churches have patterned their ministries after models that work best with people born before World War II.

These models were often quite effective in reaching the people of their day. In many places they may continue to minister well. But for an ever-increasing number of people born since 1946 (the end of the war), such models "are just not attractive," says Gary McIntosh in *Make Room for the Boom . . . or Bust: Six Church Models for Reaching Three Generations.*[27]

Each of the models below reflects a different strategy for reaching various age groups.[28] To what extent have you tested one or more of them? Which might be effective for your church in reaching a neglected age group?

Seeker-Centered

Focus: Centers on unchurched, irreligious people, helping them become fully devoted followers of Christ.

Biblical Precedent: The innovative ways Jesus fulfilled his mission to "seek and save what was lost" (Luke 19:10), such as how he reached out to Matthew the tax collector (Matt. 9:9–13).

High Visibility Example: Willow Creek Community Church, South Barrington, Illinois (Bill Hybels, senior pastor)—www.Willow creek.org.

Seeker-Sensitive

Focus: Speaks primarily to Christians, while simultaneously maintaining sensitivity to unchurched guests.

Biblical Precedent: Sermons in the Book of Acts, where congregations contained both believers and unbelievers.

High Visibility Example: Saddleback Community Church, Lake Forest, California (Rick Warren, senior pastor)—www.saddleback .com.

Blended

Focus: Combines two different philosophies of ministry to reach two target audiences, often an older and a younger one.

Biblical Precedent: Decisions of the Jerusalem Council in Acts 15, when Jews adjusted to include Gentiles, perhaps also including matters of worship.

Seven Reasons to Try a Multiple-Track Model

1. *Provides options.* Adding a new worship service is one way to provide choices in church ministry.
2. *Maximizes space.* Multiple services allow a church to use its present space to greater advantage without having to engage in an expensive building program.
3. *Allows for growth.* An overcrowded auditorium actually discourages numerical growth.
4. *Increases faith.* Churches that offer more than one worship service tend to place an emphasis on reaching newer members, which takes vision and faith.
5. *Enlarges ministry.* By adding additional services, a church nearly doubles the ministry roles and tasks where people may become involved.
6. *Reaches new people.* By adding an additional service with a differing time and style, a church can attract new people who might not normally attend.
7. *Keeps people happy.* Multiple services allow for a church to zero in on varied preferences.

Adapted from Gary McIntosh, *Make Room for the Boom . . . or Bust: Six Church Models for Reaching New Generations* (Grand Rapids: Revell, 1997), 124.

High Visibility Example: Southeast Christian Church, Louisville, Kentucky (Bob Russell, senior pastor)—www.secc.org.

Multiple-Track

Focus: Offers distinct approaches to worship at different service times, such as "traditional" at 8:30 A.M., "soft contemporary" at 9:30 A.M. and "loud contemporary" at 11:00 A.M.

Biblical Precedent: Paul's desire to "become all things to all men" so as "to win as many as possible" (1 Cor. 9:19–23).

High Visibility Example: Church of the Resurrection, Leawood, Kansas (Adam Hamilton, senior pastor)—www.cor.org, or Community Church of Joy, Glendale, Arizona (Walt Kallestad, senior pastor)—www.joyonline.org.

The bottom line in looking at these models is this: If God called your church to reach an age group that you seem unable to reach, carefully and prayerfully examine your philosophy of worship. Are there new attitudes or styles you might add that will make your worship more attractive to the target audience?

McIntosh doesn't have a clear favorite among the models. If forced to choose one, he would probably suggest the multiple-track model since that allows a church to target several different groups, but he recognizes the dangers of dividing Christ's church into segments when Jesus placed such emphasis on the oneness and unity of the church.

In McIntosh's field experience, the most difficult model to use over the long haul is the blended model. Why? Usually a church uses it as a way of trying to please everyone—which

---

Should Your Church Quit and Start Over?

In order to discern whether a rebirthing model is best for you, try this simple survey. Answer yes or no for each question.

y n Does your church have an average public worship attendance of more than fifty adults?

y n Does your church have twenty-five faithful giving units, each giving a minimum of 10 percent of their total income to your church?

y n Does your church have at least one competent lay leader for every ten adults?

y n Does your church have at least one ministry for which it is well known in your community?

y n Does your church have a positive growth rate over the past ten years?

y n Does your church demonstrate a healthy spiritual life?

y n Does your church have an average membership tenure of less than ten years?

y n Does your church talk mostly about its future goals of ministry?

y n Does your church spend at least 5 percent of its total budget on outreach to the local community?

y n Does your church have hope that God can renew its growth and vitality in its current situation?

Count the number of times you answered yes.

7–10 is excellent! Yours is a church with great potential.

4–6 Is fair. Yours is a church with unclear direction. It may grow or decline.

1–3 is poor. Your church has a limited future, and it should be rebirthed.

Adapted from Gary McIntosh, *Make Room for the Boom . . . or Bust: Six Church Models for Reaching New Generations* (Grand Rapids: Revell, 1997), 165–66.

---

can't be done. Still, for many churches the blended model is the best short-term starting point since it is just about the only way to begin moving an entire congregation from one style to another.

Each church must prayerfully assess its current methods and future goals to determine which is the best model for it to pursue.

Start a New Style Worship Service

According to Lyle Schaller, author or editor of more than eighty books on various issues of church health and growth, "Half of the congregations in North America need to expand their weekend worship services."[29] Charles Arn's book *How to Start a New Service* is the most comprehensive guide to date on how churches can reach new people by launching a new style service. After listing circumstances that would make it inadvisable for a church to launch another service, he makes a bold research-based statement: "Of the churches that add a new service eight out of ten will experience a measurable increase in (1) total

**How to Catch
the Senior Age Wave**

1. Seniors can be reached through *oikos* evangelism—networks of friends they trust.
2. Seniors can be reached by assimilation into a friendly, outward-looking, senior-adult ministry.
3. Seniors can be reached through invitations to small groups.
4. Seniors can be reached through teaching ministries that stimulate spiritual growth.
5. Seniors can be reached through church-sponsored recreational, social, and physical activities.

Adapted from Win Arn and Charles Arn, *Catch the Age Wave* (Grand Rapids: Baker, 1993).

worship attendance, (2) total giving, and (3) total number of Christian conversions."[30]

Arn boils down the process into a series of steps, beginning with a prayerful approach to the question of why start a new service. He explains how a new service will do the following:

reach the unchurched

minister to more people

reach new kinds of people

help the parent church shift its life cycle to a
   healthier point

allow for change while retaining the familiar

activate inactive members

help the parent denomination survive

After talking about the pastor's role, gifts, and "counting of the costs," Arn helps a church see who needs to gain a sense of ownership, in what order, and why. This includes key lay leaders, church staff, the entire church board, other key teams and groups, and finally the congregation itself.

The next series of decisions involve what kind of service the church wants. Who do you want to reach in terms of age group, spiritual level (believers or seekers), and cultural identity (same culture, multicultural, or cross-cultural)? These prayerful discussions include an acknowledgment that you can't reach everyone. Each decision you make will appeal, whether intentional or unintentional, to some people and not to others.

"What do *they* want?" is a more difficult question to assess. The answer requires an understanding of the spiritual needs and areas of probable responsiveness. "What are the important issues in their lives? What are their attitudes about faith, church, and God? What are their problems and dreams to which the gospel can speak?" Arn asks, then leads a church through research to find out.[31]

The final third of Arn's book offers an A to Z walk-through of when and where to meet, how to design the service, how to draw newcomers to the service, and how to evaluate your progress. He includes dozens of tips about how to keep on target and what kinds of results to anticipate.

Evangelism Strategies for Senior Adults Are Different

Criteria for Decision Making Often Followed by Older Adults	*Evangelism Strategies to Consider*
They rely on people they trust	1. Use existing networks of relationships. 2. Plan friendship-building events.
They resist a "hard sell"	1. Emphasize relationship style rather than confrontational. 2. Provide multiple exposures to the gospel message, such as books, sermons, Bible study, etc.
They must clearly understand the benefits	1. Make messages relevant to senior life issues. 2. Identify and communicate the attractive qualities of faith and community.
They require assurance of quality	1. Evaluate and improve quality of meetings and printed materials. 2. Be sure time spent in senior activities is meaningful, not superficial.
They resist dramatic change in lifestyle	1. Focus on Christian formation and discipleship. 2. Present peer role models.
They respond to personal invitations	1. Create small groups open to nonmembers. 2. Build and nurture relationships.
They base decisions on need rather than want	1. Create ministry teams to people with special needs. 2. Show how faith meets needs that seniors face.

Adapted from Win Arn and Charles Arn, *A Wake Up Call for the Church* (LIFE International, 1996), appendix A, 20–21.

From a worship style point of view, the process of launching a new service can diffuse much tension and bring about greater unity. Some people will say, "It's fine to explore new worship styles just as long as it's not at the service I attend." Others will gain a greater sense of mission, saying, "My comfort is less important than giving our neighbors a chance to have their lives put back together by Jesus Christ."

Dale Galloway, pioneering church planter, became dean of Asbury Theological Seminary's Beeson Center after more than three decades of successful pastoral ministry. He tells the story of how the relocation to Asbury enabled him to meet up with one of his mentors, someone older than himself. The man is on staff at a church that has shifted

---

Twelve Reasons Boomers Return to Church

1. Boomers are concerned about the moral training of their children.
2. Boomers are questioning the meaning of their lives.
3. Boomers are nostalgic and wish to relive earlier times.
4. Boomers are seeking security from the rapid pace of change.
5. Boomers are frustrated at living less well than they had planned.
6. Boomers are anxious about society, the environment, and materialism.
7. Boomers are realizing that the answer is not in things but in a personal faith.
8. Boomers are looking for a lifestyle that is meaningful.
9. Boomers are pursuing a new balance by looking deeper into their lives.
10. Boomers are hunting new and meaningful experiences.
11. Boomers are coping with aging parents and still-young children.
12. Boomers are turning fifty and reaching a midlife malaise.

From Gary McIntosh, *Make Room for the Boom . . . or Bust: Six Church Models for Reaching New Generations* (Grand Rapids: Revell, 1997), 33.

---

from maintenance to mission. Dale asked him, "How are you feeling about all the changes happening at your church—all these community people coming in for the first time?"

The older man affirmed that things today are indeed different. "Our pastor has transitioned our church to all this new kind of music, including drums."

"How do you like it?" Dale asked him.

"I don't like the music," he replied, "but I sure like all the new people who are coming in."

Galloway's conclusion is this: "This is the attitude we need. With people who love Jesus, you just need to help them understand why you're making changes. Once they catch it, they'll be with you whether they like it or not."[32]

What about *Your* Congregation?

What areas of "worship wars" tension is your church experiencing? Which areas would you like to break through? As Barry Liesch says:

> Nothing short of a revolution in worship styles is sweeping across North America . . . . No denomination or group can sidestep the hot debate between the benefits of hymns versus choruses, seeker services versus wor-

Hunter on Worship Variation

One of the great contributions of this chapter is the view of worship from the historical perspective. Struggles with stylistic changes in worship are a consistent part of Christian history, such as what happened in the early 1800s when George Weber, music director at Mainz Cathedral said "that new song is vulgar mischief," referring to the classic we call "Silent Night."

In my work with churches I find it helps if you can get people to distinguish between the style (the packaging) and the substance (the content). The truth of the faith should never change. The delivery system (worship styles) must change if the gospel is to remain relevant to each generation.

The emphasis in this chapter on your church's "personality" is also important. In my book, *Your Church Has Personality*, I advocate that every church should have a written philosophy of ministry. Among other aspects, your church's personality is most visibly reflected in your style of worship. To be clear and intentional will help you find your focus and maximize your mission.

The twenty-first-century church will recognize and celebrate that we live in a world of choices. I call this type of approach the Baskin Robbins Church. It's all ice cream, but there are several flavors from which to choose.

Kent R. Hunter
The Church Doctor, Corunna, Indiana
author, *Move Your Church to Action* (Abingdon, 2000)

Insights for Reaching Busters

1. Busters will attend churches that have a clear focus, narrowly defined vision, and assertive commitment to accomplish their mission.
2. Busters will attend churches where worship services are shorter, well designed, and have good flow and tempo.
3. Busters will often attend churches that have a loud, upbeat, faster pop music sound.
4. Busters will attend churches that win their loyalty every Sunday through excellent ministry.
5. Busters will attend churches that focus on local ministry more than on ministry in faraway places.
6. Busters will give money to churches where they can see their money achieving results.
7. Busters will volunteer for ministry activities that are short-term.
8. Busters will volunteer and minister to confront practical issues in their community.
9. Busters will attend churches that help them sort out the hurts in their lives through practical messages, classes, and small groups.
10. Busters will come to Christ through need-based ministries that deal with the hurts and internal issues they are facing.

From Gary McIntosh, *Make Room for the Boom . . . or Bust: Six Church Models for Reaching New Generations* (Grand Rapids: Revell, 1997), 46.

ship services, choirs versus worship teams, organs versus synthesizers, and flowing praise versus singing one song at a time.[33]

It's time to end those worship wars! Through the power of God, and gleaning insights from the writers in this chapter, you can learn how to diagnose the points of tension over worship in your congregation. You can then develop new strategies for your times of corporate worship, ones that invite as many age groups as possible to give God the worth he is due.

? APPLICATION QUESTIONS
FOR INDIVIDUAL RESPONSE OR GROUP DISCUSSION

1. In the material drawn from Elmer Towns, *Putting an End to Worship Wars*, which "personality" best describes your church? Which statement best describes your church's biggest point of tension over worship? What action step would do most to reduce feelings of "worship wars"?

2. In the material drawn from Gary McIntosh, *Make Room for the Boom . . . or Bust*, which age group is your church best at reaching? Which generation, if any, is most conspicuously absent? Why? Which of McIntosh's ideas could you explore to help your church effectively reach the total community?

3. Based on the material drawn from Charles Arn, *How to Start a New Service*, what do you see as your most likely next point of worship experimentation? What do you predict the outcome will be? How can you begin?

PASTORS 4. What age level do you relate to best? (Hint: what age bracket do the majority of your new members represent?) If that life stage doesn't represent your church's target age, then you may need to bring on a new staff member or give a lot of platform time to a lay leader who represents the age of that target group.

ten

Cash In on Two Millennia of Good Ideas

Trend #10: Christians increasingly want to participate in worship as an experience. Many appreciate feeling connected to the two-thousand-year stream of church history by the use of liturgical worship elements.

⚬⚬⚬

Suppose you were asked to take a test on denominations and how they worship. Could you match the right church group with their worship practice?

Denomination	Worship Practice
1. Episcopal	a. "Passing the peace" by affirming God's peace to the person sitting next to you.
2. Baptist	b. Saying, "The Word of God for the people of God" after reading Scripture.
3. Presbyterian	c. Participating in communion weekly (also called Eucharist or Lord's Supper).
4. Pentecostal	d. Singing a Psalm directly from the Bible or Psalter.
5. Methodist	e. Inviting the congregation to say, "Amen!" and "Yes, Lord!" during the sermon.
6. Lutheran	f. Raising one or both hands toward heaven when worshiping.

149

New Church Finds Response by Avoiding Mediocrity

Scottsdale Family Church

Denomination: Nazarene

Location: Scottsdale, Arizona (in Greater Phoenix)

Senior pastor: Alan Nelson (since 1996)

Recent goal: To organizationally structure to function as a healthy large church.

Church vision: To be the premier provider of soul growth resources to the unchurched in the northeast valley (of Phoenix).

Year founded: 1996

Attendance: 550–600 (current)

Internet address: www.scottsdalefamilychurch.org

Mediocrity is one word you won't use—or experience—when worshiping at Scottsdale Family Church, despite its limitations of being new and meeting in rented facilities. "Too often a church's publicity looks excellent, but then you show up and everything has the flavor of mediocrity," says founding pastor Alan Nelson, who with his wife, Nancy, began the congregation in 1996 without a preexisting core of people or staff. "In most subcultures across North America, mediocrity is unacceptable, whether it is inadequate sound, sloppy music, bad drama, or an uninspiring message," he says.

In studying the target community, Nelson decided that three key qualities would enable a new congregation to win a hearing with people who had given up on church: strong loving leadership, relevance, and excellence. "We want to be seen as striving for excellence for the glory of God," says Nelson, "in the same way today's businesses strive toward making a financial profit. After all, which motivating force is stronger?"

The tradeoff is that a new church can't do everything well. "Better to have less that's well done than too much that's poorly done," says Nelson.

This extreme sensitivity to people's impressions stems from Nelson's passion for outreach—and his desire for Scottsdale Family Church to be among that 1 percent of churches that genuinely grows by outreach. "I want to link with my audience, and I figure we have to grab their attention every three or so minutes," he says. "The difference between communicators and teachers is that teachers often begin with the subject, where the communicator starts with the audience." As Nelson says in *Leading Your Ministry*, one of several books he's written, "The times have never called for more and better leaders than today."*

Based on the level of life change evident in this new church, the results to date are anything but mediocre.

*Alan Nelson, *Leading Your Ministry* (Nashville: Abingdon Press, 1996), 176.
An earlier version of this case study appeared in "Leadership on the Edge," catalogue 11, January 1999, and is used by permission from The International Centre for Leadership Development and Evangelism, Winfield, BC, http://www.GrowingLeadership.com, 800-804-0777.

Most people would have a far easier time answering this question for North American denominations in 1950 than in the year 2000. Back in 1950, the worship styles of denominations and movements were much more clearly defined. Today, you can quite easily find examples of *each* worship practice in all six denominations.

Common ground for all the practices listed above, regardless of denomination, is that all of the practices move people from spectator to participant. And each practice is based on Scripture and present in church history.

Today's interest in more participatory worship goes far beyond the explosive growth of the twentieth-century Pentecostal and charismatic movements. At the same time, interest in a more historically connected liturgy goes far beyond the handful of high-visibility Christians who have "converted" to the Episcopal church or to Eastern Orthodoxy. It evidences itself everywhere from seminary classes to worship planning teams in local churches. It even shows up in seeker-driven churches that target a generation of unchurched people who are largely illiterate of both Scripture and church history. Instead of being turned off by the rich symbolism of the Christian faith, an increasing number of people find it surprisingly relevant, especially if it engages their minds and emotions.

> ### Carol Childress's Significant Changes in Worship
>
> from classical to contextual
> from performance to participation
> from music *about* God to music *to* God
> from pipe organ to percussion
> from cerebral to celebration
> from liturgy to liberty ("planned spontaneity")
> from meditation to mission
>
> ### Carol Childress's Key Worship Issues for the Future
>
> relationship not religion
> authenticity over hype
> connections and community
> burnout and balance
> growth and small groups
> soul care and spirituality
> from success to significance
> from slow transition to constant change
>
> From a live presentation at "Gathering of Church Champions" in Dallas, Texas, January 11, 1999. Sponsored by Leadership Network (www.leadnet.org).

The following insights, gleaned from a wide variety of writers, show what can happen in your congregation as you capitalize upon this worship trend.

Recognize That Today's Worship Motivations Often Stem from Spiritual Hunger

Dave Goetz, editor of *ChurchLeadership.Net*, an online publication of Christianity Today, Inc., points out how both pastors and lay leaders hunger more for experiences with the supernatural and theological,

---

Ten Great Ideas from Church History

1. Martin Luther's theology of the cross can deepen the faith of your congregation.
2. John Calvin's model of holiness can combat "me-centered" Christianity.
3. Jeremiah Burrough's denominational theory of the church can be a tremendous force for unity within your congregation.
4. William Perkin's idea of assurance through true conversion can overcome the extremes of apathy and anxiety within the church.
5. Richard Baxter's directions for delighting God can revitalize worship.
6. Jonathan Edwards's vision for revival can defend the church against the attacks of secularism.
7. John Wesley's strategy of small groups can turn slumbering churchgoers into zealous disciples.
8. William Carey's model of missions can inspire boomers and busters to fulfill the Great Commission.
9. William Wilberforce's paradigm of evangelical social action can guide Christians in opposing the evils of our times.
10. Dietrich Bonhoeffer's vision of Christian community can bring your people together and counter the tribalization and radical individualism of postmodern life.

From Mark Shaw, *Ten Great Ideas from Church History* (Downers Grove, Ill.: InterVarsity, 1997), 11–12.

---

and less for ministry methods. "During the 1980s, church growth techniques were hot and during the 90s, leadership skills have been trumpeted," he says. "But among some pastors, there's a pervasive weariness with ministry technique. People are saying, 'I want to go deeper in ministry and in my spiritual life.'"

Goetz also observes this spiritual motivation in Gen Xers, also known as Baby Busters. "In the last few years, more and more churches targeting people of Generation X—those in their twenties and thirties—have arisen. Some key qualities of Gen-X churches are spirituality, authenticity, and community. These churches also trumpet an eclectic spirituality, which combines Christian practices from Orthodox, Catholicism, and Protestantism. Themes that get emphasized in Gen-X ministry discussions: pain, silence of God, and ambiguity."[1]

Sally Morgenthaler's book, *Worship Evangelism*, likewise underscores an increasing spiritual thirst as a motivational factor. "Worship is not just for the spiritually mature. It is for the spiritually hungry, and in the last decade of the twentieth century, that includes more people than we realize," she says. "Our failure to impact contemporary culture is not because we have not been relevant enough, but because we have not been real enough."[2]

**Warren Bird's Top Ten
Reasons to Worship**

#10 Worship results in a Christian taking better care of the earth.

#9 Worship increases the Christian's vision of the greatness of God.

#8 Worship is something God desires from his children.

#7 Worship is what seems to happen whenever the Holy Spirit shows up.

#6 Worship of God helps defeat the second greatest power in the universe.

#5 Worship puts a Christian's life into perspective.

#4 Worship is what a Christian will do for all of eternity; it is the main activity of heaven.

#3 Worship stirs a Christian's evangelistic passion.

#2 Worship is at the center of everything the church believes, practices, and seeks to accomplish.

#1 Worship is unavoidable for the growing Christian.

Feed Spiritual Hunger with Solid Teaching about Worship

"Most worship wars break out because leaders have not taught their people how to worship," says Elmer Towns in his book, *Putting an End to Worship Wars.*[3] The necessary tools are readily available. If you want a worship-themed study Bible, you even have more than one variety to choose from! Plus, more books on the subject of worship are in print today than during any other era of Christianity.

What should be taught about worship that will help people meet God afresh? "The heart of worship renewal is a recovery of the power of the Holy Spirit who enables the congregation to offer praise and thanksgiving to God," says Robert Webber, longtime observer of worship trends. "My argument is that the most powerful sources of worship renewal are found first in the Scripture and second in the history of the church."[4]

Christian leaders today take several different approaches in how to instruct on worship. Pastor John Piper, of Bethlehem Baptist in Minneapolis, writes books with titles such as *The Supremacy of God in Preaching* to urge more focus on who God is and what God has done. Other Reformed leaders encourage churches to return to their confessional roots, including the usage of liturgies from previous centuries. Those in the Pentecostal and charismatic traditions tend to emphasize a more experiential approach to learning about worship, first allowing God to touch the believer's emotions and spirit. For example, Jack Hayford's *Worship His Majesty* affirms that only through worship—recognizing and praising God for who he is—can people discover who they are and who they can become.

Nine Proposals for Inviting Worship Renewal

These suggestions were first voiced almost twenty years ago by Robert Webber.

1. Educate the people about worship.
2. Acknowledge the distinction between services for worship and services for preaching.
3. Do not disregard the tradition of your denomination.
4. Orient worship toward God rather than human beings.
5. Restore a sense of awe and reverence, mystery and transcendence.
6. Recover a Christocentric focus through enactment.
7. Restore congregational involvement in worship.
8. Attain spontaneity with the proper balance on form and freedom.
9. Restore the relationship of worship to all of life.

From Robert Webber, *Worship Old and New* (Grand Rapids: Zondervan, 1982), 193–96.

Frame Corporate Worship to Invite Engagement, Not Spectatorship

As Christians discover and rediscover what it means to live "in Christ" and to be filled with the Holy Spirit, their response of wonder and thanksgiving to God can easily be guided into meaningful times of corporate and individual worship. The Bible teaches that God inhabits praise. As Scripture says, "I will declare your name to my brothers; in the presence of the congregation I will sing your praises" (Heb. 2:12). "For where two or three come together in my name, there am I with them" (Matt. 18:20). "But you are a chosen people, a royal priesthood, a holy nation, a people belonging to God, that you may declare the praises of him who called you out of darkness into his wonderful light" (1 Peter 2:9).

The bottom-line problem today, according to pollster George Barna, is that a majority of people who attend worship services at Christian churches leave church without feeling they experienced God's presence. "Enjoying or appreciating worship is not synonymous with experiencing God. Seven out of ten adults (71 percent) say they have never experienced God's presence at a church service," Barna says. According to his research, one out of ten adults (12 percent) say it "always" happens, only 5 percent say it "usually" occurs, and only 8 percent say it happens "sometimes."[5]

LaMar Boschman, academic dean of the Bedford, Texas, Worship Institute and author of *Future Worship*, observes that in most worship renewal situations he's encountered, the congregation must be actively involved in the worship process.[6] He uses theater terms to rephrase Soren Kierkegaard's analogy that God—not the congregation—is the audience in worship.[7]

"The main human players in worship are the congregation," says Boschman. "The pastors and worship leaders are the directors or stage hands, to use theater talk. God is the audience. Too often the directors and stage hands become the main players, playing all the major roles, and the people feel like they're the audience. The unintended, unfortunate result is that people begin to spectate. The worship team and choirs should be the prompters and initiators, not the central focus. The Lord, dwelling among the praise of his people, is not more attentive to the choir than to the congregation; if anything he's watching to see how the worship teams prompt and aid the main players—the *congregation*—in worshiping. . . . Those in the visual center—the band, the choir, the worship team—are the helps ministries."[8]

> *The worship team and choirs should be the prompters and initiators, not the central focus.*

Boschman concludes, "Worship renewal is something that can be attained in any church. It has less to do with music and more to do with the condition of people's hearts. It's an inward quality, and not an external thing. So musical style, skill, and new techniques are not the most important considerations."[9]

Prepare as Well for the Rest of the Service as for the Sermon

Long gone is the attitude that all the non-sermon elements of a worship service are unimportant "preliminaries." The roles of music, drama, testimony, and other events are just as meaningful to many people as the preacher's instruction and motivation from God's Word.

"One of the bigger changes today is that the church is increasingly organized around worship, more than the sermon," says church consultant and noted author Lyle Schaller. "We used to have worship services; today we have high-energy, participatory worship experiences."[10] The more value people place on the "rest of the service," the more the worship style matters to them. "Today more people choose a church primarily by its style of worship or its philosophy of ministry than on the particulars of its doctrine," says Elmer Towns in *Putting an End to Worship Wars*.[11]

Virtually every denomination is in a worship metamorphosis over this transition. Churches worldwide are in flux, trying to make sure the "rest of the service" contains meaningful, connected acts of worship. That's one reason for so much experimentation and interest in varieties of worship styles.

As the previous chapter indicated, Christians today are showing increased support for a wide variety of worship styles. For example, Biola University firmly roots its doctrine on a view of the Bible as the inerrant Word of God, authoritative in all matters of faith and practice. One of its music professors, Barry Liesch, insists that "music is relative: there is no one universal style." After citing various examples of the astonishing variety in worship that the Bible itself models, he concludes, "Scripture contains no prescribed order of service."[12]

Other scholars have reached the same conclusion. For example, when the apostle Paul says believers should "sing psalms, hymns and spiritual songs" (Col. 3:16), it's hard to imagine that he believes all music to have the same look, sound, and feel. We don't know with certainty what he meant by each category, but the *New Oxford History of Music* suggests the following:

"psalms" refer to the singing of psalms, canticles, and doxologies

"hymns" refer to the singing about new Christian experiences

"spiritual songs" refer to singing alleluias and songs of ecstasy[13]

From new approaches to biblical music to new appreciation for worship forms used across the ages, Christians today increasingly want to participate in worship as an experience. They often appreciate feeling connected to the two-thousand-year stream of church history by the use of liturgical worship elements.

Use the "Incarnational Principle" as a Measuring Stick

God's eternal plan to bring salvation to the human race is known as the incarnation. God took on human form so that we could begin to comprehend his wonderful plan of how we could be set free from our sin and brokenness. This means Jesus spoke the language of his day, interacted with the customs of his day, used illustrations that had relevance and meaning to his various audiences, and demonstrated continually that God understands and cares about each person's day-to-day concerns.

What are the implications of those facts for worship? As the sidebar on page 32 points out, "Cultural relevance is one way that we extend incarnational Christianity." George Hunter explains: "Employing culturally relevant forms is desirable because God's revelation takes place through culture. When the gospel is expressed in a people's indigenous cultural forms, then and only then do most of them perceive that Christianity is for 'people like us.'" As a result, according to Hunter, "All worship services are contemporary to *some* generation, but most are 'contemporary' to an era other than today."[14]

Bill Easum calls this idea "indigenous worship," which he defines as worship "in the everyday language of the people, in the culture of the primary target audience, and which uses the technology of the day."[15]

Why is this approach important? "Most culturally irrelevant churches cannot engage pre-Christian people meaningfully, nor do they plan to in significant numbers," says Hunter.[16]

Not only is a church's evangelism impaired if their view of worship is confused, but so is their understanding of the gospel itself. "Most people feel that in order to be true to the gospel message, they must

---

Psalms: An Argument for Variety in Song

1. God's people preserved old songs, sang contemporary songs, and looked forward to the composition of yet unwritten new songs.
   Evidence: The Psalms span some one thousand years, dating from Moses (about 1400 B.C.) to David (about 1000 B.C.) to the postexilic period (400 B.C.). Several Psalms call for a "new song."

2. God's people showed great creativity and variation in their style of music.
   Evidence: Some Psalms are short, others long. Some are historical, many are personal. Some are structurally unique (such as the acrostic psalms); some complex (such as the symmetrical Psalms); others, straightforward and repetitious.

3. God's people used many different instruments in worship.
   Evidence: Numerous musical instruments are mentioned in the Psalms. Psalm 150 alone invites at least eight different instruments to be used in praising God.

4. God's people praised God with different volumes.
   Evidence: Some Psalms call for a "loud" response of instrument or shout; others reference how God quiets the soul.

From Barry Liesch, *The New Worship: Straight Talk on Music and the Church* (Grand Rapids: Baker, 1996), 40.

keep it in the form in which they first received it," says Hunter. "Often, people can't tell the difference between form and content."[17]

Many churches today have come a long way in agreeing that ministry in the people's language is necessary to reach them, to disciple them, and to help them engage in one of the first concerns of the Christian life: worship.

> *"Most people feel that in order to be true to the gospel message, they must keep it in the form in which they first received it."*

Others agree. "Forms must be contextualized to meet the cultural situation of each worshiping congregation, but contemporary worship should not be drastically out of step with the worship heritage handed down by generations of Christians guided by the Holy Spirit," says Robert Webber.[18]

The kaleidoscope of emerging worship practices is able to be tested. Do the practices lead Christians to fulfill Jesus' great commandment of loving God with all their heart, mind, soul, and strength? Do they motivate Christians to love their neighbors as themselves? Do they prompt seekers to "fall down and worship God, exclaiming, 'God is really among you!'"(1 Cor. 14:25)?

If so, then a church's knowledge of God will deepen. If not, then poor worship will show its fruit by a malnourished view of God. Indeed, as A. W. Tozer, author of *Worship—The Missing Jewel,* has said, "I believe there is scarcely an error in doctrine or a failure in applying Christian ethics that cannot be traced finally to imperfect and ignoble thoughts about God."[19]

? **APPLICATION QUESTIONS**
FOR INDIVIDUAL RESPONSE OR GROUP DISCUSSION

1. Which idea did you most agree with in this chapter? Why? With which idea did you most disagree? Why?
2. In your own words, explain the idea of the "incarnational principle" and how it relates to worship style and content.
3. When you worship with your church, when are you most engaged? When are you mostly a spectator? How could you help worship become more participatory?

PASTORS   4. Consider preaching a series of sermons on Christianity as it relates to culture. You might look at how Jesus used different approaches with different audiences (Pharisees, farmers, etc.). You could do the same with the various gospel presentations in Acts. With each study, link your application to ideas behind worship.

Wardle on Worship and Relationship

As the author of a book on worship, *Exalt Him!* (Christian Publications, 1998), I appreciate the growing emphasis on worship in recent years. I especially cheer the many ways worship is helping people find Jesus' loving embrace.

For almost an entire decade, the Lord has been speaking one message repeatedly into my heart: "Pursue intimacy with me above all else!" For twenty years I gave all I had for Christian service. I believed mission was more important than anything else. I have learned that while the Lord certainly does desire our service, his first concern is for our hearts' devotion, as he affirmed to Mary about spending time at his feet (see Luke 10:38–42).

Woven throughout two thousand years of Christian history are numerous disciplines and role models that can help the believer's pursuit of greater intimacy with God. Nothing has changed my life for the better more than learning to discover Jesus' presence and strength in the midst of my own weakness. I have been overwhelmed repeatedly by the grace of God's loving presence.

Today's era is indeed one of heightened spiritual hunger. Through times of personal prayer as well as corporate worship, Christians are learning that God's transforming, patient love can satisfy them as nothing else could. With the psalmist, we meet God most in the broken moments and disappointments of life. And with the great heroes of the church, we are pilgrims walking with a limp as we seek to follow God to higher ground than we could ever achieve apart from his benevolence and grace.

Terry Wardle
Ashland Theological Seminary, Ashland, Ohio
author, *Draw Close to the Fire: Finding God in the Darkness* (Chosen, 1998)

Part 6

Churches Move toward Empowerment of Lay Leadership

Learn to Be a Leader-Maker

After centuries of lip service to the "priesthood of all believers," the era has arrived when the people of God are truly becoming ministers.

Look Underneath the Megachurch Movement

Large churches are learning to operate at maximum impact and to be healthy by becoming the "biggest little church around."

Make the Church Better Than a Business

Church leaders, while continuing to find valid help from secular management insights, are rediscovering the uniqueness of a church's spiritual resources and eternal mission.

eleven

Learn to Be a Leader-Maker

Trend #11: After centuries of lip service to the "priest-hood of all believers," the era has arrived when the people of God are truly becoming ministers.

cᴏᴏ

"The pastoral team, the staff of the church, is to serve the people of the church in *their* ministry—to empower *them,* to equip *them,* to give *them* tracks to run on for ministry."

This statement by Pastor Ted Haggard, author of *The Life-Giving Church* and senior pastor of New Life Church, Colorado Springs, Colorado, represents a dramatic reversal occurring in churches across North America. Here is Haggard's account of how he reached that defining moment:

> I remember when this happened to me. I was in my office. It was early one Sunday morning. I was walking around, since I like to pace when I pray.
>
> I was going to be teaching out of 1 Peter that day. I knew my outline, I knew the material, all the preparation was there. I knew that I would be speaking to roughly five thousand people that day—live, face-to-face—and I was praying.
>
> What happened next came from God. My intention had been to teach those people 1 Peter. Then the Spirit of God touched my heart about this idea. I no longer wanted to teach them 1 Peter so they would know 1 Peter.

Shared Training Experiences Lead to Shared Vision

Trinity Baptist Church

Denomination: North American Baptist

Location: Kelowna, British Columbia, Canada

Senior pastor: Tim Schroeder (since 1985)

Recent goal: To see 10 percent of our Sunday morning attendance won to Christ through evangelism.

Church vision: To help people experience a life-changing relationship with Jesus Christ.

Year founded: 1961

Attendance: 2400 (now)
                    1200 (5 years ago)
                    625 (10 years ago)

Internet address: www.trinitybaptist.net

Can an inward-focused church closely linked to its ethnic roots break free and experience explosive growth? Trinity Baptist Church in Kelowna, British Columbia, has shown that not only is this possible, but that the growth can occur in a way that honors those roots.

As the new senior pastor, Tim Schroeder quickly came to appreciate the heritage of Trinity Baptist Church. The daughter church of a German-speaking congregation, it was launched by a progressive group of young families who realized that a German language environment wouldn't be relevant to their children and community.

When Schroeder arrived on the scene, the church was twenty-four years old. "The congregation was fairly inward focused," he says, and was "searching for a clear vision." He took a team of people to a Carl George conference, which became a defining moment for Schroeder as well as for the entire church. "Within two or three years,

we had developed a unity that led to a much clearer vision to reach relevantly into our community, and to teach and equip our children for the Christian life," Schroeder says.

That renewed vision built on the church's heritage. "The key was to take that same motivation that led them to move from the German language, and to ask what it means for us to be relevant to this next generation," he says. "Half the battle was won simply because they already believed the idea; they just didn't know how to make it happen." At present one-third of Trinity Baptist's new members come by way of baptism, a percentage that is growing.

Over the years, the shared-experience concept has become the norm at Trinity Baptist. Various leadership teams regularly host or attend training events. "This isn't our idea alone," says Schroeder. "We heard it most loudly on one of our first visits to Willow Creek: 'Don't go anywhere by yourself.'" Summarizes Schroeder: "It's the shared experience that makes the difference."

An earlier version of this case study appeared in "Leadership on the Edge," catalogue 11, January 1999, and is used by permission from The International Centre for Leadership Development and Evangelism, Winfield, BC, http://www.GrowingLeadership.com, 800-804-0777.

In a split second, I started wanting to teach them so that they could teach 1 Peter to others.

I started to think of every single person in the church as a minister. *All* of them have a ministry! They're *all* called to ministry. They already have a sphere of influence outside the local church. They have a cell group. And they already have a calling on their life.

So my responsibility was to equip them to minister the principles of 1 Peter to all the people within *their* sphere of influence. I wanted them to come to church to be equipped with 1 Peter in such a way that the ideas from 1 Peter would flow through them so that they could minister to other people.

When that heart change took place in me, all of a sudden our church switched from being a place where you come and watch what happens on the platform and then participate in a program *to a place where you come and you're empowered for ministry.*[1]

Starting about twenty years ago North American churches and pastors like Ted Haggard began waking up and realizing that for centuries our focus has been terribly wrong. We had the disastrous idea that the pastors are the primary ministers.

As Scripture so clearly says, every believer is a priest and minister in a certain sense. God's purpose for pastors (as well as teachers, evangelists, prophets, and apostles) is to "prepare God's people for works of service, so that the body of Christ may be built up until we all reach unity in the faith and in the knowledge of the Son of God and become mature, attaining to the whole measure of the fullness of Christ" (Eph. 4:12–13).

Loren Mead, author of *The Once and Future Church*, is one of many people who for decades have been calling for a return of the work of God to the people of God. Referring to the struggle between New Testament values and historical traditions, he says, "In Christendom the laypeople would come to the pastor and say, 'How can I help you with the ministry?' Today, the pastor needs to come to the laypeople and say, 'How can I help you in *your* ministry?' That's the 180-degree turnaround required between clergy and laity. Clergy used to own ministry and mission, and now they're the supporters of those who own it. It's a dramatic role reversal."[2]

This chapter outlines the steps that benchmark churches are taking as they rethink ministry through the truth that God's people are *all* ministers.

Understand the New Expectations Laypeople Bring to Church

Henry Ford, revolutionary founder of Ford Motor Company, is a legend in American business history. His dream to "build a motorcar for the multitude" changed the face of twentieth-century American life. In 1903 Ford was producing nearly 50 percent of all automobiles in the United States.

According to John Maxwell, the original "Henry Ford was the antithesis of an empowering leader. He always seemed to undermine his leaders." One of those reasons was that he refused to let anyone else tinker with his Model T. As Maxwell says, "One day when a group of his designers surprised him by presenting him with the prototype of an improved model, Ford ripped its doors off the hinges and proceeded to destroy the car with his bare hands."[3]

For almost twenty years, the Ford Motor Company offered only one design. People joked that Henry Ford would provide a car in any choice of color requested, so long as the choice was black.

By 1931 Ford's market share had shrunk to only 28 percent. By the time Henry Ford stepped aside and allowed his grandson Henry Ford II to become president, the company hadn't made a profit in fifteen years. At that time, it was reported to be losing the staggering sum of a million dollars a day!

What a contrast to the year 2000, when you can drive to a full parking lot and find not one single car that is precisely identical to yours. That reality is symbolic of the fact that most people have multiple choices in every area imaginable:

attire
channels of communication
cheeses
coffee
entertainment
footwear
friendship circles
garden tools
hats
hobbies
indoor temperature

Internet sites

level of educational attainment

magazines

meals

means of cross-country travel

motels

music

mutual funds

occupation

opportunities for lifetime learning

pain killers

places of residence

postage stamps

restaurants

soft drinks

spouse

television channels

. . . and when and where to gather for corporate worship of God[4]

"Given this huge array of choices in our culture," observes Lyle Schaller, "it should not be surprising that people who have grown up in a consumer-driven culture that is organized to expand the range of available choices expect to be offered attractive choices" . . . in opportunities:

to learn more about the Christian faith;

to be engaged in meaningful fellowship experiences with other believers;

to utilize their gifts, experiences, and skills in ministry with others;

to be challenged to do what they "know" they cannot do; and

to move to a new and higher level in their own spiritual growth.[5]

What's a church to do in response to this? Schaller outlines seven possibilities:

1. *Reject culture:* Reject today's consumer-driven culture as ideologically incompatible with the Christian faith. Reach people,

primarily those born before 1930, who are comfortable with a
two-choice, "take-it-or-leave-it" approach.

2. *Wait for 1954:* Define consumerism as a passing fad and plan to
   outlive it.
3. *Reject "choices":* Be satisfied with a small congregation that reaches
   and serves those people who value the following even more than
   having choices: intimacy, community, connections, caring, pre-
   dictability, simplicity, and continuity with the past. (This is the
   alternative chosen by well over one-half of all congregations in
   American Protestantism today, representing approximately one-
   sixth of all churchgoers.)
4. *Micro niche:* Offer only one choice for each of the above, and expand the geographical area served by the congregation to a forty-
   mile radius. Draw the one-half to one percent of the population
   who find your limited array of choices to be just right—both relevant and fulfilling—for them.
5. *Expand options:* Expand the range of attractive choices as a central component of a larger strategy to reach (a) younger generations and/or (b) a broader slice of the population.
6. *Redefine roles:* Transform pastoral staff roles to that of enlisting,
   training, placing, nurturing, and supporting teams of lay volunteers who, in turn, create and staff new ministries in response
   to new needs that merge.
7. *Maximize options:* Rejoice in the fact that your congregation is
   blessed with the discretionary resources and lay leadership required to offer people an exciting array of options in learning,
   discipling, fellowship, doing ministry, and enriching one's own
   personal spiritual pilgrimage.[6]

Churches that exercise the last three options build permission-giv-
ing environments where lay ministry flourishes. Churches such as this
tend to emphasize the use of spiritual gifts, encourage people to take
initiative in ministry, make heroes of lay leaders, depend on one-another pastoral care to occur through small groups, and develop systems for raising up (apprenticing) new leaders.

Worship services in these churches tend to involve laypeople in
ways that symbolize the legitimacy of lay ministry. Usually there is a
steady mix of pastors and people involved in different aspects of worship leadership. But whatever the particular worship style, people will
regularly perceive a "growing recognition that one of the responsibilities of a worshiping community is to transform the lives of people—

and part of that process is to challenge and equip them to do what they know they cannot do!"[7]

In a lay-empowered church, people will rarely walk away with their expectations disappointed, saying, "How come only pastors get to use their God-given gifts and abilities?" or "All I keep doing is sitting and watching others minister."

Build Ministry through Lay-Led Small Groups and Teams

The vast majority of churches struggle with how to transition to a "ministry anytime, anywhere, by anyone" kind of environment, as former pastor Bill Easum of Twenty-first-Century Strategies calls it.[8] For many pastors and people, an empowered laity represents a new way of viewing church.

For some, according to Easum, the starting point for the transition is to internalize the outreach dimension of what the church is all about. As Jesus said, "You will be my witnesses in Jerusalem, and in all Judea and Samaria, and to the ends of the earth" (Acts 1:8). According to Easum, the most basic law of congregational life is that "churches grow when they intentionally reach out to people instead of concentrating on their institutional needs. Churches die when they concentrate on their own needs."[9] Growth is not concerned with numbers, but with meeting the needs of people. Both paid staff and the people of the church must value a growth-oriented, outreach-based attitude.

Assuming that value is in place, the next step is to develop a gift-based partnership between pastor, staff, and lay persons. Making this transition does not come naturally or quickly to a congregation.

According to one writer, "There must be a conscious decision on the part of existing leaders to give their leadership away and to literally push the ministry of the church out the door and into the com-

---

Driving Forces Behind Recent Lay Ministry Expansions

1. The assumption that laypeople can be trusted, rather than a distrust of local leadership and a dependence on clergy to do most ministry.
2. A context that projects high expectations of everyone seeking to become a member, rather than a low-expectation, "please-just-show-up" environment.
3. Recognition that many adults "pilgrimage" from seeker to believer to learner to disciple, instead of organizing congregational life without sensitivity to helping pilgrims progress.
4. The professionalization of a large segment of the population, not the pastor as the best-educated, most competent person in the whole community.
5. A compelling recognition that ministry is satisfying and rewarding, rather than a view of abundant committees to regulate other people's ministry.

Adapted from Lyle Schaller, *Discontinuity and Hope: Radical Change and the Path to the Future* (Nashville: Abingdon Press, 1999), 49–51.

munity. It results in the mutual empowerment of people in ministry, but it also requires the hard work of cultivating the soil of the congregation's culture to accept the changes."[10] As Easum says, "Creating the environment that will grow 'spiritual redwoods' is the primary task of leadership in our times."[11]

The story of Acts 6:1–7 indicates that the fellowship and ministry of the church can't be expanded until new workers are released into ministry. The New Testament solution was to expand the base of the church by raising up new leaders. As Carl George, former pastor and consultant to many of North America's fastest-growing churches, points out, from the time of Acts 6 until now, "Volunteers . . . do a great deal of the work of the church, if not most of the work." Therefore, he says, "the creation of pastoral, ministry-capable leadership must become the core value of the church of the future, second only to listening to God."[12]

Groups and teams of five to fifteen people, effectively networked together, are fundamental to virtually every healthy church in the world.

To be effective, lay leaders need manageable spans of care. Otherwise, they end up like Moses, trying without success to be everything to everyone. Moses became exhausted and frustrated, bordering on burnout. Meanwhile few needs were getting met.

Just as Jethro advised Moses to empower leaders who would address the needs of people through small, manageable groups, so churches today do likewise through small Sunday school classes, home groups, care circles, ministry teams, and dozens of other "cell-sized" sub-units of the overall fellowship.[13] Whatever its stated task, "If your group or team is marked by a contagious love, then . . . more and better disciples will be made," asserts George.[14]

As George affirms, changes in society have affected how the church does its ministry. "For thousands of years," he says, "the deacons took care of the crises, and 'Mom' took care of everything else."[15] In the post World War II generations, women went to work outside the house, families became smaller, and mobility tore extended families apart. "Mom" is no longer filling that nurturing, community-building role at the same level she once was.

"In response to these societal changes," says George, "a church must be very deliberate about encouraging care through groups. It can no longer assume that 'nurture' will happen automatically."[16] In fact, in too many churches, "If you're not in a small group, you've got to stand in line to be loved."[17]

According to George, "Groups and teams of five to fifteen people, effectively networked together, are fundamental to virtually every healthy church in the world."[18]

**God's Exam for Churches and Church Leaders
(based on Ephesians 4:11–16)**

What of eternal significance happens in the lives of individuals while they are in the care of your church? (v. 11)

In what ways are your members ministering? (v. 12)

What percentage of your members are involved in ministry? (v. 12)

Do your members' ministries result in the spiritual growth of faith, knowledge, and maturity? (v. 13)

Do the lifestyles of your members reflect the principles and character of Christ? (v. 13)

What percentage of your members' lifestyles reflect that of a growing Christian? (v. 13)

What percentage of your members are easily shaken in their faith and vulnerable to deceitful schemes? (v. 14)

Is there spiritual and numerical growth in your church? (v. 15)

Do your members mutually edify and build up one another? (v. 16)

See http://sites.ncsi.net/~sspt/wbp/pastors_update/pu_01_01.html.

Build Lay Leadership on Spiritual Giftedness

Another reason for the explosion of lay ministry is the growing awareness in the body of Christ of spiritual giftedness. While certain groups are focusing on the miraculous gifts, most churches are teaching that every believer should be active in serving because every believer has been given a spiritual gift, and the diversity of these gifts reflects the different ministries of believers.

There are an abundance of new books instructing believers how to find and use their gifts. Many churches are teaching giftedness in church membership classes and actually give spiritual gift inventories to help new members discover their spiritual abilities, then guide them into an area of service that makes best use of their abilities (for example, Willow Creek Community Church). There are many spiritual gift inventories distributed by publishers and churches.[19]

There is effectiveness when all members minister in the church according to their strengths and desires, "We have different gifts, according to the grace given to us," says Paul (Rom. 12:6). Each using their gifts produces synergy and unity. "God has arranged the parts of the body, just as he wants them to be" (1 Cor. 12:18).

A Team-Based Church

1. A covenant team.
2. A visionary team.
3. A culture creating team.
4. A collaborative team.
5. A trusting team.
6. An empowering team.
7. A learning team.

From George Cladis, *Leading the Team-Based Church* (Dallas: Leadership Network and San Francisco: Jossey-Bass, 1999).

The correct use of gifts should rule out competition and bring members into collaboration as they network their gifts into a larger movement.[20]

Prioritize Leader-Making as a Primary Emphasis

Popular speaker and former pastor John Maxwell conducts leadership conferences for pastors and lay leaders. In his book, *The 21 Irrefutable Laws of Leadership,* he describes an informal poll he conducted during his 1998 leadership conferences. He found that 5 percent of his respondents became leaders as the results of crisis, 10 percent because of natural gifting, and 85 percent due to influence of another leader.[21]

According to these findings, leaders are more "made" than "born." Disciples of Jesus learn to influence other people as they observe other leaders and receive coaching in how to develop their leadership abilities.

Leader-making is not a one-weekend-a-year affair. John Maxwell says, "Leadership development isn't an add-water-and-stir proposition. It takes time, energy, and resources."[22] But only when every current leader becomes a leader-maker of others will your church begin to develop the number of leaders it needs to have an adequately functioning biblical community.

Becoming a leader who develops leaders requires an entirely different focus and attitude from those who develop followers. Consider some of the differences Maxwell outlines:

Leaders Who Develop Followers	Leaders Who Develop Leaders
need to be needed	want to be succeeded
focus on weaknesses	focus on strengths
develop the bottom 20 percent	develop the top 20 percent
treat their people the same for "fairness"	treat their leaders as individuals for impact
hoard power	give power away
spend time with others	invest time in others
grow by addition	grow by multiplication
impact only people they touch personally	impact people far beyond their own reach [23]

Why do so many churches struggle for lack of lay leaders? Because most congregations have an invisible layer of untapped, untrained talent, and they've not yet built the kind of leadership culture that will

Hurston on Lay Leadership

My father, John, and I have had ample opportunity to observe the inner workings and core values of growing churches, ranging from years of direct involvement with Dr. David Yonggi Cho's congregation in Seoul (Yoido Full Gospel Central Church) to our combined seventy-five years of speaking and consulting in 525 churches in fifty-one countries on five continents, including forty-seven of fifty U.S. states.

I heartily concur with the importance Towns and Bird give to the development, modeling, empowerment, and releasing of lay leaders; and to the concept of growing bigger by excellence in becoming smaller. I see this emphasis in growing churches around the world.

Towns and Bird have captured the core values and principles practiced by churches that will thrive in the third millennium. They isolate key components to the vibrant and growing congregation.

If only all churches would heed these lay empowerment principles alone, God's kingdom would advance in a much greater measure in our need-filled world.

Karen Hurston
consultant, Gulf Breeze, Florida
author, *Growing the World's Largest Church*, (Gospel Publishing House, 1994)

Nine Keys to Effective Small-Group Leadership

Until recent years, most small-group materials focused primarily on the gathering itself. Carl George emphasizes that eight of nine group leader privileges occur *outside* the class or group's "official" meeting time:

1. Connect with the leadership network in your church.
   I will be available for debriefing interviews with the church staff.
2. Recruit a leader-in-training.
   I will recruit my replacement(s) before we begin meeting with the group, and I will help my replacement(s) develop an ability to lead.
3. Invite newcomers to your group.
   I will reach out between meetings, cultivating both old and new contacts.
4. Prepare yourself to lead the meeting.
   I will prepare my mind and heart for our meetings and will include my apprentice(s) in the process.
5. Meet together for one-another ministry.
   I will conduct meetings that encourage believers and accept seekers.
6. Bring your group to worship.
   I will bring group members to worship for the church weekend services.
7. Serve the group and others beyond.
   I will serve others with my gifts, knowledge, energy, time, and money, conscious that my greatest influence may occur as I set an example.
8. Win the world as Jesus would.
   I will make time to build acquaintances with unbelievers, serving them at their points of struggle.
9. Seek God's renewal as you meet him in secret.
   I will meet regularly with God in private prayer.

From Carl George with Warren Bird, *Nine Keys to Effective Small-Group Leadership* (Mansfield, Penn.: Kingdom Publishing, 1997), ix–x, 200.

draw it out. "I have yet to find a case where the number of potential but unrecognized leaders is not at least equal to the number of existing, identified leaders," says Carl George.[24]

Carl George also says that "churches rise and fall on the availability of trained, talented, and Spirit-gifted leadership."[25] So, "the more ministry-capable leaders there are, the more quality groups a church can sponsor."[26] It's no accident that the world's largest church has been extremely intentional about leader-making. According to an interview Warren Bird conducted with Karen Hurston, Korea's Yoido Full Gospel Central Church, the church where she grew up, has appointed one lay leader for every ten to sixteen members throughout the years. "I have tracked this since 1978—they do not intentionally keep to a ratio, but that is how it has resulted," she says. "These would not just be leaders of groups, but also deacons, senior deacons, and elders," she clarifies. The primary context for leader-making in large churches is small groups because they are so crucial to the health of the church. As Lyle Schaller says, "Megachurches survive only because they encourage attenders to bond in small groups."[27]

Bill Easum, John Maxwell, Carl George, and others offer numerous resource materials designed to help identify, recruit, train, develop, and multiply the lay leadership ability in any congregation.[28] As Carl George summarizes, "The game plan for the future is simple. The volunteer leader works with the ten, and the church staff sees to it that these lay leaders receive the necessary training and resources."[29] It's both that simple and that hard.

As that happens, a priesthood of believers will emerge that has not been seen since the time of Christ. Schaller even predicts that by the year 2050, should the Lord Jesus not return before then, today's American Christianity will take on a whole new character: "The proportion of churchgoers in American Christianity who are deeply committed disciples and apostles will be at least double or triple the proportions of 1999, while the proportion of those who are 'lukewarm' in their faith will shrink dramatically."[30]

There is no better context for that kind of evangelism and discipleship than through a lay-led, cell-sized group, class, or team.

APPLICATION QUESTIONS
FOR INDIVIDUAL RESPONSE OR GROUP DISCUSSION

1. To what extent do you agree or disagree with Schaller that God's people today increasingly expect their church will be a place that empowers them for ministry?
2. Think about John Maxwell's findings that most lay leaders are developed, not merely born that way. Describe how God has used you to develop someone else as a leader. Describe how someone has significantly mentored your hidden leadership abilities.
3. Which Carl George quote in this chapter spoke most to you? Why? What are the implications for your life in the coming week? How and when will you follow through?

PASTORS 4. How many hours in the last week did you spend actually developing lay leaders? Don't count those times you did ministry by yourself and hoped someone would learn by watching you. If you don't have a set of quality training resources, check out some of the leadership training organizations cited in the endnotes for this chapter.

twelve

Look Underneath the Megachurch Movement

Trend #12: Large churches are learning to operate at maximum impact and to be healthy by becoming the "biggest little church around."

৵

Elmer Towns wrote one of the first American church growth books in 1969. The editor of *Christian Life Magazine* described the book as "a thunder clap" that hit the evangelical world. The secular media, preoccupied with dying churches and the "God is dead" movement, had missed the story that there was a new wave of churches emerging, and that it was having a tremendous impact across the country because they were committed to the historic preaching of the gospel. This book was a boost of encouragement.

When Elmer published his book, only ninety-seven churches across the United States were known to have one thousand or more in attendance.[1] Three decades later, there are six to eight thousand such churches. One of every fifty U.S. churches is a so-called megachurch. One in every six churchgoers attends a church with overall weekend attendance of one thousand or more. As this trend continues, by the year 2050 a mere 7 percent of Protestant churches will probably account for one-half of all Protestant worshipers on a typical weekend.[2]

Growing Big by Building Small Teams

New Hope Christian Fellowship

Denomination:	Foursquare
Location:	Honolulu, Hawaii
Senior pastor:	Wayne Cordeiro (since 1995)
Recent goal:	Help every new member become a minister, discovering, developing, and deploying their gifts.
Church vision:	To present the gospel in such a way that turns non-Christians into converts, converts into disciples, and disciples into mature, fruitful leaders who will in turn go into the world and reach others for Christ.
Year founded:	1995
Attendance:	6000 (current)
Internet address:	www.newhope-hawaii.org

"God never said to build a big church," says Wayne Cordeiro, "but rather to build a big people. That's why we're planting daughter churches in the Philippines, Japan, Australia, and Sri Lanka."

New Hope Christian Fellowship, the tenth church Cordeiro has planted since 1984, exploded to an attendance of six thousand in just four years. Although their church's mailing address reads "Honolulu, Hawaii," most participants don't see their church as being in Oahu. They understand themselves to be part of a four-step movement of evangelism, edification, equipping, and extension that produces mature, fruitful leaders who will in turn go into the world and reach others for Christ.

"The best evangelists in the world are the people in our equivalent of pews, especially as they use their gifts in service," says Cordeiro. The way New Hope trains leaders and mobilizes for service is through teams. All ministry is team-based. And whatever the ministry, each leader is to reproduce four other leaders.

"Let's say a person steps forward to help with the children's ministry," explains Cordeiro. "His passion is to work with kids and he has teaching gifts and organizational skills, so he says 'yes.' In doing church as a team, his first move is not to jump in and start working with children. Instead, he builds a team of four leaders with whom he serves. As the ministry grows, he personally oversees these four primary leaders. That number never increases. In that way no one burns out."

The ministry then extends itself by doing what Cordeiro calls "growing downward." Each of the four people described above do not immediately join children's ministry. Instead each duplicates the pattern of what was just done, building a team of four other leaders with similar passions and supporting gifts.

"The phrase *doing church as a team*, which is also the title of a book I wrote, is not some original, innovative concept," says Cordeiro. "It is as old as the Bible itself."*

"God placed us here for a reason because he has a purpose for us. Every person is incredibly important to the Great Commission, and every person has a gift to contribute. They just need someone to believe in them and help those gifts be used for God's purposes."

*Wayne Cordeiro, *Doing Church as a Team* (Honolulu: New Hope Publishing, 1998).

Lyle Schaller observes, "Between 1950 and 1990 the number of Protestant congregations averaging eight hundred or more at worship has at least tripled and perhaps quintupled."[3]

This changing ecclesiastical landscape is of huge significance. "The emergence of the 'megachurch' is the most important development of modern Christian history," says Schaller.[4] Leading business writer Peter Drucker says that the emergence of the large pastoral church is "the most important social phenomenon in American society in the last thirty years."[5]

> "*The emergence of the 'megachurch' is the most important development of modern Christian history.*"

In 1999, according to research we conducted, the following North American churches averaged attendance of ten thousand or more adults and children in weekend services (listed by approximate size):

Willow Creek Community Church (nondenominational), metropolitan Chicago, Illinois, pastored by Bill Hybels

Saddleback Valley Community Church (SBC), metropolitan Los Angeles, California, pastored by Rick Warren

Southeast Christian Church (Christian), Louisville, Kentucky, pastored by Bob Russell

Calvary Chapel (Calvary Chapel), Santa Ana, California, pastored by Chuck Smith Sr.

Fellowship of Excitement/Second Baptist Church (Southern Baptist), Houston, Texas, pastored by Ed Young

Harvest Christian Fellowship (Calvary Chapel), Riverside, California, pastored by Greg Laurie

First Baptist Church (independent Baptist), Hammond, Indiana, pastored by Jack Hyles

Cornerstone Church (independent charismatic), San Antonio, Texas, pastored by John Hagee

Salem Baptist Church (National Baptist), Chicago, Illinois, pastored by James Meeks

New Birth Missionary Baptist Church (Full Gospel Baptist), Decatur, Georgia, pastored by Eddie Long

Calvary Chapel Golden Springs (Calvary Chapel), Diamond Bar, California, pastored by Raul Ries

According to megachurch specialist John Vaughan, one of the three fastest-growing U.S. churches of the century is T. D. Jakes's Potter's House church in Dallas. It grew from zero to a worship attendance of

Largest Sanctuary in World Dedicated

A 50,000-capacity church sanctuary—believed to be the largest in the world—was commissioned in Nigeria on Saturday, September 18, 1999. The country's Christian president, Olusegun Obansanjo, attended the dedication, which was the first part of a multimillion-dollar development by the Living World Outreach Center, also known as Winners Chapel.

Faith Academy, a full-boarding, coeducational secondary school, is to be commissioned along with the auditorium. The two buildings are the first phase of a seven-stage development planned for the church's Canaan Land project on more than five hundred acres on the outskirts of the country's former capital, Lagos.

The massive project is being headed by Bishop David Oyedepo, a former architect, who said that church members had made an "exceptional financial commitment" to the development. "There is

no imported technology, foreign aid, foreign consultancy. What we see here standing today is all homemade," he said.

The development has won praise from the Nigerian Institution of Structural Engineers, who called it a "feat in engineering circles." During a visit in August 1999, American evangelist T. L. Osborn described it as "awesome, prodigious and almost inconceivable." In addition to a network of churches in all major cities across the country, Winners Chapel also has ministry in more than fifty African countries through its African Gospel Invasion Project.

Adapted from Lekan Otufodunrin, daily news update, *Charisma*, 15 September 1999, newsupdate@charismanews.com.

more than five thousand in just two years.[6] Average worship attendance in 1999 was about 8,000.

Megachurches are not a North American phenomenon. In the United States, "megachurch growth began to increase after 1970," says Vaughan, while "the decade of the 1960s was the time when churches began to experience explosive growth outside the United States."[7]

In fact, U.S. growth has been consistently outflanked around the world. According to Vaughan, in 1995 the four largest churches in the world were located on three other continents:

730,000-member Yoido Full Gospel Church in Seoul, South Korea, pastored by David Yonggi Cho

350,000-member Jotabeche Methodist Pentecostal Church in Santiago, Chile, pastored by Javier Vasquez

150,000-member Anyang Assembly of God in Seoul, South Korea, pastored by Yong Mok Cho

145,000-member Deeper Life Bible Church in Lagos, Nigeria, pastored by William Kumuyi[8]

From Bigger Sunday Schools to Bigger Worship Services

How to Break Growth Barriers, by Carl George with Warren Bird* summarizes the transition window when the highest-attendance event moved from Sunday school to the worship services. Drawing from research by John Vaughan, it starts with what is generally regarded as North America's first megachurch—First Baptist Church, Fort Worth, Texas, which reported a Sunday school attendance of 5,200 in 1928. By 1969 its attendance had significantly declined, and a new record was set by Akron Baptist Temple, Akron, Ohio, which reported an average of 5,762 for Sunday school. By 1979 the Sunday school record holder was First Baptist Church, Hammond, Indiana, pastored by Jack Hyles, which reported 15,101 people in average Sunday school attendance.

From the late 1970s onwards, North America's largest church in terms of worship attendance was also First Baptist Church, Hammond, Indiana. By 1993 the top North American attendance average for on-campus weekend services was held by Willow Creek Community Church, South Barrington, Illinois, where Bill Hybels is founding pastor.

In terms of largest worship facilities, the 80,000-square-foot geodesic FaithDome, completed in 1989 as the main sanctuary for Crenshaw Christian Center in Los Angeles, California, has the largest one-room seating capacity (10,140 seats). The founder and present senior pastor of the church is Dr. Frederick K. C. Price.

Church buildings continue to outdo each other. In the year 2000, the claim for the largest seating-capacity church facility in North America will shift to Pastor Jerry Falwell and the congregation he serves, Thomas Road Baptist Church in Lynchburg, Virginia. The new sanctuary, completed in the next century at a cost of more than $20 million, will seat 12,500 worshipers.

*See Carl George with Warren Bird, *How to Break Growth Barriers* (Grand Rapids: Baker, 1993), 203–4.

Megachurches are not without controversy. Some of them have even hurt the cause of Christ. When high-visibility pastors have been caught in sexual or financial scandals, sometimes refusing to repent, the overall church has suffered. Some leaders have spent more time raising money than proclaiming Christ. Others have sacrificed their marriages and families to build huge television empires. And too many megachurches have been content to grow by transfer membership rather than reaching the unconverted or unchurched.

Setting aside these exceptions, though, what is the appeal of a megachurch? Why have they emerged? What can we learn from their good qualities? This chapter summarizes the primary distinctives of the megachurch movement.

Realize That the Driving Motivation in Most Megachurches Is Not Size

Currently, North America's most-attended, one-location congregation is Willow Creek Community Church, located in a western suburb of Chicago. Willow Creek is typical of many large churches whose launch was motivated by a dream of what God calls his church to be, not by numbers or bigness.

The genesis of Willow Creek goes back to the early 1970s, when a dynamic youth ministry was created at South Park Church in Park Ridge, Illinois. Using contemporary music, drama, and Bible teaching that was highly relevant to the lives of high school students, the services grew from a handful of teenagers to one thousand students a night. Nobody was more surprised—or inspired—by the response than the youth leaders of the ministry, including a recent college graduate named Bill Hybels.

Hybels had attended church most of his life, but was not saved until age seventeen. "I had a dramatic conversion," he says. "I went from a performance-based theology to a grace-based theology. In a moment of time, I understood I was loved so much that Christ went to the cross so salvation could be made available to me as a gift. The enormity of that shock has never left me. I have been permanently ignited by the miracle of grace."[9]

After several years of working with youth, Hybels and his group of friends in ministry felt compelled to offer their innovative and creative style of service to an adult audience, such as the parents of the teens they were reaching. On October 12, 1975, twenty-four-year-old Bill Hybels and team rented a Palatine movie theater (from which the name Willow Creek was taken) and launched the church with great optimism—only to be disappointed by the initial turnout of 125 people. Even worse, though, attendance sank the next week.

The group persisted, however, and people began to respond. In three years, attendance grew to two thousand people. Faced with standing-room-only crowds, the highly motivated congregation rallied in 1977 to buy ninety acres of farmland in South Barrington. The first service in the main auditorium was held in February 1981, and growth has continued ever since. Some one hundred ministries have been launched to serve spiritual, physical, and relational needs.

In 1988, an education wing was opened. One Saturday service was added, and then another. Later, the building was doubled in size and the property was expanded to 155 acres.

From the beginning, however, the founders' goal was not to become a big church, but to be the church to each other and the community. Authentic relationships have always been stressed, with small groups offering opportunities for people to develop spiritually while building life-long friendships. Through it all, God has changed thousands of lives and eternities, prompting Bill Hybels to reflect, "I've come to believe more deeply than ever that the local church is the hope of the world."[10]

Grow Bigger by Learning to "Do Small Well"

When feelings come up about megachurches, the most widespread fear is the idea that as a church grows, it may become impersonal, and that precious human beings will fall through the cracks or be lost in the shuffle. But healthy large churches are capable of "doing care" as well if not better than any other size of church.

The key is a well-coached system of small groups focused on quality of care. People find their primary identity in a small Sunday school class, home Bible study, women's prayer team, or any number of other groups, rather than in the entire congregation as a "single cell."

Most large churches go out of their way to emphasize that the life of the body is in the cell. The world's largest church had twenty groups in 1964 and today has 23,000 home cell groups.[11] Likewise, Saddleback's Rick Warren continually encourages people to join a small group, affirming, "The church must grow larger and smaller at the same time."[12] Dale Galloway, pioneer in the American small-group movement, grew a church that had five thousand present in worship and five thousand in pastoral care through "Tender Loving Care" groups.[13] As with many other large-church pastors, Bill Hybels of Willow Creek is continually involved in one of the church's small groups that includes nurture and one-another pastoral care. He says, "Every Tuesday the eight people who report directly to me . . . sit around a table in my office. We have food brought in and for the first hour and a half we ask each other one question: 'So, how are you doing, really?'"[14]

George Hunter has studied churches large and small for years. He says, "The church of the future will not be a church with small groups,

Potential Strengths of Larger Churches

1. Large churches develop, just like in the Book of Acts (2:41; 4:4; 5:14, 28, 42; 6:1, 7), when a church reaches out to more and more people who are put in right relationship with God.
2. The large church is able to evangelize an entire metropolitan area.
3. The large church provides all the spiritual gifts to the local church.
4. The large church can be a conscience to the community and can speak out on social issues in a community.
5. The large church can be self-supporting, without needing ongoing subsidy from a denomination, such as by sponsoring missionaries or by self-funding its own buildng programs.

From Elmer Towns, *America's Fastest Growing Churches: Why Ten Sunday Schools Are Growing Fast* (Nashville: Impact Books, 1972), 190–91.

but it will be a church of small groups where membership in a small group will be more primary than church membership."[15]

Increase Health by Empowering Lay Ministry

The previous chapter explores the significance of lay ministry. The vast majority of larger churches have learned how to release ministry to lay leaders. In doing so they diffuse leadership throughout the congregation. Rather than serving as doers of ministry, staff then "become equippers of others in ministry and facilitators of ministry teams."[16] For example, at Frazer Memorial United Methodist Church, Montgomery, Alabama, more than 80 percent of the people are involved in ministry, so the staff spends its energies resourcing them.

As Bill Easum explains, "Healthy churches do not pay staff to do ministry. They equip the laity to do ministry. Staff do not replace volunteers. Staff identify laity for ministry, recruit and deploy laity into ministry, and equip laity for ministry."[17]

Empowerment builds an increased dependency on the Holy Spirit. The need to be intentional in allowing the Holy Spirit to work is only one reason why a disproportionate amount of today's faster-growing and larger churches are connected with the charismatic or Pentecostal movements.

Change with the Times to Ensure Relevance and Effectiveness

The megachurch movement, while apparently here to stay, is not monolithic. Worship and preaching styles vary. Some emphasize television or radio ministry while others focus

---

Of Entire World Population Today, 1 in 12 Are Pentecostals

In 1999, the world population was 6 billion, including 2 billion adherents to Christendom. In the breakdown that follows, note that 540 million (1 in 4) members of Christendom are Pentecostal/charismatic:

1.	Roman Catholics	1 billion
2.	Pentecostals/charismatics	540 million
	Denominational Pentecostals	215 million
	Catholic charismatics	92 million
	Protestant charismatics	71 million
	Mainline Third Wavers	110 million
	Chinese Pentecostals	52 million
3.	Anglicans	73 million
4.	Baptists	60 million
5.	Lutherans	58 million
6.	Presbyterians	50 million
7.	Assemblies of God	35 million
8.	Methodists	33 million

Figures come from researchers David Barrett and Vinson Synan, "Pentecostal Trends of the 90s," *Ministries Today*, vol. 17, no. 3, May/June 1999, 64. These statistics are debatable (e.g., overlapping categories), but they are useful for illustration and discussion.

---

on the surrounding community. Some are known for the amount of missionaries they've sent out, while others are known as training centers for missionaries who come to them. And locations vary from center city (Abyssinian Baptist Church in the Harlem section of Manhattan) to suburban (Calvary Chapel, Santa Ana, California) to small-town (Thomas Road in Lynchburg, Virginia) to semi-rural (Ginghamsburg, twenty miles north of Dayton, Ohio).

Bob Buford, founder and chairman of Leadership Network, observes three phases in megachurch development. "The first wave of American Christianity was one of *replication*," he says. "The church in the United States started as an import from Europe. Immigrants from British Methodist, German Lutheran, and other parishes simply relocated them onto American soil."[18] Many of those transplants are still with us today. Their central values include tradition, ritual, and preservation of their rich heritage. They are readily recognized by their European architecture, classical music, and similar liturgy to what was being used in England.

"The second wave, now at its apex, is *proclamation*," Buford says. Churches like this create an experience that is analogous to a concert or sports gathering. The big-crowd event itself is a main thing, whether

America's Megachurches Continue Growth: A Church of 50,000 Soon?

The number of extra large churches—congregations numbering 2,000 or more—nearly doubled during the 1990s to an estimated five hundred today, *The Los Angeles Times* reported in its June 9, 1999 issue. These churches have transformed religion in America, partly because they have rejected traditional Sunday morning forms and adapted the use of elaborate stage productions, contemporary music, mini-dramas, and practical sermons offering life lessons for families.

Some experts contend that megachurches have passed their prime and will eventually lose popularity. Yet other trend-watchers are confident that the biggest churches in the United States are on the verge of making a quantum leap. "The first churches to hit 50,000 will do it in the next decade," said leading independent church growth expert Carl George.

Scott Thumma, a megachurch observer at the Center for Social and Religious Research in Hartford, Connecticut, said megachurches have been most popular in suburban areas because the areas offer the space needed as well as the type of people they try to serve—mobile, well-educated, middle-class families.

Among the challenges these churches face are the need for space and conflicts with neighbors over traffic, noise and development. For example, Saddleback Valley Community Church in Lake Forest, California, faced a knotty traffic problem surrounding the sole entrance to its premises. Traffic was so bad that attendance growth was stunted during 1998. By building a $4.5 million bridge, the church created a second street entrance and its attendance growth resumed.

Experts say that some churches have seen even more dramatic growth after investing in expansion. Southeast Christian Church in Louisville, Kentucky, moved in December from a 2,500-seat auditorium to a gargantuan 9,100-seat sanctuary. The church's attendance shot up by 3,500 to almost 14,000 in only a month.

In addition to spacial needs, growing megachurches must find a way to keep congregants from feeling disconnected, partly because it's easy for an individual to get lost in a crowd of thousands. Megachurch pastors recognize that their turnover rate can be fairly large.

(continued) ⟶

a Billy Graham preaching mission, Robert Schuller's *Hour of Power* telecast, or a worship service at one of today's megachurches. "The proclamation wave is like a broadcast medium for the most part," says Buford. "The message travels primarily one way as the central person plays the role of the great communicator: preacher, actor, musician, or teacher. It's enthusiastic and participatory. It's a grand and very high-quality public performance."

The third wave, according to Buford, is *demonstration*. "Christianity in this context is more pastoral and more hands-on. Community is one of its primary values, but it's not tied to a building. Authenticity is its other primary value as it's more open and spontaneous than most other ways of doing church. It's more like a relationship over time, with a lot of involvement by the Holy Spirit. Like e-mail and the In-

America's Megachurches Continue Growth: A Church of 50,000 Soon? (continued)

Small groups, or gatherings of six or more believers, is not a new concept for churches. But for megachurches the small group becomes a necessity.

"The bottom line is that if you don't figure out how to get smaller as you're getting larger, growth will definitely peak," said Brett Eastman, membership pastor at Saddleback. "If you don't keep a sense of heart and family and connectedness, then growth tends to level off."

Some experts predict that future megachurches will resemble the decentralized churches of Korea, where twenty-four of the fifty largest churches in the world are located. In many Korean churches, "cell groups" are the basic components of the church. Members meet in homes for regular services and attend the Sunday worship service every two or three weeks.

Some experts believe that megachurches could inevitably fade with the aging of baby boomers. Saddleback pastors realize that failing to meet the needs of Generation X could ultimately doom their church growth. Said executive pastor Glen Kreun: "There's going to be a day real soon we're going to start losing an entire generation if we don't design a service for them."

Another way for megachurches to keep spreading their mission and message is through planting daughter churches. Several movements and denominations, such as Hope Chapel, grow primarily by sending out their members to start new churches.

Other large churches spread their influence through loose-knit fraternal organizations. Willow Creek Community Church in South Barrington, Illinois—the largest megachurch in the country—now counts more than 4,000 churches as part of its Willow Creek Association. Churches join the group at a rate of three a day.

From Leigh DeVore, *Charisma Online* news service, 9 June 1999. See http://www.charismanews.com.

Baergen on Small Group Ministry

This chapter grabbed my attention because it identifies both what is already happening today and what must happen for tomorrow. I found it encouraging and motivating.

The information is insightful and affirming as it helps Christians understand the changing face of the church. It is important to understand what a church might look like as it becomes healthy, growing, and vibrant.

I especially want to underscore the section entitled, "Grow Bigger by Learning to 'Do Small Well'" (see page 183). As I have worked with the largest churches across Canada, experience has shown that healthy small groups are one of the essential marks of what has been called natural church development. Soul care often happens best in a small-group context, and tomorrow's church won't have the spiritual vitality it needs without both pastors and people being part of life-changing small groups.

I speak also from personal experience, as a long-time member or leader of various small groups. If churches want to make a marked difference for eternity, small groups are often the center of both conversions and discipleship.

John Baergen
executive director, The International Centre for Leadership Development and Evangelism, Winfield, British Columbia, Canada

---

Core Values in Growing Churches

If churches, whether below the 200 barrier or approaching the 20,000 barrier, "are serious about growth, they could do well to emulate as many of these characteristics as possible," says Peter Wagner.

1. Evangelical theology . . . of aggressive outreach.
2. Strong pastoral leadership.
3. Participatory worship.
4. Powerful prayer.

5. Centrality of the Holy Spirit.
6. Abundant finances . . . through tithing.
7. Lay ministry.
8. Practical Bible teaching.
9. Direct missions involvement.
10. Low denominational profile.

From Elmer Towns, C. Peter Wagner, and Thom S. Rainer, *The Everychurch Guide for Growth* (Nashville: Broadman & Holman, 1998), 67–68.

---

ternet, it's democratic and one-on-one. It's an anywhere and anytime connection.

Buford predicts that the majority of megachurches will participate in a movement towards a deeper, more intense discipleship. He cites Lyle Schaller's 1999 release, *Discontinuity and Hope*, which reviews American Christianity from the vantage point of the year 2050. Schaller predicts that, among other things, "the proportion of churchgoers in American Christianity who are deeply committed disciples and apostles will be at least double or triple the proportions of 1999, while the proportion of those who are 'lukewarm' in their faith will shrink dramatically."[19]

?

APPLICATION QUESTIONS
FOR INDIVIDUAL RESPONSE OR GROUP DISCUSSION

1. What has been your personal experience with a megachurch? What did you learn about megachurches in this chapter that was the greatest surprise to you? Why?
2. How has the emergence of megachurches affected the church you serve, both positively and negatively? Why?
3. How does your church—regardless of its size—ensure that everyone has the opportunity to be cared for?

PASTORS
4. When was the last time you visited a megachurch that serves as a teaching center (i.e., that offers an on-premises conference)? Your visit was not to copy it but to glean ideas that would be healthy and helpful to your own ministry. What did you learn? How did you feel? What did it do to your vision?

thirteen

Make the Church Better Than a Business

Trend #13: Church leaders, while continuing to find valid help from secular management insights, are rediscovering the uniqueness of a church's spiritual resources and eternal mission.

∽

Ever heard the slogan, "If it ain't broke, don't fix it?" If everyone had bought into that principle, the United States would never have made it to the moon. Thomas Edison would never have invented the electric lightbulb, and Steve Jobs would never have developed the Macintosh computer.

Why not? Because none of those things were broken; they were nonexistent. Discovery and invention brought them into existence because people challenged the status quo.

A similar revolution is occurring in how leaders shepherd today's church. They are increasingly dissatisfied with mediocrity and status quo. They are looking for better, more effective ways to proclaim Christ and to train Christ's followers.

In the process they're searching everywhere for ideas that work, from the church across town to the business community downtown. They don't want to do anything that would violate Scripture, but they

Church Rediscovers Prayer's Unique Role Prayer in Evangelism

Georgian Hills Baptist Church

Denomination:	Southern Baptist Convention (SBC)
Location:	Memphis, Tennessee
Senior pastor:	Gregory R. Frizzell (since 1985)
Recent goal:	Engage a larger percentage of the church in the evangelistic prayer ministry.
Church vision:	To be part of the spiritual awakening necessary to reach the world for Jesus Christ.
Year founded:	1958
Attendance:	300 (now)
	250 (5 years ago)
	200 (10 years ago)
E-mail:	gfrizzell@earthlink.net

What would happen if a church made organized, evangelistic prayer meetings a major ongoing strategy? Many churches give lip service to the idea that prayer is the central work of the church; what if those words were clearly lived out? In 1989, Gregory R. Frizzell, senior pastor of Georgian Hills Baptist Church, Memphis, Tennessee, led his congregation to make such a commitment. "To my knowledge no denomination has ever organized and seriously promoted such focused prayer as a sustained, nationwide strategy," he says.

The evangelistic prayer group met each Monday evening. It prayed intensely for lost people name by name. Unlike prayer meetings in many churches, this prayer group prayed fervently for one or two hours, and then committed to pray for these same people in each participant's daily prayer times. In addition to praying for the lost, the group also prayed for deep personal repentance and sweeping revival in the church.

The results were absolutely astounding. According to Frizzell, "The evangelistic prayer group began with a list of sixty lost people and within four months, forty-five of the sixty people had been saved!" That year alone, a congregation of about 250 in Sunday morning worship saw nearly a hundred people publicly pray to receive Christ. More than 90 percent had been prayed for on the Monday night prayer list.

Over time, the evangelistic prayer groups were combined with the teams represented by the church's Evangelism Explosion lay witness training and its Continuous Witness Training program (an emphasis in many Southern Baptist churches).

Frizzell points to some of the significant benefits of this prayer emphasis: "The first year, the number of our baptisms nearly tripled and a much higher percentage of the converts proved genuine and lasting. Second, the repentance and spiritual growth of prayer group members far surpassed any of their previous discipleship experiences.

"The intense combination of prayer and evangelism is biblically based, theologically sound, and historically central to all great moves of God," he concludes. "If it can happen in our community of severe economic decline and exploding crime rates, then *any* church can grow through fervent, evangelistic prayer groups."

Portions of the material in this case study are adapted with permission from Gregory R. Frizzell, *Prayer Evangelism for the Local Church* (privately published, 1999). For copies, phone 901-357-5333, fax 901-357-5349, or e-mail gfrizzell@earthlink.net.

are also driven by a pragmatism that says, "Hey, there's got to be a better way. If it works elsewhere, maybe there's something our church could learn from it."

This chapter looks at both the upside and the downside of today's pragmatic approach to leading and managing the church. It acknowledges the dangers of confusing a church with a business. But it also finds encouragement in the fact that church leaders, while finding valid help from secular management insights, are rediscovering the uniqueness of a church's spiritual resources and eternal mission.

Accept Leadership as a Permanent Addition to the Role of Pastor

Noted Christian educator Howard Hendricks serves as chairman of the Center for Christian Leadership at Dallas Theological Seminary. He tells how a thoughtful layman once challenged him by saying, "I'm convinced the typical evangelical church is doomed to mediocrity."

Hendricks flinched in response, but hesitatingly probed, "What is your evidence for that?"

The man shot back, "The average evangelical church does not plan to be in business very long."

Hendricks meditated on that pronouncement for years and then concluded, "I am convinced he is correct." The evidence? When Hendricks asks pastors, "What is your church planning to do in the next ten years?" too often he receives the response, "I don't know what I'm planning to do next Sunday, let alone the next decade!"[1]

Years ago, a church could remain stable without proactive leadership. All the pastor needed was a congenial personality and basic skills at maintaining the status quo.

No longer. As Dave Goetz, editor of *Churchleadership.Net*, writes, "In a post-Christian culture, church work is more like overseas missions work . . . . More and more pastors need to function as missionaries who try to understand culture and re-create local church ministry with new assumptions."[2]

Ministry in the third millennium requires the ability to respond to a rapidly changing world, where the church is quick to be sidelined or marginalized. Effective ministry today demands leadership skill. It also requires a sense of innovation and risk. In most cases, it is also helped by a dose of entrepreneurial and managerial savvy.

How Much Business Skill Does a Pastor Need?

Each of the following perceptions deals with the "business" side of being a pastor. To what extent do you agree with each?

	Disagree			Agree		Disagree			Agree

"Many pastors no longer see their role as a shepherd of souls but as business persons managing the store for a consumeristic society."—Donald Boyd, professor of preaching and worship at Asbury Theological Seminary.   1 2 3 4

"It's possible to build a large church with nothing more than marketing skills, hype, and charisma. It goes on all the time. (The interesting thing is that some people are genuinely converted to Christ as a result of these ministries. I suppose the answer to this intriguing phenomenon is the greatness of God's grace.)"—Peter Nanfelt, president of The Christian and Missionary Alliance.   1 2 3 4

"Contemporary evangelicalism has made a god in its own image. That god is relevant and user friendly. You might say that it's a designer god . . . . No one wants to admit that the normal Christian life has been redefined and downgraded to accommodate culture, but on a practical basis I am afraid that such is the case."—Bill Hull, former pastor and author of *Can We Save the Evangelical Church?*   1 2 3 4

"In a church era that has favored expansion over compassion, efficiency over ministry, and a business model over that of a caring shepherd tending his flock . . . if we have become business executives in the pulpit, then we've lost our sense of identity and calling."—Glenn Wagner, pastor and author of *Escape from Church, Inc.*   1 2 3 4

"A business-driven response may only make things worse. In the long run, if we train people to be consumers instead of communers, we'll end up with customers instead of disciples. It might fill up an auditorium, but it'll never turn the world upside down for Christ."—Greg Laurie, pastor of Harvest Christian Fellowship, Riverside, California.   1 2 3 4

Quotes are from Donald C. Boyd and Ronald K. Crandall, "Designing Worship for the 21st Century," *The Asbury Herald,* winter 1999, 8; Peter Nanfelt, "Leadership Skills for an Emerging Movement," Completing Christ's Commission newsletter (Christian Missionary Alliance), June/July 1999, 1; Bill Hull, *Building High Commitment in a Low-Commitment World* (Grand Rapids: Revell, 1995), 7, 29; Glenn Wagner, *Escape from Church, Inc.: The Return of the Pastor-Shepherd* (Grand Rapids: Zondervan, 1999), advertisment; and Greg Laurie, *The Upside Down Church* (Wheaton: Tyndale, 1999), 42.

As a result, a generation of pastors with little or no training in management matters are looking anywhere and everywhere to be coached in the new roles they need. The danger to be avoided, as Bill Hull warns in *Building High Commitment in a Low-Commitment World*, is that "many a pastor takes the plunge into such a belief system without running it through his scriptural grid."[3]

Rediscover the Uniqueness of Your Church's Spiritual Calling

North Americans are increasingly interested in spiritual matters, but not just matters limited to Christianity. Hit television shows such as *Touched by an Angel* and best-sellers such as Deepak Chopra's *Seven Spiritual Laws of Success* underscore the public's curiosity about supernatural explanations for day-to-day life. A visit to secular bookstores reveals that the "Christianity" section has been exchanged for the broader "spirituality." The Top-10 list of most popular books in that section are usually a mix of Christianity, New Age spirituality, Eastern mysticism, and cafeteria-style, create-your-own-religion titles.

This mixed-pickles trend in spirituality shows no sign of letup. *A Generation of Seekers* summarizes the findings of Wade Clark Roof, a University of California at Santa Barbara sociologist and past president of the Society for the Scientific Study of Religion.[4] Roof affirms the spiritual character of the rising generation, both its churched and unchurched counterparts.

Many churches are capitalizing on today's openness to spiritual quest. "Tomorrow's vital church will help people find their place in the universe, making sense out of the confusions of life," says Tom Bandy, coauthor of *Spiritual Redwoods*. "Churches will be known for their sense of community as they resource people in their journeys of discovery."[5]

The challenge, as earlier chapters in this book have pointed out, is for churches to bring the good news of Jesus Christ to a generation that is arguably history's most illiterate in terms of biblical concepts and values. As theologian John Stackhouse says, "Most Americans and Canadians are ignorant of even the basics of authentic Christian faith. And second, most people think that they do understand Christianity and thus feel entitled to dismiss it out of hand."[6]

Southern Baptist leadership development consultant Reggie McNeal finds the most effective response in churches that have returned to spiritual formation as the primary work of the church's educational ministries. He says, "The wrong question to ask is 'How do we make better church members?' The tough question to ask instead is, 'How do we develop people who think and act like Christ and who have a vibrant, living relationship with him?'"[7]

Who will be setting the pace in that direction? Is it the parachurch ministries? seminaries and Bible colleges? Christian television or radio networks? Not according to Lyle Schaller. "The newest kid on the block is the self-identified teaching church," he says, referring to high-visibility, outreach-oriented congregations around the country. "This teaching church may turn out to be the most effective way to resource congregations in the twenty-first century."[8]

The movement by churches to identify their specific mission statement and vision for ministry has had many positive effects. While the process has been influenced and popularized by the business community, its overall effect has been to remind churches of the uniqueness of their spiritual mission. They are now positioned, as perhaps never before, to answer the cries of the soul being voiced by many who are turned off by perceptions of an "institutional" church, but who are open to a living, vital, life-changing relationship with Christ and with Christian community.

Make Prayer a Central Priority in Every Ministry

E. K. Bailey has a big dream: He wants to see the United States evangelized by the conclusion of the year 2000.

Bailey, pastor of Concord Missionary Baptist Church in Dallas, believes the task begins by praying for neighbors. After Bailey shared this vision with lay leaders at the church, more than 1,500 of the church's 2,100 attenders agreed to pray for their neighbors.

Attendance at the church's Wednesday night prayer meeting jumped from 200 to 500. The youth group holds regular "prayer walks" through the church's economically diverse neighborhood of South Oak Cliff. Of the five neighbors Bailey was praying for, three began attending his church. "It's started a whole prayer wave in our congregation," Bailey says.

Bailey's church is one of 185,000 participating in Celebrate Jesus 2000 (CJ2K), a movement "to pray for and to share Christ with every person in our nation by year-end 2000." The effort is directed by Mission America, with collaborators AD 2000 and Beyond and the Na-

---

American Christians Putting More Energy into Prayer

America has been prayed for as never before in history as an unprecedented partnership of dozens of denominations, hundreds of parachurch groups and prayer ministries, and thousands of churches joined to mobilize a million Christians to "Pray America Back To God." The initiative has been championed by Campus Crusade founders Bill and Vonette Bright and Christian Broadcasting Network (CBN) founder Pat Robertson in calling for forty days of prayer and fasting for revival and spiritual awakening concluding Palm Sunday each year.

The synchronized prayer uses a forty-day prayer calendar that each day outlines prayer need for a different segment of American society. Bill Bright has stated, "There has never been a greater need in all of history for Christians to fast, pray, repent, and seek the face of God."*

As one example, pastor Mike Bickle, who founded Metro Christian Fellowship of Kansas City, Missouri, stepped down as senior pastor to focus on building a twenty-four-hour citywide prayer ministry in Kansas City. The new ministry is called the International House of Prayer. Bickle's vision is for a twenty-four-hour house of prayer, in the spirit of the tabernacle of David, to be established in every city and prison in the world.

*Alice Smith, ed., PrayerNet Newsletter (Houston: U.S. Prayer Track), 1 February 1999.

---

tional Association of Evangelicals. More than sixty-five denominations and two hundred parachurch organizations support the movement.

CJ2K is mobilizing families to pray for twenty-one homes in their neighborhoods. Organizers estimate 3 million such families will be able to reach every person in the country.[9]

"Prayer evangelism is speaking to God about your neighbors before you speak to your neighbors about God," says Dave Thompson, vice president of ministries for Harvest Evangelism and director of the City Reacher Schools, which train families to become "lighthouses of prayer."

"The goal is to change the spiritual climate from nominal Christianity to authentic Christianity," says Mission America chair Paul Cedar. The situation is "akin to other historical spiritual awakenings," he said.[10]

This scenario is increasingly common, as churches are rediscovering the power of prayer and are recommitting themselves to it. As they bathe every concern and need in prayer, they are believing God for breakthrough results, the kind that can be attributed only to the miraculous intervention of heaven.

Jim Cymbala, pastor of the Brooklyn Tabernacle, tells the remarkable story of what can happen when a church truly builds its momentum around its times of corporate prayer. *Fresh Wind, Fresh Fire* and the sequel, *Fresh Faith,* show the transforming power of God's love—strong enough to convert prostitutes and drug addicts, strong enough to draw all races and social classes together in worship, and strong enough to rekindle dull hearts and flagging spirits. When this church earnestly sought God in prayer, God's Spirit invaded the hearts of his people and lit a fire that couldn't be quenched.[11]

Ben Patterson comments that "secularization, the process by which things like prayer are losing their practical social significance, is at the root of most of our difficulties with prayer."[12] But thankfully many churches are rediscovering today what can happen when prayer becomes a central priority in every ministry.

From prayer closet to pulpit to popular authors, the concept of prayer is receiving perhaps unprecedented attention. A typical testimonial comes from Peter Wagner, a leader in the field of church growth and spiritual warfare, with more than forty books to his credit. "The decade of the 1970s focused on the *technical* side of church growth," he says. "I organized courses and wrote books about such things as the vital signs of healthy churches." But by the 1980s he wanted to better integrate the science of church growth with the kind of passionate spirituality that includes powerful prayer. "During the 1980s, my focus shifted to the *spiritual* side of church growth, teaching courses and writing books about power evangelism, divine healing, demonic deliverance, . . . prayer, and spiritual warfare."[13]

We predict that the new focus on leadership has pointed the church in the right direction, the new approach to shepherding the flock has provided new glue to keep people in the church, and the new passion for prayer will open wide doors of ministry and outreach.

? APPLICATION QUESTIONS
FOR INDIVIDUAL RESPONSE OR GROUP DISCUSSION

1. What concept most encouraged you in this chapter? Why? Assuming the idea you named is a positive development, when and where could it be more effectively applied at the church you serve?

2. In the sidebar entitled, "How Much Business Skill Does a Pastor Need?" which quote seemed most troublesome to you? What can you do to help ensure that these patterns or perceptions don't occur in your church?

3. What is the hardest problem your church is facing right now? What can you do to prioritize a season of intense prayer around it?

Smith on Equipping Churches

In the 1960s, *pastor* meant someone who preached, taught the Bible, and cared for the "flock." The 1980s added the role of vision-caster and chief executive officer for leading the church to new influence in the world. Recently the pendulum has swung again so that the pastor must be the spiritual director of the church environment—sort of a cultural incarnation of spirituality and health.

Yet, with each change of expectations, previous roles are not really removed. The new ones are just added on with each new visit by a church consultant and each new blockbuster book on church leadership.

On top of that, experts are saying that social paradigms are changing and present structures are becoming obsolete. Greg Ogden has described this era as "pastoring between the paradigms."

What is the lasting identity of a pastor that goes beyond role *de jour?* The underlying role is that of equipper. Fortunately, today's "lay" empowerment movement is also a "clergy" empowerment movement—returning the role of the pastor to what God intended for that individual.

An equipping church knows how to surround its pastor with people who are gifted in areas where the pastor is not. In the equipping church, the lead pastor has a key role to create a *culture* of empowerment that encourages all people to discover and use their gifts.

Pastors in equipping churches say it was much harder than they ever imagined to change their culture, build the teams, and change their own and others' expectations. But those who make it also say the end result is much sweeter than they had ever dreamed.

Brad Smith
president, Leadership Network, Dallas, Texas
coauthor, *Starter Kit for Mobilizing Ministry* (Leadership Training Network, 1997)

PASTORS   4. Is prayer one of your church's highest priorities in ministry? What would your schedule look like if the church's prayer life was everything you would like it to be? What can you do in the coming week to shape the church's schedule in that direction?

Part 7

Churches Move toward New Stewardship Motives

Free People to Give from the Heart

People will not give money because of emotional appeal or fund-raising emphasis, so much as in direct proportion to the benefit they're receiving from it, the confidence they have in its use, and the training they have received in biblical stewardship.

fourteen

Free People to Give from the Heart

Trend #14: People will not give money because of emotional appeal or fund-raising emphasis, so much as in direct proportion to the benefit they're receiving from it, the confidence they have in its use, and the training they have received in biblical stewardship.

❧

Dear Pastor Cushman:

I started attending this church in March of 1996, during the darkest period of my life. I became part of a divorce recovery group in addition to attending services. God used Princeton Alliance Church to help me put my life back together.

Laypeople were the ones who helped me most directly, not members of the pastoral staff. I later learned that this was by design.

Six months later I attended Promise Keepers—a pivotal point for me. Shortly afterward I became involved in both a care circle and a PK group study. I came to appreciate the way we do church. I believe it's the way a church should be. I became a member.

A Church That Sends Its People to Rebuild the Community

Windsor Village United Methodist Church

Denomination: United Methodist

Location: Houston, Texas

Senior pastor: Kirbyjon Caldwell (since 1982)

Recent goal: Offer numerous, relevant, and creative options to worship God, serve the community, and learn about the Christian faith.

Church vision: To represent God's kingdom on earth as it is in heaven by serving as a scripturally fruitful and obedient church of Jesus Christ for persons and institutions throughout the Greater Houston community.

Year founded: 1958 as Southmont UMC; became Windsor Village in 1968

Attendance: 6200 (now)
5200 (5 years ago)
2900 (10 years ago)

Internet address: www.kingdombuilder.com/index.htm

Houston's Fiesta supermarket food chain owned a rat-infested, empty K-Mart property in a transitional neighborhood on the southwest part of town. Hearing that Windsor Village United Methodist Church had grown over the last decade from twenty-five people to become a significant community center of influence, they offered to lease some of the acreage to the congregation.

That was 1994, during Kirbyjon Caldwell's twelfth year as pastor. Instead, the MBA-educated, former Wall Street bond-trader-turned-gospel-minister proposed that Fiesta give the entire property to the church, take a $4.4 million tax write-off, and receive a lot of positive community publicity. That's exactly what happened.

Today the Power Center—its new name—houses more than one hundred community outreach ministries, including a medical clinic to offer quality medical care for families in need, a 450-child school (pre-K to eighth grade), a pharmacy, a local business technology center, twenty-seven executive suites, a bank branch, a huge banquet facility, and an eyecare center. "Churches being led by God to minister among African-American people in the twenty-first century must embrace solid theology, identify problems, and deliver solutions, which is to say, spiritually, economically, and holistically," says Caldwell.

The Power Center, according to *Urban Churches, Vital Signs,* "models black economic enterprise, stimulates entrepreneurial vision, and promotes community confidence."*

Pastor Caldwell continually trains the church in a biblical view of stewardship, from tithing to the church to investing in the local community. As a result, the church has also inspired a 237-acre master-planned community including 454 affordable homes, a twenty-four-hour shelter for abused children and AIDS ministry, and a multi-million dollar prayer center for deploying a powerful team of intercessory prayer warriors.

Windsor Village Church draws people from all socioeconomic levels. Over 70 percent of the members come from within twenty minutes of the church facility. The neighborhood is clearly a better place today because of the presence of the church.

"Jesus met needs; he met people where they are," says Caldwell. "The days are long gone when the church can be high on creeds and low on deeds and expect the pews to be filled."

*Niles Harper, *Urban Churches, Vital Signs* (Grand Rapids: Eerdmans, 1999), 228.

In late 1996 I met Sue, who would later become my wife. We married a year later with you officiating and several friends from Princeton Alliance Church participating in the ceremony and reception.

God had given me a fresh start.

During this time God had been speaking to me about stewardship. He has materially blessed me and one appropriate response was to be a better steward of what he has given to me.

Shortly after our marriage I followed Sue's example by dramatically increasing my financial offering to the church. Sounds easy, but for me it was a step of faith.

I give because I want to see more lives put back together and changed for eternity like mine was.[1]

This letter, written to the pastor of the church where Warren Bird is on staff, underscores the future of Christian stewardship—a future that is already present in many places. Christians no longer tithe automatically, and when they do, their motive is usually not one of duty or denominational loyalty. Rather, they give as an investment, both in themselves and in others. And they want to see the results of their giving.

Tithe = 2.6%?

In fat and prosperous America, "giving has been declining as a portion of income for almost thirty years" and "dramatic change" will be necessary if believers are to live out God's mandates and promises. These are the conclusions of John and Sylvia Ronsvalle, who head Empty Tomb, Inc. (www.emptytomb.org), a Christian service and research organization based in Champaign, Illinois.

The study finds that members gave only 2.58 percent of their income in 1996. This is a 17 percent decrease from the 3.12 percent average in 1968, generally considered to be harder times. *The State of Church Giving through 1996* was released in 1999 and uses the most recent data available, which is data from 1996. It includes data from twenty-nine Protestant denominations, representing more than 100,000 congregations, that published statistics in the Yearbook of American and Canadian Churches.

From John and Sylvia Ronsvalle, *Behind the Stained Glass Windows: Money Dynamics in the Church* (Grand Rapids: Baker, 1996), 36.

American Philanthropy: People Give to Church

Philanthropy is as American as apple pie. Americans donated $175 billion to nonprofit organizations in 1998, reports the *AARFC Trust for Philanthropy/ Giving USA 1999.* The 11 percent increase in giving significantly outpaced inflation. This is the third year in a row that charitable giving is up, according to their report entitled Giving USA 1999.

The lion's share of contributions, 77 percent, came from individuals, many of whom are spreading the good fortune they've enjoyed because of a strong national economy. The rest comes from foundations (17 billion), bequests (14 billion), and corporations (9 billion).

On the receiving end, 44 percent of the total giving went to religious organizations. The second most popular recipient area was education, followed by health, foundations, and human services.

"Simply put," comments George Barna, "More people give to religious organizations than to any other kind; more gifts are given to religious organizations; and the greatest amount of money is given to faith entities."

From George Barna, *How to Increase Giving in Your Church* (Ventura, Calif.: Regal, 1997), 59–70.

Church must more meaningfully engage this emerging mindset. Understanding where people are allows you to do a better job of leading them to where God is calling them to be. As you take the steps highlighted in this chapter, you free people to give generously from their hearts.

Debunk Common Myths about Giving

Churches are one of the most popular recipients of charitable donations. Donations of almost $200 billion a year can do a lot of good if wisely used.

However, according to a Christian Stewardship Association survey, financial giving by Christians in America has experienced a twenty-six-year decline with "only one or two out of ten Christians" giving 10 percent of their income to the Lord's work.[2] Researcher George Barna found that less than 5 percent of the U.S. churchgoing population tithes in this way.[3]

Further, the average annual amount of money donated to churches, per person, is declining. Giving to religious causes, in general, is declining, and overall giving to churches is also declining. Finally, fewer people give habitually; instead more and more donors carefully evaluate every gift they give.[4]

This less-than-rosy news raises the question of why people give. Barna finds that only one out of six or seven churchgoing adults has a healthy, biblical view of stewardship. Americans appear to be either hardened to, or ignorant of, the fundamental precepts of being "God's trustee" of their time, talents, and treasures. "Perhaps the most startling outcome of the research about people's motivations for church giving," says Barna, "is how few of them give money to their church because they feel a spiritual compulsion to return to God what he has entrusted to them."[5]

It is important to remember that most people have never fully or critically thought through their charitable giving in terms of what motivates them at the deepest level. No single reason adequately describes what moves the typical follower of Christ to give away money. In fact, the reasons may change with each project or need. For example, someone may have one reason for helping sponsor the youth trip to Chicago's rescue missions and another motivation for an increased pledge to the building fund.

Overall, says Barna, six primary motivations compel a person to give money to a church. "Although most churches need not trigger all six motivations to inspire a person to donate to the church, the more of these reasons the church can stimulate, the better are its chances of . . . having that person develop into a long-term supporter."[6] The following are the motives Barna identifies:[7]

1. *Shared Cause*. Nine out of ten people give when they are convinced the church believes in and stands for the same thing as the donor. This concept is often problematic for churches; few churched adults think of the church they attend as representing a specific, compelling cause. A general concept, such as "the cause of Christ," is generally not focused and passionate enough to motivate most people to give financially.

> ### Top Reasons Why People Give to Nonprofit Organizations
>
> 1. They have a great reputation for being reliable and trustworthy.
> 2. You feel good about yourself when you know that you have helped others.
> 3. The organization is involved in a type of work that is of great interest to you.
> 4. You have seen or studied the work of the organization firsthand and know they're trustworthy.
> 5. The organization is highly recommended by people you know personally and trust.
> 6. The organization has helped you, or people important to you, in the past.
> 7. The organization serves people in a geographic area that is of interest to you.
>
> From George Barna, *How to Increase Giving in Your Church* (Ventura, Calif.: Regal, 1997), 172.

2. *Ministry Efficiency*. Eight out of ten people said they will give only if they are persuaded the church uses people's money carefully and wisely. Church donors need continual evidence that they are giving money to a financially efficient ministry. Barna specifically studied those who regularly attend a church but do not give anything financially to it. He learned that, unless they encounter convincing evidence to the contrary, they assume that any donor-funded organization—even their church—is of average or below-average efficiency.

3. *Ministry Influence*. Many donors, especially older ones, are searching for a channel of influence. People no longer give to the church simply because it is a church. Today four out of five church support-

ers actively search for evidence that their money has made a difference in people's lives. The church must prove it is worthy of someone's financial gifts through the mark it leaves on the world.

4. *Urgent Need.* Six out of ten church donors admit they are more likely to give when they become aware of an urgent need. In many places, so-called church fund-raising has become the art of honestly and convincingly describing the many, ongoing needs of the church in terms of the urgency of those needs.

5. *Personal Benefit.* Many people give to a church because they have received identifiable benefits from the church, or because they hope the church will provide certain benefits to them and their loved ones in the future.

6. *Relationship with the Ministry.* People generally understand that their financial assistance is integral to the health and vitality of the church. Six out of ten adults said they gave to their church out of a feeling of responsibility or moral obligation to the Christian community to which they belong and to the ministries in which they participate.

> **Janitor Leaves $1.1 Million to Bible College and Church**
>
> Christian Thomsen worked as a janitor for Northwestern Bell Telephone before retiring in his eighties. When he died November 5, 1998, at age 101, he left $1.1 million to Faith Baptist Bible College, Ankeny, Iowa, and a substantial amount to his home church, Campus Baptist.
>
> "We're reaping the benefits of a man who dedicated his life to the Lord for 101 years," said Craig Hastings, executor of the will. According to Hastings, Thomsen was "faithful to the Lord and on top of that he was a millionaire. We just couldn't believe it." Thomsen never attended the Bible college, but was a faithful member of Campus Baptist, one of several churches that support it.
>
> See http://www.ReligionToday.com, 4 January 1999.

Teach People to Respond to Biblical Concepts of Stewardship

"When all is said and done," suggests veteran church consultant Lyle Schaller, "there are only two good reasons why anyone should be asked to contribute money to the church. The first is to help promote the giver's spiritual growth . . . . The second reason is even simpler. Christian discipleship is Christian stewardship . . . . How else do God's people grow in grace?"[8]

Stewardship, according to Doug Carter, "is not humanity's way of raising money, but rather God's way of raising people into the likeness of His Son."[9] Fred Wood made a similar comment: "The most important aspect of tithing and stewardship is not the raising of money for the church, but the development of devoted Christians."[10] Regrettably, not much intentional training on stewardship is happening in churches today. In a study of denominational funding, church finance author J. David Schmidt was asked what surprised him most about his research discoveries. He replied, "The biggest surprise was how little stewardship education is really going on in denominations today."[11] Instead, church members have changed from stewards into consumers. They demand a higher level of comfort and services from their congregations than did previous generations. The commonly perceived definition of stewardship is one of "meeting the financial budget."[12]

Training can and does make a difference. Princeton sociologist Robert Wuthnow, author of *The Crisis in the Churches: Spiritual Malaise, Fiscal Woe,* studied church members who attend services at least once a week. He found that giving was substantially higher among those who had heard a sermon about stewardship within the past year than among those who had not heard a sermon on this topic. Further, he underscored the importance of church-wide stewardship: Of every one thousand dollars received by churches, nine hundred comes from people who work in middle-class occupations.[13]

> *Stewardship is successfully managing your time, talents, and treasures for the glory of God.*

Stan Toler and Elmer Towns, who wrote *Developing a Giving Church* to deal with this larger stewardship issue, use the following definition: Stewardship is successfully managing your time, talents, and treasures for the glory of God.[14]

Using Jesus' parable of the laborers and the vineyard (Matt. 20:1–16), they describe the heart attitudes that shape an environment of stewardship:[15]

1. *We were useless until we were found in the marketplace.* The workers had nothing to do until the owner issued them a call.
2. *The field belongs to the owner (God) and not to us.* The place where we work, whether in the church, in secular employment, or in any other place of ministry, is God's field.
3. *The fruit (results) we harvest belongs to the owner (God) and not to us.* When we work for Jesus Christ, we must remember the fruit belongs to Jesus Christ.
4. *We are among many that serve the owner (God).* The field is not exclusively ours; many are working with us in it.
5. *The owner judges us by our faithfulness; we demonstrate our productivity by our faithfulness.* If we do the best that can be done with the tools we have, within the time allotted, the owner is satisfied with that effort.

Teachings that Result in a Giving Church

1. *God deserves my best.* "Honor the LORD with your wealth, with the firstfruits of all your crops" (Prov. 3:9).
2. *God will get my best every week.* "On the first day of every week, each one of you should set aside a sum of money" (1 Cor. 16:2).
3. *God will get a minimum of 10 percent as each person gives* "in keeping with his income" (1 Cor. 16:2).
4. *God will be glorified through my gifts,* "always giving thanks to God the Father for everything, in the name of our Lord Jesus Christ" (Eph. 5:20).
5. *God will be praised through my gifts.* "Each man should give what he has decided in his heart to give, not reluctantly or under compulsion, for God loves a cheerful giver" (2 Cor. 9:7).

From Stan Toler and Elmer Towns, *Developing a Giving Church* (Kansas City: Beacon Hill, 1999), 43–44.

6. *The worst thing we can do is to be nonproductive.* God doesn't want his people to be idle while there is much to do in the field.
7. *The owner (God) has total control over the field, the fruit, and the time of harvest.* It is our responsibility to yield to him, and he will guide us and direct us.
8. *The owner's plans (God's plans) for us are "generous" (v. 15) and good.* Our lack of faith in God's goodness causes us to mistrust his purpose. Part of his purpose is for us to prosper.

A church develops a giving environment by recognizing that God is the ultimate source of all things. The resulting stewardship of his resources becomes an act of worship for the true follower of Christ.

As evangelist Billy Graham said, "If a person gets his attitude toward money straight, it will help straighten out almost every other area in his life."[16]

Don't Limit Your Congregation's Stewardship Options

The idea of stewardship addresses *why* Christians should contribute to advancing God's work. Only then are you ready to prayerfully assess *how* to ask your members to support the ministry and outreach of their church.

Lyle Schaller, whom *Leadership* journal has called "America's foremost authority on the dynamics of church life," suggests that most congregations would benefit from having more choices in their financial stewardship. In doing so, he challenges what sometimes prove to be faulty operational assumptions on which the financial program at a church is based. The principles Schaller notes deserve consideration:

1. *How many special offerings should be taken?* "In general, the more limits the governing board places on what [the church] will ask of its members, the larger the proportion of total member giving that will

be directed to *other* charitable causes."[17] In fact, during a typical year, churches and other religious organizations receive almost half the total gifts to nonprofit organizations.[18]

2. *Is our congregation a "fixed-sum society" in which raising money for one cause guarantees that some other committee or need will be shortchanged?* "The evidence indicates people respond to perceived needs, not to what they have been accustomed to giving," says Schaller.[19]

3. *Should we hang on to the idea of a unified budget (one budget that includes all causes and needs, including missions and building programs)?* Historically, this practice was widely applied in the 1930s and 1940s, but over time churches tended to experience several downsides. As a result "people began to question the wisdom of the concept."[20]

4. *How many sources of income are available?* Some people identify only two: special offerings and regular contributions. That generalization was true for many congregations in 1955, but it is obsolete in most churches today. Other potentially significant financial boosts include bequests, non-member gifts, income from investments, income from money-raising projects, and rental or user fees (weddings, weekday nursery or day schools, counseling services, etc.). To neglect these oversimplifies the financial picture and neglects to look for ways to expand the church's financial base.[21]

5. *Is a deficit always to be avoided?* Some numerically declining congregations pay all their bills on time and never run a deficit. Other "vigorous, vital, dynamic, enthusiastic, numerically growing, and apparently healthy congregations . . . respond readily and often eagerly to new challenges in ministry, even when the money does not appear to be readily available to finance those new ventures. . . . and encounter two to five financial crises year after year." Schaller suggests the latter is often preferable.[22]

6. *Will everyone give the same amount?* Do you think everyone should and will contribute about the same? Or do you believe that in a typical healthy congregation one-third of the members will contribute approximately two-thirds of all contributions?[23]

7. *Will contributions depend on members' income?* Sometimes a well-intentioned person examines the median family income for your area and projects what a church's stewardship level could be and should be. This tactic, according to Schaller, assumes that all charitable contributions go to the church. "That often is not true. The higher the income level, the more likely that person or household will distribute their charitable giving to a variety of causes." Also, an even more misleading assumption is the idea that people contribute to charitable

Heresies of Fund Raising

1. *Don't lower God to your own standards.* Claiming that God's blessing will come to those who give to your cause is presumptuous and it lowers God to a supporting role in achieving your objectives.
2. *Don't use a prosperity gospel motive.* People should give as an act of devotion to God, not because they expect to profit from their largess.
3. *Don't claim a false crisis.* Don't talk about a financial emergency unless one truly exists.
4. *Don't play a "shell game" with the money.* Funds raised to support a specific ministry should be used for that purpose, no matter how pressing other expenses may be.

5. *Don't neglect proper business practices.* Accounting sleight-of-hand which may be legal but of questionable ethics has no place in church.
6. *Don't raise funds to cover inefficient management.* Contributions should not be used to subsidize poor management practices.
7. *Don't substitute slogans or traditions for Scripture.* Every campaign must be willing to submit to scriptural scrutiny.

From Norman Shawchuck, Philip Kotler, Bruce Wreen, and Gustave Rath, *Marketing for Congregations: Choosing to Serve People More Effectively* (Nashville: Abingdon Press, 1992), 350–51.

causes out of their current income. "That was true for the overwhelming majority of Americans in 1950," says Schaller. But today "it is not at all unusual for over one-half of the money received in a congregation's special building fund campaign today to come out of the savings of accumulated wealth of their members."[24]

8. *What will happen as people understand the idea of stewardship?* "A good stewardship education program not only will motivate people to increase their level of giving, it also will teach them the responsibility of being good stewards of what God has given them and then need to be discriminating in where they direct their increased level of giving," declares Schaller.[25] However, not all congregations earn the right to be perceived as good stewards of the church's gifts. Inadequate communication and low levels of trust sometimes result in people contributing only a modest proportion of their total charitable contributions to the congregation of which they are members.

Explore the Benefits of Financial Freedom for Your Congregation

As of 1998, Americans are collectively $1.3 trillion in debt. In 1997 1.35 million Americans filed for bankruptcy.[26] Like consumers, churches and Christian ministries often get themselves into financial trouble.

They go into debt for new buildings, unbudgeted programs, or even to meet operating expenses. Then weeks, months, or years later they wake up to the harsh reality of long-term payments. They realize only too late that their effectiveness and ability to meet needs are jeopardized by the burden of debt they must shoulder.

Two recent books offer significant help toward climbing out of the debt trap. Ray Bowman and Eddy Hall underscore the consequences of church debt in *When Not to Borrow: Unconventional Financial Wisdom to Set Your Church Free.*[27]

1. *By presuming on the future, borrowing puts the church at unnecessary risk.* "Most borrowing is based on presumptuous financial predictions . . . that a new building would lead to higher attendance and more giving," says Bowman.
2. *Borrowing tends to undermine contentment.* "The main reason people borrow is because they are not content to live within their income."
3. *Borrowing can deprive us of God's timing.* "If God has directed us to pursue a particular ministry or project, we can confidently ask Him to supply the resources to make it possible."

Warning Signals: When Loyalty Shifts from God to Possessions
1. When you go from managing your money to being anxious about it.
2. When envy and jealousy creep into your life.
3. When you lose appreciation for what God has already given you.
4. When you lose the joy of cheerful giving.
5. When you seek things more than God.
6. When you think that things will make you happy.
7. When enough is not enough.
From John Maxwell, *Leadership Wired*, December 1998 (www.injoy.com).

4. *Borrowing can blind us to people's needs.* "When the church as a whole is committed to living within God's provision, emergencies that threaten to create involuntary indebtedness for church members are seen for what they are—opportunities for the church to demonstrate caring and to protect fellow members' financial freedom through generous sharing."

Bowman does recognize situations when borrowing is advisable. He lists three: (1) when renting would cost more, (2) to buy income-generating property that provides space for future growth, and (3) during transition from a debt economy to a provision economy.[28]

Jeff Berg and Jim Burgess wrote *The Debt-Free Church: Experiencing Financial Freedom while Growing Your Ministry* to help ensure long-term financial health in churches. They identify fifteen scriptural, practical, and creative strategies to employ when trying to move a ministry away from dependence on borrowing:

1. *Prayer and fasting.* Prayer is the church's most powerful resource.
2. *Commitment from church leadership.* Are each of them trying to reduce personal indebtedness?
3. *Scriptural giving.* Are God's people being taught about joyful, sacrificial, regular giving?

How Debt Affects Freedom to Minister	
Level of Debt	*Effects on Freedom to Minister*
Modest Debt (does not hinder existing ministries)	Tendency to overlook possibilities to expand existing ministries.
	Tendency to overlook possibilities for creating new ministries.
	May overlook financial needs of people in the church and community.
Substantial Debt (makes it a struggle to maintain effectiveness of existing ministries)	Some existing ministries operate on less than optimum funding.
	Seriously limits funds available for intentional local outreach.
	Limits funds available for meeting financial needs within the church body.
	Makes it almost impossible to launch new ministries.
Heavy Debt (debt becomes church's focus, dominating the budget and the time and energy of church leaders)	Cannot hire needed pastoral or support staff.
	Ministry programs handicapped by underfunding.
	Facility maintenance eventually neglected, unloved appearance of building an embarrassment and a barrier to outreach.
	May cut support staff.
	May lay off pastoral staff in desperate situations.
	Worst case: Foreclosure, bankruptcy, or dissolution of church.

From Ray Bowman and Eddy Hall, *When Not to Borrow: Unconventional Financial Wisdom to Set Your Church Free* (Grand Rapids: Baker, 1996), 29.

4. *A written plan.* Without a written plan, you may never reach your goals.
5. *Loan prepayment.* The sooner you pay off an existing loan, the more resources can be freed up for true ministry.
6. *No additional borrowing.* Simply put: If you don't borrow any more money, you won't get any deeper in debt.
7. *Involvement of everyone.* Is the church seeking to involve as many of its people as possible in its debt-elimination plans?
8. *"Smallest First" loan repayment strategy.* Concentrate surplus resources on paying off the smallest loan balance first. When it is paid off, tackle the next smallest.
9. *Spending cuts.* When you reduce spending, you can apply more money to paying off loans.
10. *Sale of assets.* You may have unneeded resources that could be liquidated, such as real estate or excess supplies.
11. *Cooperation with other ministries.* Are there ways you can share facilities, thus reducing costs for both parties?
12. *Fund-raising events.* This is suggested only for churches that feel the freedom to do so, such as asking the youth group to help raise the costs for their summer missions trip.
13. *Innovative giving opportunities.* Creatively think outside the box of standard ministry practices.
14. *Open communication.* Effective, open, clear communication of ministry needs and strategies is vital to the success of a debt-free initiative.
15. *Teaching, training, and counseling.* The church needs to be at the forefront of training people to manage the resources God has entrusted to them.[29]

Berg and Burgess summarize by affirming, "God has decreed few specific ministry methods; and the same old, tired methods of the past can be increasingly ineffective as we approach the new millennium."[30]

In this chapter, we've attempted to remove some of the "stew" from "stewardship" to use a John Maxwell expression. We have emphasized some core values: churches are raising money for life transformation, rather than organizational survival; people give to people and causes, not to institutions or programs; repeat donors must be both inspired and persuaded; there is no substitute for absolute integrity; a visionless church is an impoverished church; and people give to winners in response to shared stories. Underneath each of these concepts is a larger spiritual issue. "The financial crisis we are approaching is

---

America's Leading Religious Charities

The Salvation Army raised $1.2 billion in private donations during 1998, the most of any charity for the seventh straight year said the *Chronicle of Philanthropy*.* "We are grateful for the public's generosity," Army spokesperson Theresa Whitfield said, noting that needs are increasing because many people are moving off welfare and into low-paying jobs.

Other nonprofits among the top one hundred recipients include Catholic Children's Fund, World Vision, Campus Crusade for Christ, Habitat for Humanity, Feed the Children, Lutheran Services in America, Trinity Broadcasting Network, Christian Children's Fund, Christian Broadcasting Network, Catholic Relief Services, Focus on the Family, MAP International, Wycliffe Bible Translators, Young Life, Billy Graham Evangelistic Association, and Covenant House.

*See News Summary, 2 November, 1999, religiontoday.com.

---

part of a larger spiritual problem we have in America's churches," says church consultant Loren B. Mead.[31]

Indeed, fund-raising is a means to an end. Focusing on the end facilitates the means. As the church enters a new millennium, you can equip your church to let love, compassion, and servanthood—not dollar goals—be your motivations. As a result, God may enable you to dream bigger, pray bigger, ask bigger, and minister bigger—"immeasurably more than all we ask or imagine, according to his power that is at work within us" (Eph. 3:20)—for Jesus' sake.

? APPLICATION QUESTIONS
FOR INDIVIDUAL RESPONSE OR GROUP DISCUSSION

1. Review George Barna's list of six reasons why people give money to their churches. Which of the six are the most important motivators for you? Why?
2. How have you been trained in concepts of biblical stewardship? Which contexts were most effective? What can you do to help train other "stewards" at your church?
3. Lyle Schaller warns, "Be careful not to limit your congregation's stewardship options." Why is that important, according to Schaller? Which of his concepts most applies to your church? Where and when can that concept be useful to your church?

PASTORS   4. When was the last time you led a discussion about being debt-free? Try conducting a "dream" session with your

Maxwell on Biblical Stewardship

I founded Injoy Stewardship Services to partner with growing churches by providing them with the most innovative, effective program for capital funding. The key to the ISS strategy is a unique, biblically-based strategy of mobilization without manipulation and a customized approach to each of its partner's needs, whether to raise money for building and relocation projects or retire debt.

The stewardship perspectives in this chapter are consistent with our findings and experiences. I especially agree with the statement that "not much intentional training on stewardship is happening in churches today."

That doesn't have to be the case! Amazing things happen when leaders direct stewardship training toward people's hearts. My book, *The 21 Indispensable Qualities of a Leader: Becoming the Person Others Will Want to Follow,* points out that money is only a means to an end. Generosity starts in the heart. As I teach in what I call the Law of Connection: "Touch a heart before you ask for a hand."

John C. Maxwell
founder, The Injoy Group, Atlanta, Georgia
author, *Failing Forward: Turning Mistakes into Stepping Stones for Success* (Nelson, 2000)

elders, board, or finance team. List the benefits of being debt-free and suggest what steps would be necessary to get there. Then talk about what God would need to do for that to happen.

Conclusion

You have now read through excerpts from nearly one hundred different books, almost all of them written by Christians who have invested considerable research and prayer into discerning the way of the future. Each hopes to provide a partial picture of what the future church will look like and advice on what your church could do today to prepare for that future. Our goal has been to give you the tools your church needs to help this next decade—and century—bear as much fruit as possible.

Some writers we've cited might be right in their assessment; others might be wrong. Prayerfully note what you consider to be the best suggestions made in this book. Glean those ideas that will make your church stronger and more effective in carrying out the Great Commandment and Great Commission.

After prayer, the skills most needed for effective twenty-first-century ministry are those of adaptation and life-long learning. The social structures and values that impact your church are shifting at an ever-accelerating rate, much like the channel of a rapidly changing river. If "change is the one constant on which the leaders of tomorrow's church can rely," then "the key is to train yourself for change itself," says Robert Dale.[1]

Not every idea in this book will work at every place. The church is Christ's body, and like a human body the body of Christ must adjust to the climate and culture that surrounds it.

No human authority has all the answers you need. We are simply God's servants believing, as Henry Blackaby has so wonderfully stated, that God invites us to become involved with him in his good work. "You come to know God by experience as you obey him and he accomplishes his work through you: the incarnation of God through you to bless the world."[2]

Evangelist John Wesley said it a different way: "What we need is a desire to know the whole will of God, with a fixed resolution to do it."[3]

Summary of Trends Your Church Is Facing		
Chapter Topic	Yesterday's Trend	Tomorrow's Trend
1. Overall focus	church growth	church health
2. Social impact	cautious role	increased role
3. Effective communication	primarily verbal	multi-sensory
4. Attention grabbers	start with truth claims	start with relevance claims
5. Program strategy	one size fits all	targeted needs and interests
6. Evangelistic strategy	measurable outreach goals	more use of prayer evangelism
7. Spiritual discussions	basic general knowledge	total Biblical illiteracy
8. Apologetic discussions	logic directed	relationally directed
9. Worship styles	easier to stereotype	acceptance of diversity
10. Worship planning	focus on the sermon	integration of entire service
11. Priesthood of believers	lip service to lay ministry	best lay empowerment yet
12. Church size	bigger is better	grow big by doing small well
13. "Business" side of church	corporate model	spiritual distinctiveness
14. Motives for giving	duty, habit, and loyalty	deeper grasp of stewardship

According to evangelist Billy Graham, the specter of third millennium population growth merely points us to a bigger challenge. "Decay in the societies of the world, consternation in the governments, and a deep heart-cry for revival throughout the church of our Lord Jesus Christ all point to the need of the world for our Savior," says the famed evangelist.[4]

World evangelization must be "fresh in every generation," according to John Corts, president and chief operating officer of the Billy Graham Evangelistic Association. The gospel doesn't change but "the methods and delivery systems will be different," Corts says. "We can neither count on past victories or look ahead to anticipate how evangelism will be done in the future," he continues. "But there is an urgency for us to meet and encourage one another in a task that seems more daunting every day."[5]

Because God is greater than anything we've ever imagined, the greatest work for God is yet to be done by the one who allows God to work through him or her. Remember the old slogan, "The world has yet to see what can be accomplished by one person completely dedicated to God."

We conclude by leaving the arena of trends and predictions to offer you a handful of current facts. Each reminds us of the huge task ahead, and each urges us to make the best possible use of every moment, every opportunity, and every resource for the glory of God through the church. (See the apostle Paul's affirmation of this in Ephesians 5:16.) Consider the following:

Untrained Christians—Nine out of ten pastors call their churches "evangelistic." However, less than one out of three church attenders has shared his or her faith in Christ with a non-Christian within the past twelve months.[6] *What is the church you serve doing about it?*

Warehoused Christians—Despite the efforts of church leaders to integrate spiritual efforts into people's daily experience, involvement in ministry remains the exception to the rule among Protestants. According to pastors, only about four out of every ten adults who attend the church's services are actively involved in the church's ministry efforts. Just one out of every three churches claim that at least half of the congregation participates in active ministry.[7] *What is the church you serve doing about it?*

Undercultured Christians—Chicago has more Polish-Americans than San Francisco has people. Los Angeles is now the second-largest Iranian city in the world. One-third of the world's Jewish people live in North America. There are more Buddhists in the U.S. than Episcopalians. Muslims now outnumber Presbyterians. In California's school system, 239 languages are spoken; in New York, 184; in Washington, 181; in Texas, 169.[8] Yet the vast majority of churches still offer worship and training in only one language to a congregation that is far less multicultural than its surrounding community. *What is the church you serve doing about it?*

Undercompassionate Christians—Of a world population just crossing the 6 billion mark, approximately 1.8 billion could be considered the urban poor, 1.1 billion more live in slums, and a total of 1.4 billion are illiterate.[9] The urban poor and slum dwellers comprise 48 percent of the world's population, up from 24.6 percent in 1970.[10] *What is the church you serve doing about it?*

Underchallenged Christians—Islam is growing more quickly than Christianity. The world's second largest religion expanded from 15 percent of the world's 1970 population to almost 20 percent today. Since 1970, Hinduism grew from 13 to 14 percent of the world's population. Meanwhile growth in Christendom (Catholic, Protestant, Orthodox) is only keeping pace with world population growth.[11] As late as 1960 more than half of all professing Christians still lived in North America and Europe. By

Wrong Predictions

The common thread in the following somewhat humorous list of assessments is that each was remarkably wrong!

"Louis Pasteur's theory of germs is ridiculous fiction."

—Pierre Pachet, Professor of Physiology at Toulouse, in 1872

"Everything that can be invented has been invented."

—Charles H. Duell, Commissioner, U.S. Office of Patents, in 1899

"The wireless music box has no imaginable commercial value. Who would pay for a message sent to nobody in particular?"

—David Sarnoff's associates in response to his urgings for investment in radio in the 1920s

"I'm just glad it'll be Clark Gable who's falling on his face and not Gary Cooper."

—Gary Cooper on his decision not to take the leading role in *Gone With the Wind*

"I think there is a world market for maybe five computers."

—Thomas Watson, chairman of IBM, in 1943

"Computers in the future may weigh no more than 1.5 tons."

—*Popular Mechanics*, forecasting the relentless march of science, in 1949

"There is no reason anyone would want a computer in their home."

—Ken Olson, president, chairman and founder of Digital Equipment Corp., in 1977

"So we went to Atari and said, 'Hey, we've got this amazing thing, even built with some of your parts, and what do you think about funding us? Or we'll give it to you. We just want to do it. Pay our salary, we'll come work for you.' And they said, 'No.' So

then we went to Hewlett-Packard, and they said, 'Hey, we don't need you. You haven't got through college yet.'"

—Apple Computer Inc. founder Steve Jobs on attempts to get Atari and HP interested in his and Steve Wozniak's personal computer

"640K ought to be enough for anybody."

—Bill Gates, in 1981

"We don't like their sound, and guitar music is on the way out.'

—Decca Recording Co. rejecting the Beatles, in 1962

"The concept is interesting and well-formed, but in order to earn better than a 'C,' the idea must be feasible."

—a Yale University management professor in response to Fred Smith's paper proposing reliable overnight delivery service. (Smith went on to found FedEx Corporation.)

"A cookie store is a bad idea. Besides, the market research reports say America likes crispy cookies, not soft and chewy cookies like you make."

—response to Debbi Fields's idea of starting Mrs. Fields' Cookies

"If I had thought about it, I wouldn't have done the experiment. The literature was full of examples that said you can't do this."

—Spencer Silver on the work that led to the unique adhesives for 3M "Post-It" notepads

We hope the fourteen trends identified in this book fare a bit better!

Many of these quotes can be found in Howard G. Hendricks, *Color Outside the Lines: A Revolutionary Approach to Creative Leadership* (Nashville: Word, 1998).

1990, only 38 percent of all Christians lived in Western nations, and by 2000, the figure is probably down to 31 percent.[12] *What is the church you serve doing about it?*

Underappreciative Christians—Less than 1 percent of the world's Jewish population believes Jesus is the Messiah, according to the U.S. Center for World Missions. More than 10 million Jews live outside Israel, mostly in nations where Christianity is the dominant faith. Seventeen nations have a Jewish population of over 50,000. About 14,785,000 total people in eighty-one countries consider themselves to be Jewish. About 75 percent of those do not follow the Torah or attend synagogue and many are atheists.[13] *What is the church you serve doing about it?*

Underinformed Christians—Each day, over 200 million people in dozens of countries risk being beaten, raped, imprisoned, or even killed simply because they dare to follow Christ. There were close to 100 million martyrs during the so-called "modern" twentieth century.[14] More Christians were martyred in the past century than in the nineteen prior centuries *combined*.[15] Some 160,000 Christians are martyred for their faith each year, many killed in cruel, painful, gruesome ways. That's seventeen Christians being murdered every hour![16] Others are sold into slavery, denied education or employment, and rejected from their families because of their refusal to deny Christ.[17] *What is the church you serve doing about it?*

Underinvolved Christians—The USA has more than 1.6 million people incarcerated and another 4 million under parole, probation, home confinement and other forms of correctional supervision. In spite of all the efforts made to create an environment of rehabilitation, 74 percent of those released from prison are arrested again within four years of their release. The annual economic impact of our correctional system is more than $18 billion.[18]

> **Third World Missionaries Will Soon Outnumber Anglos**
>
> More than 75 percent of the earth's evangelical Christians live in developing nations. As a result, by the year 2000 there will be more missionaries from the Third World than from Anglo-Saxon backgrounds, according to international speaker Federick Bertuzzi, a member of PM International, a missions project to the Muslim world.
>
> In 1975 Anglo-Saxon missionaries outnumbered others 100,000 to 85,000, Bertuzzi said. By the year 2000 there will be 120,000 Anglo-Saxon missionaries and 150,000 missionaries from other backgrounds.
>
> The United States continues to field the largest single-country missionary force with 50,000.
>
> From Rev. Jesus M. Huertes, "Religious News," *Alliance Life*, 27 January 1999, 7.

Christendom's Two Billion in 2000

More than 2 billion people worldwide—about one-third of the world's population—claim allegiance to Christianity in the year 2000, according to researchers David Barrett and Todd Johnson. This includes Roman Catholics with more than 1 billion members, followed by 845 million Protestants (mainline, 321 million; Anglican groups, 75 million; and charismatics and Pentecostals, including independents and others who belong to denominations, about 449 million), followed by the world's Orthodox churches claiming 222 million believers.

Islam is the second largest religion with 1.19 billion adherents, followed by Hindu (774 million), non-religious (768 million), Buddhists (359 million), tribal religions (252 million), atheists (151 million), new religions (101 million), Sikhs (22.7 million), and Jews (14.2 million), Barrett said.

From Current News Summary, 26 April 1999 (www.religiontoday.com).

In Matthew 25:43–44 and Hebrews 13:3 the Bible stresses the importance of visiting those in prison. *What is the church you serve doing about it?*

Indeed, let us continually call upon the God we serve, "who alone does marvelous deeds. Praise be to his glorious name forever, may the whole earth be filled with his glory. Amen and Amen" (Ps. 72:18–19). We close this book with the following evidence of God's amazing handiwork:[19]

• Worldwide, three thousand new churches are opening every week.

• Worldwide, Christianity is growing at the rate of ninety thousand new believers every day.

• More Muslims in Iran have come to Christ since 1980 than in the previous one thousand years combined.

• In 1900, Korea had no Protestant church; it was deemed "impossible to penetrate." Today Korea is 35 percent Christian with seven thousand churches in the city of Seoul alone.

• In Islamic (Muslim) Indonesia, the percentage of Christians is so high the government won't print the statistic—which is probably nearing 15 percent of the population.

• After seventy years of oppression in Russia, people who claim allegiance to Christ number about 85 million—56 percent of the population. In one Siberian city people are being baptized twenty-four hours a day!

• God is creatively sending Chinese believers to reach Tibetans, Hondurans to reach North African Muslims, and Navajos to reach Laplanders. There are currently more than sixty thousand non-Western missionaries from over one thousand non-Western mission agencies. Many of these are serving in places that are hostile to Western missionaries.

Where the church has been planted, it's growing like wildfire. The good news is breaking loose worldwide. In A.D. 100, only one in every 360 people in the world was an active believer. Today one in ten people is an active believer. In A.D. 100 there were twelve unreached people groups per congregation of believers. Today, with six million churches worldwide, there are six hundred congregations for every remaining unreached people group!

That's what your God is doing. So what are you and your church doing to exploit the trends you've read about for the glory of God?

Notes

Introduction

1. Michael Slaughter with Warren Bird, *Real Followers*, (Nashville: Abingdon Press, 1999), 38.

2. Eldon Trueblood, quoted by Bob Briner, "Roaring Lambs," Xenos Christian Fellowship Conference speech, summer 1998, tape XSI=t980717a. See www.xenos.org.

3. Len Sweet, "A Dream Church for the Twenty-first Century," *Pastor's Update*, vol. 76, 1998. Audiocassette. Produced by Fuller Theological Seminary, Pasadena, CA.

Chapter 1: Get Help Becoming More Healthy

1. Tom Verducci, "Man on a Mission," *Sports Illustrated*, 23 March 1998, 78.

2. Haddon Robinson in foreword to Stephen Macchia, *Becoming a Healthy Church* (Grand Rapids: Baker, 1999), 10.

3. Ibid., 13–14.

4. Ibid., 16.

5. Christian Schwarz and Christoph Schalk, *Natural Church Development* (Kelowna, B.C.: International Centre for Leadership Development and Evangelism, 1998). Available at 800-804-0777, 250-766-0907, or www.GrowingLeadership.com.

6. Christian Schwarz and Christoph Schalk, *Implementation Guide to Natural Church Development* (Carol Stream, Ill.: Church Smart, 1998), 200. See also "The Strong Little Church: An Interview with Christian A. Schwarz," *Leadership* (fall 1999), 53.

7. Dale Galloway, "Ten Characteristics of Healthy Churches," *Net Results*, April 1998, 20–22.

8. Luis Palau, *Luis Palau Responds*, 15 June 1999, available from www.lpea.org.

9. George Barna, *Evangelism That Works* (Ventura, Calif.: Regal, 1996), video cassette.

10. George Barna, *Evangelism That Works* (Ventura, Calif.: Regal, 1995), 127.

11. Billy Graham, "Recovering the Primacy of Evangelism," *Christianity Today*, 8 December 1997, 27.

12. Ibid.

13. Dann Spader and Gary Mayes, *Growing a Healthy Church* (Chicago: Moody, 1991), 9–10.

14. Ibid., 210.

15. Ibid., 19.

16. Ibid., 180.

17. Rick Warren, *The Purpose-Driven Church* (Grand Rapids: Zondervan, 1995), 30.

18. Ibid., 102, 107.

19. Ibid., 17.

20. Ibid., 119.

21. Quoted in Spader and Mayes, 258.

22. Warren, *The Purpose-Driven Church*, 56.

23. Ibid., 61.

24. George Hunter, *Making Church Relevant*, ed. Dale Galloway (Kansas City: Beacon Hill, 1999), 113.

Chapter 2: Keep the Bible in One Hand and a Cup of Cold Water in the Other

1. George H. Gallup and Timothy K. Jones, *The Saints Among Us* (Harrisburg, Penn.: Morehouse Publishing Company, 1992), 12–16.

2. William G. McLoughlin, *Revivalism in the Rise of Adventism*, ed. Edwin Scott Gaustad (New York: Harper and Row, 1974), 132.

3. Some of the thoughts in these opening paragraphs were inspired by Charles Colson, "A Breed Apart: Christian Faith in Society," 19 October 1998, *Breakpoint with Chuck Colson,* ©1998 Prison Fellowship Ministries. Reprinted with permission. *BreakPoint with Chuck Colson* is a radio ministry of Prison Fellowship Ministries.

4. Stephen L. Carter, *The Culture of Disbelief: How American Law and Politics Trivialize Religious Devotion* (New York: Anchor Books/Doubleday, 1994), 23–43. See also the monthly *Mars Hill Audio Journal* (www.marshillaudio.org or 800-331-6407) in which host Ken Myers shows the subtle ways secularism has diluted the power of Christian living and has redefined Christianity to fit secularist assumptions.

5. Tim Stafford, "The Criminologist Who Discovered Churches," *Christianity Today*, 14 June 1999, 35–39.

6. Michael G. Maudlin, "God's Contractor," *Christianity Today*, 14 June 1999, 45. See also www.habitat.org/how/millard/html.

7. Richard Niebuhr, *Christ and Culture* (New York: Harper and Row, 1951).

8. In a later interview Carl Henry said, "The book was a critique of fundamentalism in terms of its own positioning in the cultural arena. Fundamentalists had largely withdrawn from societal outreach. As far as I was concerned, *The Uneasy Conscience of Modern Fundamentalism* was an effort to restate where fundamentalism ought to be in the light of its own heritage" (*Christianity Today*, 26 August 1996, 28). For more current rationale for Bible-based Christians, see John Eldredge, "A Biblical Case for Social and Political Involvement," *Citizen Link* published by Focus on the Family, at www.family.org/cforum/tempforum/A000 0997.html.

9. Os Guinness, *Dining with the Devil: The Megachurch Movement Flirts with Modernity* (Grand Rapids: Baker, 1993), 90, 89.

10. Philip D. Kenneson and James L. Street, *Selling Out the Church: The Dangers of Church Marketing* (Nashville: Abingdon Press, 1997), 164.

11. Douglas D. Webster, *Selling Jesus: What's Wrong with Marketing the Church* (Downers Grove, Ill.: InterVarsity Press, 1992), back cover.

12. H. B. London and Neil Wiseman, *The Heart of a Great Pastor* (Ventura, Calif.: Regal Books, 1994), 94.

13. Paul Basden, *Worship Maze* (Downers Grove, Ill.: InterVarsity Press, 1999), 94.

14. Guinness, *Dining with the Devil*, 90.

15. Elmer L. Towns, "What Are the Main Boundaries for the Evangelical Church and How Can We Best Address Our Major Issues?" Lecture delivered at the annual conference of the American Society for Church Growth, November 13–14, 1998.

Chapter 3: Enter the World of *Cheers, Friends,* and *Seinfeld*

1. This is a compilation of three accounts: Charles Colson, "Reaching the Pagan Mind," *Christianity Today*, November 1992, 112; Gene Edward Veith, *Postmodern Times* (Wheaton: Crossway Books, 1994), 15–16; and Chuck Colson, "A Tale of Two Cities: Apologetics for a

Post-Christian World," 25 August 1998, *BreakPoint with Chuck Colson,* © 1998 Prison Fellowship Ministries. Reprinted with permission. *BreakPoint with Chuck Colson* is a radio ministry of Prison Fellowship Ministries.

2. Len Sweet, "A Dream Church for the 21st Century," *Pastor's Update,* vol. 76. Audiocassette.

3. Chuck Colson, "A Taste of Grace—*Les Miserables,*" *BreakPoint with Chuck Colson,* © 1998 Prison Fellowship Ministries. Reprinted with permission.

4. Gene Edward Veith, *State of the Arts: From Bezalel to Maplethorpe* (Wheaton: Crossway Books, 1991), 154, quoted in Colson, "A Taste of Grace."

5. Colson, "A Taste of Grace."

6. Jimmy Long, *Generating Hope: A Strategy for Reaching the Postmodern Generation* (Downers Grove, Ill.: InterVarsity Press, 1997), 50, 147–48.

7. John Naisbitt, *Megatrends* (New York: Warner Books, 1982), 39–53.

8. Long, *Generating Hope,* 148.

9. Ibid., 112–13.

10. Ibid.

11. Ibid., 133. See also Tim Celek and Dieter Zander, *Inside the Soul of a New Generation: Insight and Strategies for Reaching Busters* (Grand Rapids: Zondervan, 1996); Kevin Ford, *Jesus for a New Generation* (Downers Grove, Ill.: InterVarsity Press, 1995); Ralph Moore, *Friends: How to Evangelize Generation X* (Honolulu: Straight Street Publishing, 1997); and Thom Rainer, *The Bridger Generation: America's Second Largest Generation, What They Believe, How to Reach Them* (Nashville: Broadman and Holman, 1997).

12. Tex Sample, *The Spectacle of Worship in a Wired World* (Nashville: Abingdon Press, 1998), 15.

13. Ibid., back cover.

14. Abraham Mehrabian, *Silent Messages: Implicit Communication of Emotions and Attitudes* (Belmont, Calif.: Wadsworth Publishing, 1971), 43–44.

15. Jana Childers, *Performing the Word: Preaching as Theatre* (Nashville: Abingdon Press, 1998), 57.

16. Suzette Haden Elgin, *How to Turn the Other Cheek and Still Survive* (Nashville: Thomas Nelson, 1997), 116.

17. Gene Edward Veith Jr., *Postmodern Times* (Wheaton: Crossway Books, 1994), 191.

18. Michael Slaughter with Warren Bird, *Real Followers* (Nashville: Abingdon Press, 1999), 191.

19. Luis Palau and David Sanford, *God Is Relevant* (New York: Doubleday, 1997), xxiv.

20. R. C. Sproul, in a press release about Luis Palau's *God Is Relevant.*

21. Leith Anderson, *A Church for the 21ˢᵗ Century* (Minneapolis: Bethany House, 1992), 24–25.

22. Ibid.

23. A. J. Conyers, *The Eclipse of Heaven* (Downers Grove, Ill.: InterVarsity Press, 1992), 175.

24. Long, *Generating Hope,* 125.

Chapter 4: Learn the Language That Connects with Postmoderns

1. Walter Truett Anderson, *Reality Isn't What It Used to Be: Theatrical Politics, Ready-to-Wear Religion, Global Myths, Primitive Chic and Other Wonders of the Postmodern World* (San Francisco: Harper and Row, 1990), 71.

2. J. Richard Middleton and Brian J. Walsh, eds., *Truth Is Stranger Than It Used to Be* (Downers Grove, Ill.: InterVarsity Press, 1995), 31.

3. For more information about these three views, read Millard Erickson, *Postmodernizing the Faith* (Grand Rapids: Baker, 1998). This book by a Protestant theology professor help-

fully explains the relationship between premodernism, modernism, and postmodernism. Erickson explores the views of seven theologians, three of whom believe that postmodernism is totally incompatible with Christianity (David Wells, Thomas Oden, and Francis Schaeffer). The other four (Stanley Grenz, J. Richard Middleton, Brian Walsh, and B. Keith Putt) hold that "postmodernism is a development that needs to be accepted, and Christian theology done in light of it."

4. Allan Bloom, *The Closing of the American Mind* (New York: Simon and Schuster, 1987), 25.

5. Brian McLaren, *Reinventing Your Church* (Grand Rapids: Zondervan, 1998), 178–92.

6. Lesslie Newbigin, *The Gospel in a Pluralist Society* (Grand Rapids: Eerdmans, 1996), 22.

Chapter 5: Turn On Your Daytime Running Lights

1. John Naisbitt, *Megatrends* (New York: Warner, 1982), 39–53.

2. Norman Shawchuck, Philip Kotler, Bruce Wrenn, and Gustave Rath, *Marketing for Congregations: Choosing to Serve People More Effectively* (Nashville: Abingdon Press, 1992), 22.

3. Aubrey Malphurs, *Strategy 2000* (Grand Rapids: Kregel, 1996), 90.

4. Mark Galli, "Learning to Be Some Things to Some People," *Leadership*, Fall 1991, 37.

5. George Barna, *A Step-by-Step Guide to Marketing the Church* (Ventura, Calif.: Regal Books, 1992), 124.

6. Ibid., 121.

7. Summarized from *Church Leaders Handbook* 4th ed., (South Barrington, Ill.: Willow Creek, 1997), 45–47, and Lynn and Bill Hybels, *Rediscovering Church* (Grand Rapids: Zondervan, 1995), 57–62.

8. Leonard A. Schlesinger and James Mellado, *Harvard Business Review,* 23 February 1999.

9. Peter Drucker, *Management: Tasks, Responsibilities, Practices* (New York: Harper and Row, 1973), 64–65.

10. Shawchuck, et. al., *Marketing for Congregations,* 22.

11. G. A. Pritchard, *Willow Creek Seeker Services: Evaluating a New Way of Doing Church* (Grand Rapids: Baker, 1996), 249.

12. John MacArthur, *Ashamed of the Gospel: When the Church Becomes like the World* (Wheaton: Crossway, 1993), 121.

13. Barna, *Marketing the Church,* 1.

14. George Gallup Jr. and Sarah Jones, *One Hundred Questions and Answers: Religion in America* (Princeton, N.J.: The Princeton Religion Research Center, 1989), 164–78.

15. John Pearson and Robert Hisrich, *Marketing Your Ministry: Ten Critical Principles* (Brentwood, Tenn.: Wolgemuth and Hyatt, 1990), 16, 23.

Chapter 6: Set Benchmarks for Reaching the Unchurched

1. C. Peter Wagner, ed., *The New Apostolic Churches: Rediscovering the New Testament Model of Leadership and Why It Is God's Desire for the Church Today* (Ventura, Calif.: Regal Books, 1998), inside dust jacket.

2. Ibid., 25.

3. George G. Hunter III, *Church for the Unchurched* (Nashville: Abingdon Press, 1996), 13, 29.

4. Ibid., 12.

5. Ibid., 43–44.

6. Rick Warren, *The Purpose-Driven Church* (Grand Rapids: Zondervan, 1995), 144.

7. Ibid., 132–34.

8. Ibid., 32.

9. Henry Blackaby and Claude V. King, *Experiencing God: How to Live the Full Adventure of Knowing and Doing the Will of God* (Nashville: Broadman and Holman, 1994), 129.

10. Warren, *The Purpose-Driven Church*, 13.

11. Ibid., 14–16.

12. T. D. Jakes, "Preachers and Pray-ers," *Ministries Today*, May/June 1999, 89–90.

13. Ibid., 89.

14. Go to www.globalharvest.org and click its link about prayer ministries.

15. See www.harvestevan.org. Silvoso is head of Harvest Evangelism and author of *That None Should Perish: How to Reach Entire Cities for Christ through Prayer Evangelism* (Ventura, Calif.: Regal Books, 1997). Call 1–800–835–7979 for resources and more information on Lighthouses of Prayer.

16. Contact Houses of Prayer Everywhere (HOPE) at P.O. Box 141312, Grand Rapids, MI 49514. Phone: 800-217-5200. Fax: 616-791-9926. Web address: www.missionindia.org.

17. Hunter, *Church for the Unchurched*, 19.

18. Donald McGavran, foreword to *Church Growth Survey Handbook*, by Bob Waymire and C. Peter Wagner (Colorado Springs: OC International, 1984), 2.

Chapter 7: Make More Room for Truth

1. Chuck Colson, 24 August 1998, radio commentary, *BreakPoint with Chuck Colson*. © 1998 Prison Fellowship Ministries. Reprinted with permission.

2. Leonard Sweet, *SoulTsunami* (Grand Rapids: Zondervan, 1999), 60.

3. George Barna, *The Second Coming of the Church* (Ventura, Calif.: Regal Books, 1998), 21–28.

4. Sweet, *SoulTsunami*, 59.

5. George Barna, *Index of Leading Spiritual Indicators* (Nashville: Word, 1996).

6. Colson, 24 August 1998, radio commentary.

7. Ibid.

8. Challenge Weekly, *chalpub@iconz.co.nz*, and cited in Friday Fax, 31 July 1997.

9. Os Guinness, *Fit Bodies, Fat Minds: Why Evangelicals Don't Think and What to Do About It* (Grand Rapids: Baker, 1994), 14.

10. Christian Smith, *American Evangelicalism: Embattled and Thriving* (Chicago: University of Chicago, 1998).

11. Bruce Shelley, "Charles E. Fuller: Taking Risks on Radio," *Eternity*, May 1976, 25. The first gospel television program sent coast-to-coast took place October 9, 1949, with evangelist Percy Crawford. On that date, a Sunday evening, Percy and Ruth Crawford's "Youth on the March" (subtitled "The Young People's Church of the Air, Inc.") went on the air over the ABC network, broadcast from the WFIL-TV station in Philadelphia and carried by most of its eleven affiliates. The day marked a milestone in the history of the television segment of the electronic church. The Crawfords' use of a variety-type format, as well as skits and dramatic presentations, was based on their radio broadcasts, which had been on the air in Philadelphia since 1931. Their show and the changes they introduced to it over the years served as a model to other religious television broadcasters who were to follow. (Walter Maier, the popular Lutheran radio evangelist, had previously made a television broadcast of *The Lutheran Hour* at a local station on January 1, 1949. A few other preachers also made local broadcasts, going out to the audience of a single station. But the costs and the still-developing technical requirements of the new medium had discouraged any nationwide broadcast of a Christian evangelistic program, until October 9, 1949.) For more information, see www.wheaton.edu/bgc/archives/crawford.htm.

12. Thom S. Rainer, *High Expectations* (Nashville: Broadman and Holman, 1999), 171.

13. "Study: More Than 100 Million Americans Use Net," CNET's News.com, 9 November 1999. See http://news.cnet.com.

14. William Romanowski, *Pop Culture Wars: Religion and the Role of Entertainment in American Life* (Downers Grove, Ill.: InterVarsity Press, 1996), 33.

15. See also the JESUS Film Project, 910 Calle Negosio, Suite 300, San Clemente, CA 92673-6251. Phone: 714-361-7575. Fax: 714-361-7579. Internet: www.jesusfilm.org/.

16. Lyle Schaller, *Discontinuity and Hope* (Nashville: Abingdon Press, 1999), 132.

17. *Charisma News Service* online, vol. 1, no. 104, 26 July 1999.

18. See, for example, George Cladis, *Leading the Team-Based Church* (San Francisco: Jossey-Bass, 1999).

19. Leith Anderson, *Dying for Change* (Minneapolis: Bethany House, 1998), 57. See also pages 17 and 134.

20. Elmer Towns and Stan Toler, *Leading Your Sunday School into the 21ˢᵗ Century* (Ventura, Calif.: Gospel Light, 1998), video.

21. Cited in J. P. Moreland, *Love Your God with All Your Mind: The Role of Reason in the Life of the Soul* (Colorado Springs: NavPress, 1997), 19.

Chapter 8: Go Confidently to Mars Hill

1. Mark Noll, *The Scandal of the Evangelical Mind* (Grand Rapids: Eerdmans, 1994), 3.

2. Allister McGrath, *Evangelicalism and the Future of Christianity* (Downers Grove, Ill.: InterVarsity Press, 1995), 139, and John Wilson, "*Christianity Today* '98 Book Awards," *Christianity Today*, 27 April 1998, 26.

3. Gene Breitenbach, *The IVY Jungle Report 2* (Spring 1994): 1, quoted in J. Mack Stiles, *Speaking of Jesus* (Downers Grove, Ill.: InterVarsity Press, 1995), 120.

4. Max Lucado, foreword to Ravi Zacharias, *Cries of the Heart: Bringing God Near When He Feels So Far* (Nashville: Word, 1998), vii–viii.

5. See these titles by Ravi Zacharias: *Cries of the Heart: Bring God Near When He Feels So Far* (Word, 1998), *Can Man Live without God?* (Word, 1994), *A Shattered Visage: The Real Face of Atheism* (Baker, 1993), and *Deliver Us from Evil* (Word, 1996).

6. Ibid., 329.

7. Adapted from Marie Chapian, *Of Whom the World Was Not Worthy* (Minneapolis: Bethany House, 1978), 122–23.

8. "Leadership in the Political Arena, Part 6," broadcast of *Let My People Think*, 13 October 1998, RZIM (Ravi Zacharias International Ministries), www.rzim.com.

9. Jonah Blank, "The Muslim Mainstream," *US News & World Report*, 20 July 1998, 22.

10. Leonard Sweet, *SoulTsunami* (Grand Rapids: Zondervan, 1999), 56–57.

11. Tom Phillips and Bob Norsworthy, *The World at Your Door: Reaching International Students in Your Home, Church, and School* (Minneapolis: Bethany House, 1997), Winfried Corduan, *Neighboring Faiths: A Christian Introduction to World Religions* (Downers Grove, Ill.: InterVarsity, 1998), William Saal, *Reaching Muslims for Christ* (Chicago: Moody, 1993), and James W. Sire, *The Universe Next Door: A Basic Worldview Catalog*, third edition, (Downers Grove, Ill.: InterVarsity, 1997).

12. See, for example, Josh McDowell and Don Stewart, *Handbook of Today's Religions* (Nashville: Thomas Nelson, 1983); Walter Martin, *Kingdom of the Cults* (Minneapolis: Bethany House, revised 1997); and Norman Geisler and Ron Rhodes, *When Cultists Ask* (Grand Rapids: Baker, 1997).

13. J. Budziszewski, *How to Stay Christian in College: An Interactive Guide to Keeping the Faith* (Colorado Springs: NavPress, 1999).

14. James Emery White, *A Search for the Spiritual: Exploring Real Christianity* (Grand Rapids: Baker, 1998).

15. Josh McDowell and Bob Hostetler, *The New Tolerance* (Wheaton: Tyndale, 1998), 15–20.

16. See Bill Myers and David Wimbish, *The Dark Side of the Supernatural* (Minneapolis: Bethany House, 1999).

17. Go to www.religiontoday.com, click the news story archives, and find the news summary for July 28, 1999.

Chapter 9: Maximize the Strong Points of Your Worship Service

1. List adapted from Elmer Towns, *Putting an End to Worship Wars* (Nashville: Broadman and Holman, 1997), 2–3, 53.

2. Donald P. Hustad, *True Worship* (Wheaton: Harold Shaw, 1998), 7, 20.

3. Gary Tangeman, *Disciplemaking Church* (Ft. Washington, Penn.: Christian Literature Crusade, 1996), 164–65. Also see Edward S. Ninde, *The Story of the American Hymn* (Nashville: Abingdon, 1921), 94–97. A similar story in that book relates another tense scene in the history of church music:

> The church should be a place of purity and holiness, separate from the world and its secular entertainment. How could good Christians conceive of welcoming this worldly instrument into the Lord's house." The wealthy churchman did all he could to thwart the efforts of the "misguided" group that had conceded to accept the sinister gift, beseeching them with tears and even offering to refund the entire price if someone would only dump the ill-fated cargo—a musical instrument—overboard during its transatlantic voyage. Just what was this instrument of such vile associations and shady history? . . . The churchman's pleas were left unheeded; the instrument arrived safely in the New World, and the Brattle Street Church of Boston made room for the controversial instrument: the organ.

4. Barry Rose in *Heavenly Voices*, Gateway Films/Vision, 1998, video.

5. *Eerdmans' Handbook to the History of Christianity* (Grand Rapids: Eerdmans, 1977), 216.

6. Andrew Wilson-Dickson, *Story of Christian Music* (Minneapolis: Fortress, 1996), 28.

7. *Eerdmans' Handbook*, 140.

8. Wilson-Dickson, *Story of Christian Music*, 36. See also Harry Eskew and Hugh McElrath, *Sing with Understanding* (Nashville: Broadman/Church Street Press, 1995), 86–87.

9. Steve Miller, *The Contemporary Christian Music Debate* (Wheaton: Tyndale, 1993), 109.

10. Wilson-Dickson, *Story of Christian Music*, 30.

11. *Eerdmans' Handbook*, 216.

12. Wilson-Dickson, *Story of Christian Music*, 33. See also Donald Hustad, *Jubilee II*, second edition (Carol Stream, Ill.: Hope Publishing Company, 1993).

13. Wilson-Dickson, *Story of Christian Music*, 34.

14. Eskew and McElrath, *Sing with Understanding*, 91–92.

15. Wilson-Dickson, *Story of Christian Music*, 52.

16. Ibid., 46.

17. Ibid., 56.

18. *Heavenly Voices*, video.

19. *Eerdmans' Handbook*, 363.

20. Eskew and McElrath, *Sing with Understanding*, 99.

21. Wilson-Dickson, *Story of Christian Music*, 81.

22. J. D. Douglas, Walter Elwell, and Peter Toon, *Concise Dictionary of Christian Tradition* (Grand Rapids: Zondervan, 1989), 259.

23. Wilson-Dickson, *Story of Christian Music*, 76.

24. *Eerdmans' Handbook*, 426–27, 448.

25. Wilson-Dickson, *Story of Christian Music*, 139. Some sources attribute the concept to Martin Luther. See Richard Friedenthal Luther, *His Life and Times*, trans. by John Nowell (New York: Harcourt Brace, 1967), 464.

26. Towns, *Putting an End to Worship Wars,* 136–37.

27. Gary McIntosh, *Make Room for the Boom . . . or Bust: Six Church Models for Reaching Three Generations* (Grand Rapids: Revell, 1997), 100.

28. Models are adapted from McIntosh, *Make Room for the Boom,* 60–136. McIntosh offers two additional models, the satellite congregation (a church plant) and the rebirthed congregation (one that has started over). In both cases the worship style could be, and often is, different from the parent church.

29. Lyle Schaller, endorsing Charles Arn, *How to Start a New Service* (Grand Rapids: Baker, 1997), back cover.

30. Arn, *How to Start a New Service,* 14.

31. Ibid., 117.

32. Based on conversation between Dale Galloway and Warren Bird.

33. Barry Liesch, *The New Worship: Straight Talk on Music and the Church* (Grand Rapids: Baker, 1996), 13.

Chapter 10: Cash In on Two Millennia of Good Ideas

1. Dave Goetz, ed., *ChurchLeadership.Net,* an online publication of Christianity Today, Inc., issue 11, 2 June 1999, www.christianity.net/cln.

2. Sally Morgenthaler, *Worship Evangelism* (Grand Rapids: Zondervan, 1995), 85, 30.

3. Elmer Towns, *Putting an End to Worship Wars* (Nashville: Broadman & Holman, 1997), 135.

4. Robert Webber, *Worship Old and New* (Grand Rapids: Zondervan, 1982), 196, 14.

5. George Barna, *The Index of Leading Spiritual Indicators* (Waco: Word, 1996), 50–53.

6. LaMar Boschman, *Future Worship* (Ventura, Calif.: Regal Books, 1999), 179. Also see LaMar Boschman, "Leading Your Church into Worship Renewal," *Pastor's Update,* vol. 70, audiocassette. Produced by Fuller Theological Seminary, Pasadena, CA.

7. Søren Kierkegaard, *Purity of Heart Is to Will One Thing,* Douglas Steeve, trans. (New York: Harper, 1948), 160–66.

8. Adapted from "Leading Your Church into Worship Renewal," *Pastor's Update,* no. 70. Audiocassette.

9. Ibid.

10. Lyle Schaller, "Changes in Staff Configuration," Asbury Seminary–sponsored Beeson Institute for Advanced Church Leadership, 4 June 1998.

11. Towns, *Putting an End to Worship Wars,* 10.

12. Barry Liesch, *The New Worship: Straight Talk on Music and the Church* (Grand Rapids: Baker, 1996), 245, 242.

13. Egon Wellesz, *The New Oxford History of Music,* vol. 2 (London: Oxford University Press, 1957), 2.

14. George Hunter, "The Culturally Relevant Congregation," American Society for Church Growth, November 1996. Audiocassette.

15. William Easum, *Growing Spiritual Redwoods* (Nashville: Abingdon, 1997), 66.

16. Hunter, "The Culturally Relevant Congregation."

17. Ibid.

18. Webber, *Worship Old and New,* 11.

19. A. W. Tozer, *Knowledge of the Holy* (San Francisco: Harper, 1978), 10.

Chapter 11: Learn to Be a Leader-Maker

1. Based on an interview with Ted Haggard, conducted by Warren Bird in 1999.

2. Loren Mead, "The Future of the Church," Change Conference, Prince of Peace Lutheran Church, Burnsville, Minnesota, 1997. Audiocassette.

3. John Maxwell, *The 21 Irrefutable Laws of Leadership* (Nashville: Thomas Nelson, 1998), 122.

4. Lyle Schaller, *Discontinuity and Hope: Radical Change and the Path to the Future* (Nashville: Abingdon Press, 1999), 137.

5. Ibid., 138

6. Ibid., 138–39.

7. Ibid., 51.

8. William Easum, *Sacred Cows Make Gourmet Burgers: Ministry Anytime, Anywhere, by Anyone* (Nashville: Abingdon Press, 1995). Also see Easum's extensive Internet site: www.easum.com.

9. William Easum, *The Complete Ministry Audit: How to Measure 20 Principles for Growth* (Nashville: Abingdon Press, 1996), 11.

10. "Effective Churches and Team Leadership," *Next*, vol. 5, no. 2, April-May 1999, 1.

11. William Easum, *Growing Spiritual Redwoods* (Nashville: Abingdon Press, 1997), 17.

12. Carl George with Warren Bird, *Nine Keys to Effective Small-Group Leadership* (Mansfield, Penn.: Kingdom Publishing, 1997), 22, 46.

13. For more information on the Jethro model, see Carl George, *Prepare Your Church for the Future* (Grand Rapids: Revell, 1991), 121–49. Also see Carl George with Warren Bird, *The Coming Church Revolution* (Grand Rapids: Revell, 1994), 53–61.

14. George with Bird, *Nine Keys*, 8.

15. Ibid., 34.

16. Ibid.

17. Ibid., 80.

18. Ibid., 7.

19. Larry Gilbert, *Spiritual Gift Inventory* (Lynchburg, Virg.: Church Growth Institute, P.O. Box 4404, Lynchburg, VA 24502). This is the largest selling inventory with over 2.5 million sold. To order, call 1-800-553-GROW. Willow Creek pioneered the ministry-finding approach called Network, available from Network Ministries International, 27355 Betanzos, Mission Viejo, CA 92692, 800-588-8833 or 714-854-3530 (phone), 714-854-1268 (fax), www.networkministries.com. Other Willow Creek tools are available from the Willow Creek Association, 800-570-9812 (phone), 847-765-5046 (fax), www.WillowCreek.com. Rick Warren supplements his SHAPE idea for gift deployment with Mels Carbonell's "Uniquely You" series, which can be obtained from The International Centre for Leadership Development and Evangelism, 800-804-0777, www.GrowingLeadership.com. The Towns Spiritual Gift Questionnaire is available free at www.elmertowns.com.

20. George Cladis has written the theological and practical basis for employing gifts. See George Cladis, *Leading the Team-Based Church* (San Francisco: Jossey-Bass, 1999).

21. Maxwell, *21 Irrefutable Laws*, 133.

22. Ibid., 210.

23. Ibid.

24. George with Bird, *Nine Keys*, 54.

25. George with Bird, *The Coming Church Revolution*, 49.

26. George with Bird, *Nine Keys*, 6.

27. Lyle Schaller, "Every Part Is an 'I,'" *Leadership* (fall 1999): 29.

28. See William Easum's extensive Internet site at www.easum.com. Contact John Maxwell at Injoy Group, P.O. Box 7700, Atlanta, GA 30357-0700, 800-333-6506, www.Injoy.com. For Carl George training materials, call 800-9DOCENT or 909-396-6843, fax 909-396-6845, email CarlGeorge@metachurch.com, or check out www.metachurch.com online.

29. George with Bird, *Nine Keys*, 192.

30. Schaller, *Discontinuity and Hope*, 226.

Chapter 12: Look Underneath the Megachurch Movement

1. Elmer Towns, C. Peter Wagner, and Thom S. Rainer, *The Everychurch Guide to Growth* (Nashville: Broadman and Holman, 1998), 120.

2. Lyle Schaller, "Solo Practitioner or Team Member?" *Net Results,* July 1996, 27.

3. Lyle Schaller, *The Seven-Day-A-Week Church* (Nashville: Abingdon Press, 1992), 28.

4. Quoted in Norman Shawchuck, Philip Kotler, Bruce Wrenn, and Gustave Rath, *Marketing for Congregations: Choosing to Serve People More Effectively* (Nashville: Abingdon Press, 1992), 166.

5. Peter Drucker, "New Paradigms," *Forbes,* 5 October 1998, www.forbes.com.

6. John N. Vaughan, *Megachurches and America's Cities* (Grand Rapids: Baker, 1993), cited in Vinson Synan, "Pentecostal Trends of the '90s," *Ministries Today,* vol. 17, no. 3, May/June 1999, 61. For information on Vaughan's writings, including a monthly fax on the megachurch movement, contact Church Growth Today, P.O. Box 47, Bolivar, MO 65613, 417-326-3826 (phone), 417-326-3827 (fax), JV@ChurchGrowthToday.com.

7. Vaughan, *Megachurches and America's Cities,* 50.

8. Vaughan, *Megachurches and America's Cities,* cited in Synan, "Pentecostal Trends," 61.

9. Interview with Bill Hybels, "Beyond the Summit," *Leadership,* Summer 1999, 29.

10. The material about Willow Creek is adapted from www.willowcreek.org /wccc/txt/w2.html. Also see Lynne Hybels and Bill Hybels, *Rediscovering Church* (Grand Rapids: Zondervan, 1995).

11. Paul David Yonggi Cho with Harold Hostetler, *Successful Home Cell Groups* (Plainfield, N.J.: Bridge, 1991). Also see Karen Hurston, *Growing the World's Largest Church* (Charisma, 1994).

12. Rick Warren, *The Purpose-Driven Church: Growth without Compromising Your Message & Vision* (Grand Rapids: Zondervan, 1995), 325–27.

13. Dale Galloway, *20/20 Vision: How to Create a Successful Church with Lay Pastors and Cell Groups* (Portland: Scott Publishing, 1986).

14. Interview with Bill Hybels, "Beyond the Summit," *Leadership,* Summer 1999, 30.

15. George Hunter and Dale Galloway, eds., *Making Church Relevant* (Kansas City: Beacon Hill Press, 1999), 152

16. "Effective Churches and Team Leadership," *Next,* vol. 5, no. 2, April–June, 1999, 1.

17. William Easum, *The Complete Ministry Audit: How to Measure 20 Principles for Growth* (Nashville: Abingdon Press, 1996), 32.

18. Bob Buford, in foreword to Michael Slaughter with Warren Bird, *Vital Christianity* (Nashville: Abingdon, 1999), 15–18.

19. Lyle Schaller, *Discontinuity and Hope: Radical Change and the Path to the Future* (Nashville: Abingdon Press, 1999), 226, cited by Robert Buford in foreword to Michael Slaughter and Warren Bird, *Real Followers* (Nashville: Abingdon Press, 1999).

Chapter 13: Make the Church Better Than a Business

1. Howard G. Hendricks, *Color Outside the Lines: A Revolutionary Approach to Creative Leadership* (Nashville: Word, 1998), 214.

2. David Goetz, *Churchleadership.Net,* 20 May 1999.

3. Bill Hull, *Building High Commitment in a Low-Commitment World* (Grand Rapids: Revell, 1995), 29.

4. Wade Clark Roof and Bruce Greer, *A Generation of Seekers: The Spiritual Journeys of the Baby Boom Generation* (San Francisco: HarperSanFrancisco, 1994), 243.

5. Thomas Bandy, "Coaching Clergy to Transform Leadership," *Growing Leaders for the 21ˢᵗ Century,* 12–15 May 1998. Audiocassette.

6. John Stackhouse Jr., "Why Our Friends Won't Stop, Look, and Listen," *Christianity Today*, 3 February 1997, 49.

7. Reggie McNeal, *Netfax*, Leadership Network fax newsletter, 30 March 1998. The two-part article begins with issue 93, 16 March 1998. Also see Reggie McNeal, *Revolution in Leadership: Training Apostles for Tomorrow's Church* (Nashville: Abingdon Press, 1998).

8. Lyle Schaller, *Discontinuity and Hope: Radical Change and the Path to the Future* (Nashville: Abingdon Press, 1999), 65.

9. For more information check www.prayusa.com, call 1-888-PRAYUSA, or fax-on-demand by dialing 713-466-6392 from the handset of a fax machine. When using the fax line, follow the voice instructions and request document #900. When instructed to do so, press start on your fax machine. You will receive seven pages of information. The PrayUSA! coordinator is Eddie Smith.

10. The Cedar quote comes from "'Prayer, care, share' Strategy Reaches Neighbors," www.ReligionToday.com, 27 July 1999, current feature story. The Bailey story was adapted from Christine J. Gardner, "Churches Join 'Prayer Evangelism,'" *Christianity Today*, 11 January 1999, 13.

11. Jim Cymbala with Dean Merrill *Fresh Wind, Fresh Fire* (Grand Rapids: Zondervan, 1997), and Jim Cymbala with Dean Merrill, *Fresh Faith* (Grand Rapids: Zondervan, 1999).

12. Ben Patterson, "Whatever Happened to Prayer Meeting," *Leadership*, Fall 1999, 121–22.

13. C. Peter Wagner, *Churchquake!* (Ventura, Calif.: Regal, 1999), 14.

Chapter 14: Free People to Give from the Heart

1. Helen Baker, *The Church at the Crossroads: A History of Princeton Alliance Church* (Westfield, N.J.: Ministry Press, 1999), 94. Letter updated by permission of original writer.

2. Stan Toler and Elmer Towns, *Developing a Giving Church* (Kansas City: Beacon Hill, 1999), back cover.

3. George Barna, *The Habits of Highly Effective Churches* (Ventura, Calif.: Issachar Resources, 1998), 139.

4. George Barna, *How to Increase Giving in Your Church* (Ventura, Calif.: Regal Books, 1997), 21.

5. Ibid., 70.

6. Ibid.

7. Ibid., 59–70.

8. Lyle E. Schaller, *Forty-four Ways to Expand the Financial Base of Your Congregation* (Nashville: Abingdon Press, 1989), 11.

9. Toler and Towns, *Developing a Giving Church*, 59.

10. Ibid., 17.

11. Ibid., 11.

12. John and Sylvia Ronsvalle, *Behind the Stained Glass Windows* (Grand Rapids: Baker, 1996), 31, 39, 121.

13. Ibid., 190.

14. Toler and Towns, *Developing a Giving Church*, 19.

15. Ibid., 21–22.

16. Barna, *How to Increase Giving in Your Church*, 12.

17. Schaller, *Forty-four Ways*, 20.

18. Norman Shawchuck, Philip Kotler, Bruce Wrenn, and Gustave Rath, *Marketing for Congregations: Choosing to Serve People More Effectively* (Nashville: Abingdon Press, 1992), 349.

19. Schaller, *Forty-four Ways*, 21.

20. Ibid., 28.

21. Ibid., 29, 30.

22. Ibid., 31–32.

23. Ibid., 34.

24. Ibid., 35.

25. Ibid., 24.

26. *Your Money,* December/January 1999, 16.

27. Ray Bowman and Eddy Hall, *When Not to Borrow: Unconventional Financial Wisdom to Set Your Church Free* (Grand Rapids: Baker, 1996), 33–35.

28. Ibid., 37–40.

29. Jeff Berg and Jim Burgess, *The Debt-Free Church: Experiencing Financial Freedom while Growing Your Ministry* (Chicago: Moody, 1996), 107–18.

30. Ibid., 113.

31. Loren B. Mead, *Financial Meltdown in the Mainline?* (Bethesda, Md.: Alban Institute, 1998), 82.

Conclusion

1. Robert Dale, *Leadership for a Changing Church* (Nashville: Abingdon, 1998), back cover.

2. Henry Blackaby and Claude V. King, *Experiencing God* (Nashville: Broadman & Holman, 1994), 50.

3. John Wesley, quoted in Robert Logan and Tom Clegg, *Releasing Your Church's Potential* (Carol Stream, Ill.: Church Smart Resources, 1998), 4–7.

4. Billy Graham Evangelistic Association press release, "Billy Graham Announces Amsterdam 2000," 15 September 1999.

5. Ibid.

6. "How Pastors View the Church," *Barna Report,* September/October 1997.

7. Ibid.

8. "Mosques on Main Street," *Charisma,* vol. 23, no. 3, October 1997,

9. David Barrett, quoted by Brandt Gustavson, NRB, February/March 1998, 14.

10. "Christianity Is Growing Slowly Worldwide," *Religion News Today,* 21 January 1997, www.religiontoday.com.

11. Ibid.

12. Patrick Johnstone and David Barrett, quoted by Kim Lawton, "Faith Without Borders," *Christianity Today,* 19 May 1997, 42.

13. Cited material by David Bogosian, news summary, *Religion Today,* 12 August 1998, www.religiontoday.com.

14. Nina Shea, *In the Lion's Den: A Shaking Account of the Persecution and Martyrdom of Christians Today and How We Should Respond* (Nashville: Broadman & Holman, 1997), 1.

15. Literature on "International Day of Prayer for the Persecuted Church," 15 November 1998, distributed by *www.persecutedchurch.org.* Also see World Evangelical Fellowship Religious Liberty Commission.

16. See http://members.aol.com/brskeeper/links1.htm for an annotated listing of sites that monitor religious persecution. Also see David C. Barrett, "Annual Statistical Table on Global Mission," *International Bulletin of Missionary Research,* January 1997, 25.

17. See www.wingnet/net~icc/index.phtml, www.lightsource.net/liberty/index.shtml, and www.iclnet.org/pub/resources/text/vom/vom.html.

18. Rev. Jesus M. Huertas, editorial titled "Prison Outreach," *The Alliance Life,* vol. 134, no. 2, 27 January 1999, 4.

19. "1996 Mission Frontier," November-December 1996.

Subject Index

absolutes, 76
AD 2000 and Beyond, 194
African (and Christian) Method. Episcop., 123
American Bible Society, 58
American Orthodox, 123
American Society for Church Growth (ASCG), 42, 85
apologetics, 119–28
Armenian Church, 123
artists, 120
Asbury Theological Seminary, 33
atheists, 222
auditory learner, 59
authenticity, 74

baby boomer, 146, 187
baby busters. *See* Generation X
Baptist, 123
Baylor University (Waco, Texas), 49
Bible, 17, 39, 42–52, 55, 57, 64, 72, 87, 97, 98, 107–18, 109, 110, 111, 115, 116, 155, 163
billboards, 114
Billy Graham Evangelistic Association, 214
blended worship model, 141. *See also* worship, styles of
blessability boundary, 47

body life church, 139. *See also* worship, styles of
Buddhist, 123, 219, 222

Campus Crusade for Christ, 214
Canada, 25, 126, 164
cantor, 136
Catholic Children's Fund, 214
Catholic Relief Services, 214
changes, 13, 91
charismatic movement, 41, 153, 184, 185, 222
charities, leading religious, 214
Christian and Missionary Alliance, 123, 192
Christian Broadcasting Network, 214
Christian Children's Fund, 214
Christian churches, 123
Christian experience boundary, 46
Christian Sanitation Commission, 37
Christianity, essence of, 18
church
    business aspects, 189–97
    church planting, 126
    commercialization of, 40
    expectations, for lay contribution, 166

growth, 9
    health, 15, 19, 20, 23–34, 50, 177, 183
    history, 149–60
    larger, 177–200
    mega-, 177–200
    planting, 222
    teaching, 194
    team-based, 171
Church of Christ, 123
Church of the Nazarene, 123
church growth, 23, 42, 51, 222
church growth movement, 40, 104
community, 17, 60, 62, 64, 97, 103, 135, 139, 182, 183
community churches, 123
compassion, 35, 37–38, 48–50, 95, 97, 109
congregational church, 139. *See also* worship, styles of
conscience, 57
consumerism, 17, 40, 103
contemporary culture, 57
core-teaching barriers, 45
Covenant House, 214
crime, 38
cults, 83, 124
cultural identity, 144
culturally relevant ministry, 32
culture, 39, 66, 111, 112, 167

debt, 209, 210–14
denominations
    Evangelical Lutheran
        Church in America, 24
    Evangelical Missionary
        Church (EMC), 132
    Foursquare, 178
    independent, 36
    Nazarene, 150
    nondenominational,
        108
    North American Bap-
        tist, 164
    Presbyterian Church of
        America PCA), 94
    Southern Baptist Con-
        vention (SBC), 120, 190
    United Methodist, 68,
        202
    Vineyard, 56
    Wesleyan, 82
despair, 66
Disciples of Christ, 123
discipleship, 31, 40, 97,
    109, 189
doctrine, 45
donors, 205–6

e-mail, 61
Eastern Orthodox church,
    123
Eastern Orthodoxy, 151
electronic culture, 62
empowerment, 184
Empty Tomb, 203
entertainment, 115
Episcopal church, 123
ethics, 35
Evangelical Church in
    America, 24
evangelical churches, 123
Evangelical Free Church,
    123
Evangelical Lutheran
    Church in America, 24
Evangelical Missionary
    church (EMC), 132
evangelism, 9, 13, 19-20,
    27, 28, 31, 38, 40, 51,
    55, 57, 59, 85, 93-104,

116, 125, 139, 144, 173,
    183, 219
evangelistic church, 139.
    See also worship, styles
    of
excellence, 88
experience God, 27, 66
expositional church, 139.
    See also worship, styles
    of

faith,
    boundaries of, 41
    essentials of, 17
Feed the Children, 214
fellowship, 31
finances, 201–15
    debt and, 209, 210–14
    fund-raising and, 210
    giving and, 95, 137, 144
    money and, 88
    offerings and, 89
    tithing and, 98
    worldly goods and, 20
First Great Awakening, 42
Focus on the Family, 214
forgiveness, 58
Foursquare, 178
Friends, 60
Fuller Theological Sem-
    inary, 85
fundamentalist-modernist
    disputes, 39
fundamentalists, 64
fund-raising, 210

Generation X, 60, 97, 147,
    152, 187
gifts, 20
giving, 137
    joyful, 95
    total, 144
Global Harvest Ministries
    (Colorado Springs, Col-
    orado), 102
God-centered, 26
good deeds, 17
good works, 48
gospel boundary, 44
grace, 44–46, 59, 182

Great Commandment, 15,
    30
Great Commission, 15, 28,
    30, 217
guilty, 88

Habitat for Humanity, 38,
    214
Harvard University, 119
hedonism, 17
heresy, 42–43
high school shootings, 38,
    90
Hindu, 123, 222
holiness, 42, 104, 109
Holocaust, 66
Holy Spirit, 16, 42, 46–48,
    49, 50, 51, 76, 83, 95,
    109, 116, 153, 158, 163,
    174, 186
hope, 64, 103
Houses of Prayer Every-
    where, 103
humanism, 17, 38
hypocrisy, 74

illiterate, 219
immorality, 136
incarnational principle, 156
independent churches, 36
Internet, 61, 113, 114, 116,
    127, 167
irrelevance, 87
Islam, 123, 124, 219, 222

Jehovah's Witnesses, 123
Jesus boundary, 43
Jesus video, 115
Jews, 123, 221
justice, 57, 109

kinesthetic learner, 59

larger churches, 27
leadership, 41, 95, 97
    development of, 163–76
    as pastoral role, 191
    small group, 173
Leadership Network, 185,
    197
Leading Ideas, 19

learners, kinds of, 59
liberal conservative, 41
Lighthouse of Prayer, 102
limits of Christianity
  blessability boundary,
    47
  Christian experience
    boundary, 46
  core-teachings barrier,
    45
  gospel boundary, 44
  Jesus boundary, 43
liturgical church, 139. *See
  also* worship, styles of
love, 17, 33, 35, 38, 46, 48,
  49, 51, 58
Lutheran church, 123
Lutheran Services in America, 214

MAP International, 214
marketing, 41, 81–92
  advertising and, 85
  of the gospel, 40
  television, 86–87
Mars Hill, 57, 121
martyrs, 221
materialism, 17, 211
maturity, 29, 165
megachoices, 83
Methodist church, 123
methods, 32, 40
ministry teams, 184
mission, 13, 14, 85
Mission America, 194
mission statement, 84
missionaries, 221
modernists, 64
modernity, 41
monastery, 136
money, 88
Mormon church, 123
multiple-track worship,
  142. *See also* worship,
  styles of
multisensory framework,
  55–66
music, 136, 138, 167
  harmony in, 136
  instruments and, 138

spiritual songs as, 156
stanzas in, 136
Muslims, 124, 219

narcissism, 17
National Association of
  Evangelicals, 194–95
natural church develop-
  ment, 27
Nazarene, 150
New Age spirituality, 55
New Apostolic Reforma-
  tion, 95, 96
new apostolic church, 41
new barbarians, 33
nominalism, 17
nondenominational, 108
North American Baptist,
  164
nuclear bomb, 90
nuclear destruction, 66

outreach, 95

passion, for reaching the
  lost, 28
passionate spirituality, 27
pastor, role of, 197
Pentecostal church, 123
Pentecostal movement,
  153, 184, 185, 222
philanthropy, 35, 37
pluralism, 17
Polish National Catholic
  church, 123
political correctness, 112
poor, 35, 37–38, 48–50,
  219. *Also see* social issues
population, 184
postmodern, 9, 19
postmodernism, 65, 67–78
pragmatism, 17
Prayer Book, 138
prayer, 9, 16, 17, 18, 85,
  95, 100, 101, 173, 217
  and fasting, 17
  central priority of,
    194–97
preaching, multimedia culture in, 62
Presbyterian, 123

Presbyterian Church of
  America (PCA), 94
priesthood of believers,
  163, 174
priorities, 28, 81–92
Prison Fellowship, 55
prison ministry, 221
privatism, 17
prostitution, 136
public square, 107, 112
Puritan, 119
purpose-driven church, 30

radio, 113, 114
Reformed churches, 123
relational communication,
  55–66
relativism, 17
religious groups, U.S.
  largest, 123
renewal, 17, 153
renewal church, 139. *See
  also* worship, styles of
revival, 9, 42
Roman Catholic, 123, 222

Salvation Army, 123, 214
science, 119–28
Second Great Awakening,
  42
secular management in-
  sights, 189
secularism, 17, 19, 107–18
secularization, 37
seeker, 41, 125, 135, 141
seeker-centered worship
  model, 141. *See also*
  worship, styles of
seeker-sensitive worship
  model, 141. *See also*
  worship, styles of
Seinfeld, 60
self-centeredness, 17
self-evaluation, 25
senior adults, 144, 145
sermon, 155
Seventh-Day Adventist,
  123
sex, 112
small groups, 97, 98,
  169–74, 182, 183, 187

smaller churches, 27
social issues, 35–53
    social change, 35, 37
    social compassion, 51
    social expectations, 83
    social gospel, 38
    social justice, 109
    social reform, 39
Southern Baptist Convention (SBC), 120, 190
spiritual awakening, 9
spiritual gift, 97, 98, 140, 171, 183, 219
spiritual hunger, 151–53
spiritually-driven ministry, 16
status quo, 13
stewardship, 201–15
story, 121, 122
Sunday school movement, 113–16

television, 86–87, 114
tolerance, 48, 125
traditions, man-made, 14
transfer Christians, 27
trend summary, 5–6, 21, 53, 53, 79, 105, 129, 161, 199, 218
Trinity Broadcasting Network, 214
truth, 20, 67–78, 107–18

unchurched, 93–104. *See also* evangelism
ungodliness, 42
Unitarian Universalist, 123
United Methodist, 68, 202

values, 71
Vineyard, 56
vision, 17, 85
visual learner, 59

watered-down gospel, 38
Wesleyan, 82
Word, (God's) 39, 85
World Prayer Center, 102
World Vision, 214
worldliness, 17, 135
worldviews, 123
worship, 17, 20, 31, 40, 62, 63, 83, 95, 131, 149–60
    indigenous, 157
    liturgical, 149
    services, 168
    styles of, 131–48
wrong predictions, 220
Wycliffe Bible Translators, 214

YMCA, 38
Young Life, 214

Name Index

Abyssinian Baptist Church (Manhattan, New York), 185

Akron Baptist Temple (Akron, Ohio), 181

Allen, Woody, 57

Ambrose of Milan, 136

Anderson, Leith, 9–10, 65–66, 116

Anderson, Walter Truett, 69

Anyang Assembly of God (Seoul, Korea), 180

Arn, W. Charles, 51, 143–45

Baergen, John, 187

Bailey, E. K., 194

Bandy, Tom, 193

Barna, George, 28, 41, 85, 89, 90, 110, 133, 154, 204, 205

Barnhouse, Donald Grey, 139

Barrett, David B., 113, 185, 222

Basden, Paul, 40

Baxter, Richard, 152

Berg, Jeff, 211, 213

Berger, Peter, 41

Berguson, Johnny, 2

Bethlehem Baptist (Minneapolis), 153

Blackaby, Henry, 26, 27, 101, 217

Bloom, Allan, 71

Bonhoeffer, Dietrich, 152

Booth, William, 139

Boschman, LaMar, 154

Bowman, Ray, 211

Boyd, Donald, 192

Buford, Bob, 185-186, 188

Burgess, Jim, 211, 213

Burrough, Jeremiah, 152

Caldwell, Kirbyjon, 202

Calvary Chapel (Calvary Chapel), (Santa Ana, California), 179, 185

Calvary Chapel Golden Springs (Calvary Chapel), Diamond Bar, California), 179

Calvin, John, 138, 152

Carter, Doug, 206

Carter, Stephen L., 37

Cedar, Paul, 195

Centre Street Evangelical Missionary Church (Calgary, Alberta, Canada), 132

Childress, Carol, 151

Cho, David Yonggi, 11, 173, 174, 180

Cho, Yong Mok, 180

Chopra, Deepak, 193

Church of the Resurrection (Leawood, Kansas), 142

Churchill, Winston, 30

Cladis, George, 171

Clegg, Tom, 103

Colson, Chuck, 55, 57–60, 110

Community Baptist Church (Manhattan Beach, California), 77

Community Church of Joy (Glendale, Arizona), 24, 142

Concord Missionary Baptist Church (Dallas, Texas,), 194

Copan, Paul, 69

Cordeiro, Wayne, 178

Cornerstone Church (independent charismatic), (San Antonio, Texas), 179

Corts, John, 218

Cowles, H. Robert, 11

Crenshaw Christian Center (Los Angeles, California), 181

Crichton, Michael, 71

Criswell, W. A., 11

Cushman, Robert (Bob), 11, 201

Cymbala, Jim, 195

Dale, Robert, 217

Dawn, Marva, 135

Deeper Life Bible Church (Lagos, Nigeria), 180

DeGeneres, Ellen, 69

Dewey, John, 38

Dilulio, John, 38

Drucker, Peter, 89, 179

Eastman, Brett, 187
Eastside Foursquare
    Church (Kirkland,
    Washington), 33
Easum, Bill, 157, 169, 184
Edison, Thomas, 189
Edwards, Jonathan, 42,
    152
Elgin, Suzette Haden, 63

Falwell, Jerry, 11, 181
Fellowship Bible Church
    (Little Rock, Arkansas),
    36
Fellowship of
    Excitement/Second
    Baptist Church (South-
    ern Baptist), (Houston,
    Texas), 179
Ficken, Jock, 91
First Baptist Church (Fort
    Worth, Texas), 181
First Baptist Church (inde-
    pendent Baptist),
    (Hammond, Indiana),
    179, 181
First Great Awakening, 42
Ford, Henry, 166
Foster, Richard, 109
Francis of Assisi, 37
Frazer Memorial United
    Methodist Church
    (Montgomery, Al-
    abama), 184
Frizzell, Gregory R., 190
Fuller, Charles E., 113, 139
Fuller, Millard, 38

Galli, Mark, 84
Galloway, Dale, 11, 27–28,
    49–50, 145–46, 183
Gallup, George H. Jr., 35,
    85, 116
Gandhi, Mahatma, 111
Garlow, Jim, 82
George, Carl, 2, 11, 170,
    173, 174, 181
Georgian Hills Baptist
    Church (Memphis, Ten-
    nessee), 190

Ginghamsburg Church
    (Tipp City, Ohio), 16,
    68, 185
Goetz, Dave, 151, 191
Graham, Billy, 28, 110, 218
Green, Michael, 28
Grove City Church of the
    Nazarene (Grove City,
    Ohio), 51
Guinness, Os, 39, 40–41,
    111

Habitat for Humanity, 38
Hagee, John, 179
Haggard, Ted, 102, 163,
    165
Hall, Eddy, 211
Hamilton, Adam, 142
Harvest Christian Fellow-
    ship (Calvary Chapel),
    (Riverside, California),
    179, 192
Hayford, Jack, 11, 153
Heber, Reginald, 135
Hendricks, Howard, 11,
    191
Henry, Carl F. H., 39
Hisrich, Robert, 92
Hodges, Cecil, 11
Hofstede, Geert, 32
Hope Community Church
    Network (Seattle,
    Washington), 33
Hope, Bob, 113
Hugo, Victor, 58
Hull, Bill, 193
Hunter, George, 32, 33–34,
    96, 157–58, 183
Hunter, Kent R., 147
Hurston, Karen, 173
Hustad, Donald P., 133, 174
Hybels, Bill, 11, 41, 87–90,
    100, 141, 179, 181-183
Hyles, Jack, 179, 181

Jacobus, Bob., 86-87
Jakes, T. D., 101, 179
Jankowski, David, 11
Jenkins, Jerry, 116
Jobs, Steve, 189
Johnson, Kevin, 124

Jotabeche Methodist Pen-
    tecostal Church (Santi-
    ago, Chile), 180

Kageler, Leonard M., 65
Kallestad, Walt, 24, 142
Keep, Doug, 126
Keller, Tim, 94
Kennedy, John F., 127
Kierkegaard, Soren, 154
King Henry VIII, England,
    138
Kreun, Glen, 187
Kumuyi, William, 180

LaHaye, Tim, 116
Laurie, Greg, 127, 192
LeFever, Marlene, 59
Leno, Jay, 110
Lewis, C. S., 57
Lewis, Robert, 36
Liesch, Barry, 146–48, 156
Living Word Outreach
    Center (Winners
    Chapel), (Nigeria), 180
London, H. B., 40
Long, Jimmy, 60, 75
Lucado, Max, 121–22
Luther, Martin, 138, 152

MacArthur, John, 90
Macchia, Steve, 25
MacLaine, Shirley, 45
Maier, Walter A., 113
Malphurs, Aubrey, 84
Marble Collegiate Church
    (New York, New York),
    31–32
Martin, Glen S., 77
Maxwell, John C., 11, 41,
    166, 172, 215
McCarthy, Charlie, 113
McGavran, Donald, 11, 104
McGraph, Alister, 110, 121
McGwire, Mark, 23
McIntosh, Gary, 141–45.
McLaren, Brian, 71, 73, 74
McLean Bible Church
    (Tysons Corner, Vir-
    ginia), 108

McLoughlin, William, G., 35

McNeal, Reggie, 127, 193

Mead, Loren, 165, 214

Meeks, James, 179

Mehrabian, Albert, 63

Milosevic, Slobodan, 38

Moerman, Murray, 126

Moreland, J. P., 121

Morgenthaler, Sally, 152

Mosaic (Los Angeles, California), 120

Mother Teresa, 49

Murren, Doug, 33

Nanfelt, Peter, 192

Nelson, Alan, 19, 150

New Birth Missionary Baptist Church (Full Gospel Baptist), (Decatur, Georgia), 179

New Hope Christian Fellowship (Honolulu, Hawaii), 178

New Hope Community Church (Portland, Oregon), 27–28, 49–50

New Life Church (Colorado Springs, Colorado), 102, 163

New Song Church (West Covina, California), 97

Newbigin, Lesslie, 76

Niebuhr, Richard, 39

Noll, Mark, 119

Osborn, T. K., 180

Palau, Luis, 28, 65

Patterson, Ben, 196

Pawley, Dan, 11

Pearson, John, 92

Pensacola Revival, 41

Perkins, William, 152

Peterson, Eugene, 71

Peterson, Tom, 49

Phipps, Bill, 126

Piper, John, 153

Porter, Doug, 11

Potter's House, 101, 179

Price, Frederick K. C., 181

Princeton Alliance Church (Princeton, New Jersey), 201

Prison Fellowship, 55

Quakers, 37

Rainer, Thom, 2, 114, 188

Rauschenbusch, Walter, 39

Redeemer Presbyterian Church (New York, New York), 94

Ries, Paul, 179

Robertson, Sara, 11

Robinson, Haddon, 23

Romanowski, William, 115

Ronsvalle, John and Sylvia, 203

Roof, Wade Clark, 193

Russell, Bob, 142, 179

Ryrie, Charles, 11

Saddleback Community Church (Lake Forest, California), 30–31, 32, 97–99, 141, 179, 186

Saint Augustine, 73

Saint Francis of Assisi, 37

Saint Nicholas (Santa Claus), 37

Saint Patrick, 37

Saint Valentine, 37

Salem Baptist Church (National Baptist), (Chicago, Illinois), 179

Salvation Army, 37, 139

Sample, Tex, 62

Sayers, Dorothy, 60

Schalk, Christoph, 27

Schaller, Lyle, 115, 143, 155, 167, 169–70, 174, 179, 188, 194, 206, 208–10

Schmidt, J. David, 207

Schorr, Henry, 132

Schroeder, Tim, 13, 164

Schuller, Robert, 186

Schwarz, Christian, 27

Scifres, Mary, 63–64, 88

Scottsdale Family Church (Scottsdale, Arizona), 19, 150

Second Great Awakening, 42

Seifert, Dave, 11

Shaw, Mark, 152

Shawchuck, Norman, 99, 210

Shelley, Marshall, 115

Silvoso, Ed., 102

Sjogren, Steve, 56

Skyline Wesleyan Church (Lemon Grove, California), 82

Slaughter, Michael, 2, 11, 16, 64–65, 68

Smith, Brad, 197

Smith, Christian, 111

Smith, Chuck Sr., 179

Smith, Julie, 11

Solomon, Lon, 108

Southeast Christian Church (Louisville, Kentucky), 142, 179, 186

Spader, Dann, 29

Sproul, R. C., 32, 65

St. Paul's Lutheran Church (Aurora, Illinois), 91

Stackhouse, John, 193

Sweet, Len, 20, 58, 124

Synan, Vinson, 185

Thomas Road Baptist Church (Lynchburg, Virginia), 181, 185

Thompson, Dave, 195

Thomsen, Christian, 206

Thumma, Scott, 186

Toler, Stan, 2, 207–8

Tolstoy, Leo, 57

Toronto Airport Vineyard Church, 41

Tozer, A. W., 158

Trinity Baptist Church (Kelowna, British Columbia), 13, 164

Troeger, Thomas, 62

Trueblood, Eldon, 18

United Church of Canada, 126

Valjean, Jean, 58
Vander Griend, Alvin, 103
Vasquez, Javier, 180
Vaughan, John, 179–80
Veith, Gene Edward, 60, 64, 69
Vineyard Community Church (Cincinnati, Ohio), 56
Vision New England, 25
von Harnack, Adolph, 39

Wagner, C. Peter, 2, 41, 95, 96, 95, 102, 188, 196
Wagner, Glenn, 192
Wardle, Terry, 159

Warren, Rick, 11, 29–31, 97-99, 101, 141, 179, 183
Watkins, William, 112
Watts, Isaac, 134–36, 138
Webber, Robert, 153, 154, 158
Weber, George, 147
Wesley, Charles, 135, 138
Wesley, John, 42, 152, 217
White, James, 124
White, James Emery, 125
Wilberforce, William, 37, 152
Willow Creek Community Church (Palatine, Illinois), 87–90, 100, 141, 171, 179, 181–83, 187

Windsor Village United Methodist Church (Houston, Texas), 202
Wiseman, Neil, 40
Wood, Fred, 206
Wooddale Church (Eden Prairie, Minnesota), 9–10, 116
Wuthnow, Robert, 207
Wycliffe, John, 138

Yoido Full Gospel Central Church (Seoul, Korea), 173, 174, 180
Young, Ed, 179

Zacharias, Ravi, 122, 123

Elmer Towns is cofounder of Liberty University and is dean of the School of Religion there. He has lectured at more than fifty theological seminaries in North America and abroad. He has edited two encyclopedias and has written more than seventy books, including four best-sellers on the Christian Bookseller Association list. He has also penned some two thousand magazine articles. Elmer and his wife reside in Virginia and have three grown children.

Warren Bird, on staff with a large, cutting-edge church in Princeton, New Jersey, works with numerous pacesetting church leaders. He has served as researcher for Carl George, Dale Galloway, Michael Slaughter, and several other pioneering innovators. He has edited or collaboratively written seven books and over one hundred magazine articles. Warren and his wife have two children, and they live in a suburb of New York City.

The authors would like to talk with readers about ideas for the twenty-first-century church. After reading this book, send your comments via e-mail to: etowns@elmertowns.com